Photos on the front cover are of patients receiving their special requested dreams.

Photos starting from the top left:

Nolan Ryan from the Texas Rangers gives Cody a few pointers right before the baseball game starts in Arlington, Texas.

Floyd is checking out his new ride; a battery powered Jeep Safari.

Daniel meets the Phantom of the Opera on Broadway in New York.

Chase is playing on the beach during his dream vacation to Florida.

T. C. is excited about learning to use his new computer.

Five patients posed together at the Little Rock National Airport. The patients and their families are leaving on a dream vacation to Disney World and other theme parks in Florida. All families flew together on the same plane.

Jimmy is getting to know his dream; a horse!

April is having her dream granted; a shopping spree in Memphis, TN. Assisting her is a volunteer (Ken) from our organization as they try on sunglasses together in the mall.

Experience The Miracles
of Giving

V. O'C. Davis

Preface

This book was compiled from all different aspects of the dream granting process including views from parents, patients, siblings, friends, and volunteers. In most of these stories, the names have been changed to protect the family members and the patients.

Sadly, around 70% of the parents who have experienced having a child diagnosed with a life threatening illness end up divorced. If their child died the percentage raised to 90%. Many times they either blamed one another or blamed themselves and never tried to work long enough to get through the hardest phase.

No two people grieve at the same time. One spouse may get through the worst part of the grieving period, while the other spouse has not even started grieving yet. I feel that divorce is such a tragedy because the two parents could never find anyone else to share in their lives who could fully understand the depth of their grief from losing a child.

When I asked the authors of these stories to sit down and write about their experiences before, during, and after the dream, I was not aware of the mind cleansing effect that this challenge would be for each of them. Along with the stories came letters thanking me for asking them to write down their feelings.

For some, it was like a huge sigh of relief or a release from the bad times. It gave them a chance to look back and analyze just what had happened to them. Some said that now that it was down on paper, they could somehow move on with their lives. Others said that writing their memories down allowed them to enjoy the good times all over again and experience the thrills of being with the patients when things were "fun" and remember when the pain and suffering was put on hold, just for a while.

Having feelings written down on paper can really assist a person to search their souls and later be able to come back and read it again and again. They can feel good about themselves knowing that they have done the best that they could have done under the set of circumstances that were given to them.

About the Author

U p to this point in my life at 42 years old, I was very energetic, exercised regularly, took vitamins, and my overall health was excellent. I had worked for the past 14 years as a full-time volunteer for 60 to 70 hours a week granting dreams for children diagnosed with life-threatening illnesses. I was married to a wonderful loving husband for five years. He had two sons from a previous marriage and I had three sons. My faith in God was unblemished.

During this time, I founded a nonprofit organization with a board of 14 members. We granted 833 children's dreams during that period. I was the Executive Director and had created a volunteer base of over 400 people just in our own state.

In those early years, I founded another nonprofit organization to assist children who needed transplants. Even though transplants were very costly, I was able to negotiate the fees of the hospitals, physicians, specialists, pharmacies, airlines, pilots, hotels, and apartment buildings. By doing this we were able to actually pay for 20 transplants for Arkansas patients. Involvement of our then current Governor Bill Clinton, our President Ronald Reagan, and the Arkansas Legislators were key figures in this major task.

Also early on, a third nonprofit organization was formed that was affiliated with the dream-making organization. The sole purpose of this foundation was to fund, organize, and orchestrate Christmas parties for all of our surviving dream patients, siblings, and parents. The second purpose was to fund, organize, and coordinate group trips annually for the surviving patients.

Throughout our endeavors, we raised over 3 million dollars of which no salaries were paid and where 100% of the money raised went toward the dreams, other needs and activities for the patients.

Among the services for the sick children were summer get-togethers and picnics for the patients and their entire families. Our purpose for this activity was for the families to share with one another and to attend special classes and activities to learn more about the diseases. They were taught skills to better cope with their situations.

Stories about us were featured in newspapers, magazines, talk radio programs, and television all over the country. "ABC", "NBC", "CBS", "CNN, local TV, and radio stations in many states have covered our many accomplishments. We have had news stories written about us in the "Washington Post", the "Chicago Tribune", the "San Francisco Chronicle", the "Dallas Morning News", the "Kansas City Courier", "USA Today", the "New York Times", the "Philadelphia Inquirer", and almost every paper in Arkansas, as well as in many other states, too many to name. We were on the cover of the "Mid Week" magazine in 1984. We were featured on the national afternoon program "America" with hosts Sarah Purcell and McClain Stevenson. "Good Morning America" had stories about us on two separate occasions. Even Paul Harvey spoke about one of our achievements, on his national radio broadcast. All stories were, of course, positive.

Because of our involvement in assisting children with organ transplants, President Ronald Reagan while in office in 1984 set aside one week each year for "Donor Awareness Week" which is still in effect today.

In 1986, I helped campaign for the emergency services of 911 to be implemented in our state for the good of everyone. Today, we know how important these services are for actually saving lives.

We had to fight for the rights of organ transplant patients even against our then Governor Bill Clinton. Because of our persistence, in July of 1987, a law was changed to force Medicaid to cover organ transplants even if the patient had to go to another state for the operation and treatments. Before the law was put into effect, Medicaid would only pay for medical services in-state which ultimately ended with the death of the patient since our state was unequipped for most transplants.

On April 22, 1992, President George Bush, Sr. appointed me "A Point of Light" number 752 out of 1000. I was chosen to attend a special luncheon in my honor at the White House on January 14, 1993. This was a great honor for me and my family.

Even though I did not want or need recognition of my achievements, I received numerous awards for my altruism. There are too many to count, but among them were the "Thomas Jefferson Award", "752nd Point of Light", "Service to Mankind Award", "Hometown Hero Award", the "Golden Rule Award", "Arkansas Community Service Award", "Spirit of Arkansas Award", "Volunteer of the Week Award", and many more. I attended luncheons at the Governor's Mansion that were held in my honor.

My faith in God has been my strength throughout my life. I have always believed when one person reaches out to help another, that person (the receiver) will in turn find others in need and help them.

It has taken ten years of compiling stories and data to write this book partly because of my illness and partly waiting on others to finish their stories. I still have many days of not being able to walk or use my arms but I always get back eventually to where I can type and read again. I have had many years to think about which stories to put in this book. There are so many more important stories but the book would be so large that it would defeat the purpose of writing it.

My wish is for this book to inspire others to keep going and keep a positive attitude while doing so. I want to encourage others to become involved where they are needed. Whether you are a volunteer, family member of a sick loved one, or a friend, hopefully my words can help you find a way to realize that what you do with your life counts. Everyone needs a friend. I believe that when you do become involved with assisting others, you will be much happier with yourself. I also want everyone to know how important it is to have faith in God and know that He is always with us.

Dedication

I am dedicating this book to the ones who helped me and encouraged me to keep fighting to survive my own illness.

At age 42, I had spent the past 14 years providing my voluntary services to assist others. Suddenly, my whole world turned upside down. I began having heart attacks and no physician could discover the causes. I went through many doctors and numerous tests. Finally after eleven months of being in one life threatening situation after another, I met the most amazing physician during one of my many visits to the emergency room. He was an oncologist/hematologist who was practicing locally. While standing in the emergency room on the night that we met, he asked me if he could be my hematologist. I told him, "You couldn't be any worse than the ones that I have already had! So, sure. Why not?"

God had sent this outstanding physician to me, but I didn't know that at the time. He would need to earn my trust. Eventually, I realized that I had found the right specialist who was interested enough to get to the bottom of my health issues. (Or he found me.) This doctor was very good, caring, and intelligent!

Blood clots were finally discovered. I had developed bead-like clots in every vein and vessel of my entire body. I had several locations where the bead-like clots were gathering to form larger clots. I will tell you that during those horrifying times, I was in tremendous pain. The clots burned inside my veins and felt like hot matches burning inside them. Every inch of my body was burning and nearly made it impossible for me to think straight. At times, I thought my head would explode.

How could so many "good doctors" not find that? It seemed as if knowing <u>what</u> was going on and <u>why</u> were half of the battle. Finally, the blood clots were contained to certain parts of my body. My hematologist became my overall physician sending me to specialists for tests, evaluations and treatments. He was involved with every decision that was made by all of the doctors involved.

Seven more months passed before I was diagnosed and could start receiving the proper treatments. My diagnosis was achieved through the slow process of elimination of a long list of diseases. My final diagnosis was Lupus (SLE), Ankylosing Spondilitis and Antiphospholipid Antibodies Syndrome. Many side effects accompany these diseases thus making it so hard to find all that was happening to my body. Once the diseases were found, the proper treatments could begin. Some of the treatments would be nearly as bad as the diseases.

When I wasn't hospitalized, I had to go to the hematologist four times a week to have my blood drawn and tested. Even though I was taking a blood thinner, it was very difficult to get my blood to thin properly. Most of the time, my blood would actually gel as it entered the syringe. Many times the LPNs drew my blood, rushed 30 feet to put it in the PT/INR machine and it was too thick to test. My heart was straining just to pump the thickened blood. My brain functions were slowed and it was almost impossible for me to walk without assistance.

Throughout this ordeal I had 17 heart attacks caused from blood clots passing through my heart. Some of them went to my lungs. One of those clots went to the left side of my brain where it sat for 14 months. I was blessed to have at least 95% use of the right side of my body during that time. The clot was in a place where it could not dislodge, and it eventually dissolved. Within two years of the clot going to my brain I was almost back to normal with only a few of long term minor problems. For two years it was very difficult to swallow food or drinks without choking. That did heal, also. The mild stroke has caused me to lose much of my short term memory and I still struggle with that even today.

I had another clot that my heart threw down my aorta and lodged blocking my colon. My colon began dying out and I was hospitalized so they could watch me. Nothing else could be done because I could not have surgery due to the blood clotting disease. I was very fortunate to have a Christian doctor who prayed over me while I was in my hospital bed. Many others were also praying for my recovery. God brought me through that situation and the clot dissolved and reopened my colon. I do believe it was truly a miracle because those doctors really did not believe I would ever walk out of that hospital that time. My colon was completely healed within months.

I soon realized that I could no longer work outside my home when my life became a daily struggle. I went through the same stages as many or most of the patients I had assisted over the years. I went through the rough times asking God "Why me? Haven't I done all that you have put before me? Haven't I been thankful enough for every blessing?" I, too, became the victim of anger and grief. For a brief period, I felt as if God had left me all alone to deal with my illness.

Everyone who has been in this type of situation will go through all of these stages. Now that I look back on those days, I can see some good that came from those bad times.

I have been very fortunate to have some of my patients come to me and assist me by becoming my phone buddies, sending me cards and e-mails, but most important; praying for me. In the beginning, it was very hard for me to accept assistance from others. I was the one always doing that part! I had to learn how to be humble and accept others' kindness and assistance. I also learned some hard lessons in who my true friends were.

My son Patrick and my beloved husband Keith rotated missing work to care for me since I could not be left alone. I had to be assisted to visit the bathroom, to take showers and to eat meals they had prepared for me. I know I was not the greatest patient, but I did very much appreciate the help, for I could not have survived if not for their love, assistance, patience, and understanding of the situation. At times, I was as near to death as one could be without actually crossing over.

Even though my telephone was hanging on the wall less than two feet beside my bed, I did not have the strength to answer it. The receiver was too heavy for me to lift. My family took turns answering the phone and laying the receiver on my pillow (up to my ear), so I could talk to the callers. They were my main source of strength for my faith in God. Their words were like small stepping stones that would eventually bring me back to life, and they gave me the means to keep fighting for the healing that was yet to come.

My niece Glenda lives in Texas and called me at least three times a week. She was a tower of strength for me. Her words were so powerful and her voice so sincere. She really did make a big difference in my attitude. Many times I was ready to give up and she would not let me give in to those thoughts. She would talk me through the most difficult of times.

My dear friend Judy was also one who would not let me give up. She phoned me several times a week for years. I know she must have gotten discouraged, but she never once let me know it. I don't know how she managed to keep up her strength and patience with me. Never did she utter a single negative word during all of those years! Judy will always remain one of the key people who brought me through that horrible ordeal. I am forever grateful to her, for there can be no greater friend than she. I thank God every day for sending her to me.

Judy lost her son to cancer ten years earlier. I first met them when he had a dream granted through our dream-making organization. Her son Brian was one who will never be forgotten. He had such a wonderful uplifting personality and to all who had the privilege of knowing him, he was truly a blessing to each of us. I know that he got his strength from his mother. It is her faith in God that keeps her strong.

My dearest friend Norma called me every single day, sharing her courage, strength, and her faith in God. She is a wonderful person with so much love in her heart. I am very thankful that she is my friend. She constantly sends me cards, poems, and prayers, all of which I treasure.

Vicki is another true friend in which I will be eternally thankful. She phoned me often. Her prayers brought me through so many life threatening situations, and I know that she still has me in her prayers today. A person could not ask for a better friend than one who keeps you in their prayers. She sends me wonderful greeting cards and handwritten notes of wisdom and courage. It is amazing just how much these little things can mean to another. If I get discouraged, I hear from Vicki by a card, a note or a phone call, right away. How does she always know? It seems as if God tells her when to contact me. I believe that God sends her just at the right time, and she is still there for me today.

I cannot and will not forget my loving and forever faithful dog Snowy. He was a beautiful white Cockapoo with black spots. He was half Cocker Spaniel and half Poodle and weighed 18 pounds. We rescued him from the pound years earlier when he was only eight months old. At times, it seemed as if he was almost human, and we talked to him as if he were. He was so grateful to us for giving him the run of the house, and he loved every one of us so very much. When we had visitors in our home he always thought that they were there to see him.

During my long illness, Snowy never left my side. He kept a constant vigil at the foot of my bed. He was touching some part of my body at all times and knew he had to be careful so his touch was ever so gentle. If I moved over an inch, he immediately moved over an inch. Usually it was my feet or the bend in my legs that he was up against. He had to be forced to go outside for potty breaks every couple of hours, but he would do his business and then run as fast as he could to get back in the house and onto the bed again. That was his only exercise for the day. When my family fed me meals in bed, Snowy also had his meals on the bed.

During one of my heart attacks, he knew it was coming even before I did. He came up beside me and stood on my chest with his front paws and stared down into my eyes. He alerted my family and they called an ambulance. My husband had to hold him back so that the EMTs could get the IV started and load me into the emergency vehicle.

Snowy lived to be 12 years old before he died of cancer. I know that he was a special gift from God. There can be no greater companion than a loyal pet who loves you unconditionally. There will always be a special place in my heart for Snowy. I still miss him dearly.

There are many other friends and neighbors like Coleen and Beunah who helped me by bringing food often and praying for me and my family. I cannot possibly name all of them because there were so many. It took all of them to bring us through some of the hardest times in our lives, and we thank God for each one.

When I look back on those years I was shown which people were my true friends. There were many people in my life who I thought were my friends but were the very ones who disappeared and were never heard from again. Just the thought of some of them really hurts me very deeply, even to this day.

When a person is going through such a horrific experience as a life-threatening illness where even the physicians don't have much hope of their survival, friends are needed the most! The families cannot bear the entire weight alone. Often friends disappear because they don't think they have the right words and don't want to offend the patient or family members.

The sad thing is that those people fade away, and some patients find themselves all alone. It is true that there is strength in numbers. Do you know of someone that needs to hear words of encouragement and needs to tap into your powerful faith in God? Whether you realize this or not, when you help another in need, you are also helping yourself.

Contents

PART 2. The ups and downs of having a family member diagnosed with a life threatening illness do not just affect the patient. It affects everyone around them!..51

Introduction

Many of the parents of these dying children have asked me, "Why is this happening to my child?" I do not have all of the answers, and I do not believe that anyone does. My answers to their questions have been, "Even though you may not understand why these terrible things are happening, please believe that in the near future God will reveal His purposes to you."

Sometimes as long as two years later I have had conversations with the parents who lost their child. Somehow they always remembered my words about God revealing a purpose to them. I have had them tell me how God answered their questions. I have not heard a negative response from any of these parents. They shared the good that came from the death of their special child.

Don't misunderstand me. I am not saying it was good they lost their child nor that they believed it was good. What I am saying is that good came from the death of their child. Something that could not have happened without losing their child has happened to improve the lives of the rest of the family or their children had touched another person and helped them with their death. Many different stories have been shared with me about the good that has risen from their loss.

One family that I had the pleasure to know had a 13 year old daughter diagnosed with cancer and a rambunctious 16 year old who was always in trouble at home and in school (even before her sister became ill). After her younger sister died, she changed. Her parents believed because their 13 year old daughter was always good, kind, and loving, she was taken home to be with Jesus. The 16 year old learned from the death of her sister that no one is guaranteed how long any of us have to live here on earth. She is now a sweet loving person who is trying to do the right things. She no longer has an attitude problem. She even joined our volunteers and began assisting others, and I could see she is a much happier person. She has learned to like herself and now others like her, too.

There are so many more stories just like this one, but instead of me telling you about each one, I have let others write about their experiences. As you read them you will notice that some children have died while others are still living.

Jennifer hugging Randy Travis

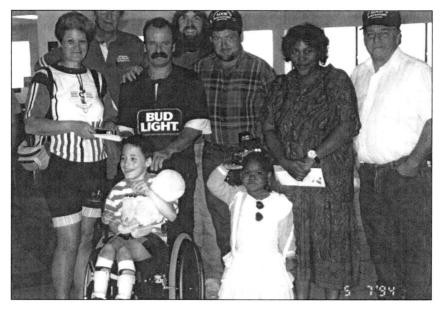

Two patients and families on their way to Florida

Brian with his new computer

The Dreams Granted

Being a volunteer within a dream-granting organization was sometimes fun and other times heart-breaking. Over 20 years ago, I started a non-profit dream-making organization for children diagnosed with life threatening illnesses, with a handful of volunteers and many prayers. We have a children's hospital in our city. From the first moment we started operations, our phones were ringing off of the hook! We were quickly swamped with requests for dreams from the doctors, the families, and even from patients.

In those humble beginnings, we were granting an average of seven dreams per month. That average carried on for about the next six years. As the Executive Director of the non-profit organization, I worked directly with the patients and families. A part of my job was working directly with the patient's physician maintaining a good relationship with every one of them.

We found volunteers to help raise the necessary funds to keep us going. We had volunteers who worked in the office and volunteers for every aspect of a functioning organization including attorneys, CPAs, travel agents, and doctors. It took all of us working together to make these dreams come true. Our non-profit organization was an all-volunteer organization with no paid persons. Our volunteer base grew to over 400 volunteers from around our entire state.

Over a 14-year period, in our state alone, we were very proud that our volunteers granted 833 patients' wishes. Of these dreams granted, around 75% requested to visit Disney World or Disneyland. The other 25% requested shopping sprees, to meet the idol of their dreams (a celebrity or TV/movie star), to see relatives who lived far away, or to receive a hard-to-find pet.

Dreams were granted only for children diagnosed with life threatening illnesses. One of the rules of the organization was that patients must live within our state. We did not have an abundance of money flowing in, and we used the funds as quickly as it came in. Many times we were granting several dreams a week and even sometimes several in one day.

Between the eighth and 14th years of service, the average had dropped to around three dreams per month. I believe the change was because of two factors. The life threatening disease rate had slowed down (maybe due to new medical procedures and cures), and there were more dream-making groups around the United States. Also, three more dream-making groups popped up just in our state alone. Regardless of how many other groups were out there, we were steadily busy granting dreams and never denied a patient their requested dream.

When we first began, the children's doctors would comment that many times after a dream was granted, the patients would have a burst of energy, enough to fight the disease even harder. The dreams would actually work as a boost for the children and their families to improve their attitudes and quiet some of their fears. In other words, having a positive attitude was very important to the patients because their outlooks became brighter, and they sometimes gathered more strength throughout the process.

Most of the patients (around 80%) were diagnosed with some type of cancer. Around 10% of our patients were diagnosed with cystic fibrosis or other types of lung diseases. The other 10% were children diagnosed with AIDS, other blood diseases, organ failures, and many types of rare disorders with no cures.

I tried to keep in touch with the families after the dreams were granted to follow the patients' conditions. It was then that I noticed that around the holiday seasons, things would start falling apart for some of those families. The patients that we assisted with dreams were from families that were already struggling to make ends meet due to the illness, the parents' lack of time spent at work, and the medical bills piling up. This could be overwhelming, even for those who were from middle-income families. We soon were aware of the depression that came with the holiday seasons. We saw a need to assist these families during the Christmas Season.

The Christmas Parties

Around the third year of our existence, we decided to put together a Christmas party for the patients, the siblings and their parents. Our organization was in the Capitol City. All of the families traveled to the Capitol which is in the center of the state to be at the party. This seemed fair and worked out great for everyone! The first party was a wonderful success and became an annual event.

Every dime raised for the parties went into the preparation for the parties and gifts for the children. We never used money raised for dreams to cover Christmas gifts. That money was kept separately. We thought that donations for dreams should be just that—used for dreams!

We started around October 1st sending letters to the families inviting them to come to the Christmas Party. We also requested a list of what each patient and their siblings were wanting for Christmas. The list had to be back in our hands by October 31st. The parents had to probe their children inconspicuously so they wouldn't know what their gifts would be on that special day. By November 1st, we searched for volunteers to raise the money for as many children as they wished to sponsor or purchase the gifts and then bring them to us (unwrapped). We only had 29 days to assign all of the patients to volunteers and to have all gifts in our hands by the deadline.

When November 30th rolled around, we had an office full of gifts stacked to the ceiling! (In the later years, we had to find an empty office in our building to store the gifts because the patient and sibling count had grown to over 400.) Assigned volunteers would come into the office and check and recheck to make sure all of the gifts were there. Then in came the volunteer wrappers! These ladies worked feverishly to get everything wrapped beautifully and labeled each gift with the proper child's name.

The party would always be on the second weekend of December, so as not to interfere with family activities closer to Christmas. A local Hilton Inn donated the use of the largest ballroom and even decorated the room with Christmas decorations. They also provided enough food to feed every single person attending, including the volunteers. The Hilton Inn and their employees were a blessing to our organization.

We had a special volunteer who was a very good Santa. He was wonderful with the children. His wife and older daughters were Santa's helpers. The Hilton donated a large room (suite) located close to the ballroom where Santa and his helpers guarded all of the gifts the night before the parties.

As the main event began, volunteers made sure that each person had a nametag and was checked in before entering the ballroom. The families got their food and were seated wherever they wished. After everyone ate, Santa would come in with "HO, HO, HO" and would be seated at a throne beside the huge decorated Christmas tree. Every year, the children would squeal and clap when they heard him coming. Children were called up, individually, to sit on his lap and receive his or her presents and have their photos taken. A professional photographer was there to take each shot.

Many of the patients were too weak to carry their own gifts. Some were in wheelchairs and some were on stretchers. There were times that we had to have an ambulance pick up a child from the hospital and bring them to the party. Of course, this was with the child's doctor's permission. Volunteers would be there to help carry the gifts to the family's table and have the children open their gifts while the volunteers took pictures of them.

The crowd count would be around 600, which included all volunteers, patients, parents and siblings. No family ever left there without feeling overwhelmed by the special attention they were given. So many families wrote thank you notes to all that were involved. Comments were mainly geared toward the excitement of the parents and the children and the good feelings and emotions that they experienced. We had many letters every year that thanked us because without our special Christmas party, there would be no Christmas gifts for their family.

Everyone who attended the parties, especially the volunteers, felt a special peace in their hearts because they had helped to make a difference in the lives of these wonderful children and their families.

The Special Trips

For the last 10 years of the organization's existence, we had special trips for the surviving patients. All survivors were from our list of dreams granted. They were invited on this special one-day arranged trip. Every year we picked a new place to go. The money raised for these trips was kept separated from the money raised for the dreams just like we did for the Christmas parties.

We had so many activities with the children because we felt if we could keep them feeling positive about their situations and themselves, the odds of them living longer were greater. We learned from experience that this is true. Even the physicians of these patients agreed.

Over those last ten years, the special trips were to the following places:

Disney World in Florida (by 747 chartered planes)
Sea World in Texas (by a 707 chartered plane)
Universal Studios in Florida (by a 747 chartered plane)
Silver Dollar City Theme Park in Branson, MO
    (by four buses)
Memphis, TN (by four buses) to the Peabody Hotel to see the
    ducks, Graceland (Elvis' home), and on to Libertyland (a
    theme park)
St Louis, MO (by a 747 chartered plane) to the Arch, to Busch
    Stadium for a ballgame, to the paddle boats to eat lunch,
    and the railways gave us our own train!

Each of these places was more than just nice to us. They opened up their parks and their towns to us. But most of all, they opened up their hearts for these special children. We were allowed to go and do things that the normal public could not do. Their employees would become involved with the children and help anywhere they were needed. We can never thank them enough for all that they did for us. We very much appreciate all of the wonderful caring people that helped us.

We worked closely with every child's physician and parents to prepare for the trips. We had all legal paperwork documented before each trip. Every patient that was ten years old or younger was allowed to bring one parent. A volunteer (and an RN, if needed) would be assigned to every patient.

Our volunteers were usually state troopers, local police officers, and medical staff. People and groups who raised a large amount of money were allowed to have a couple of volunteers from their group to come help us. On one trip, the Navy assigned 100 of their personnel to meet us in Florida to help with the patients. That year, we had around 50 patients in wheelchairs. The sailors wheeled children around and literally carried them on and off of the airplane.

They also lifted children all day long in and out of rides at Disney World. We carried walkie-talkies to communicate. We had floaters who were RNs, respiratory therapists, and physicians in case of any emergencies that might come up.

The patients were allowed to guide the volunteers to wherever they wanted to go when we were in a theme park. Every single person and child had to wear a special t-shirt and nametag made just for this day. Everyone wore the same color so we could spot "our bunch" anywhere in a crowd. Every year, we picked a different color to wear and designed a special t-shirt that displayed the trip's activities.

When we were planning the Memphis trip, Graceland allowed us to put a copyrighted picture of Elvis on the t-shirt. We gladly signed a release that we agreed not sell the t-shirts. On the day of that trip all day long people came up to our group and offered money for the t-shirts! Of course we dare not sell a one! These special t-shirts were also souvenirs for each of us to keep in remembrance of the trip. We all felt very privileged that Graceland had been so kind to us.

On each trip, our day would begin by boarding the transport vehicle(s) around 6:00 a.m. and getting back in around 12:00 a.m. (midnight). Those were long days but well worth every effort. We always filmed with video cameras and still pictures during the entire trip. We made sure that we had footage of the volunteers on the way back because they were so worn out and exhausted. You could see it on their faces. Then we would scan the patients with the video cameras and most of them were still going strong. It was a funny sight to see! It was also a blessing for us to see these very sick children acting normal again.

The positive feedback we received is what kept us going from year to year. So many good things have happened during these annual excursions. The patients could thrive on the energy produced from these special events for months at a time.

To help each patient and volunteer remember those special days, we took photos and videos every minute of these trips. A local production company volunteered their services and helped produce a video of the entire day. We had to edit around 35 hours of footage every year. Each patient and volunteer would be in the video several times. We copied the number of videotapes necessary to send one to each person involved. They would also receive copies of any still photos of themselves for keepsakes.

All fundraising groups and large donors that helped raise the money for the trips also got a copy of the video along with a letter thanking them for supporting our efforts to make these children's lives better. They were willing to take time out of their busy schedules to find ways of either donating money or working very hard to have fundraisers for these activities. We could not have had one trip, one Christmas party, or even one dream granted without the wonderful loving individuals and groups that supported us.

PART 1

Lessons everyone needs about life, death, and the grieving process.

Assisting Others in Need

There are so many different ways to assist others in need. If you truly wish to learn how to help others you should first find a worthy cause and commit your time, energy, and talents to someone or something as a voluntary act. Having positive thoughts about your commitments will help you follow through especially if you are serious about your efforts. Assisting others will also help yourself. Use today to seek ways to accomplish goals you have set for yourself.

Being fearful of getting involved with a person with a serious illness because you are afraid of losing this person to death can keep you from experiencing true love. While your inner voice screams, "Stay away! Befriending them will hurt you when they die." Think for a moment. What if it were you in their place? What if you were the one needing a friend at a time when you were the one facing a fatal or debilitating disease? How would you feel if you were all alone trying to deal with a devastating illness?

Everyone needs someone to love them and care about them. Why not give some of your time to help others? Only good can come from your efforts. One day you might find yourself in their shoes. All of us at some time during our lives will need assistance from others. Love is a very powerful word. When we experience love for others, we will find love for ourselves. We will be much happier and content and people will want to be around us.

Pray each day for strength and courage to help you through your trials, to carry the message of love to others, and to help you forgive and have compassion for others. Thank Him for the love and support you receive from others. Pray that God will lead you in the right direction to assist those who need you in their lives. God will richly bless you for your endeavors.

Listening Carefully to Others

Listening with undivided attention and being nonjudgmental is probably the greatest gift that we can give one another. Your inner voice, conscious, or voice of God will lead you to choose the right path and the words to say when needed. Praying beforehand will insure that the proper words will come from you.

Listening can be very beneficial when we are committed to helping another person. Listening does not mean that we must agree with everything being said. We should listen without attacking, blaming, or judging them. We should learn to listen without having any demands or expectations of this person.

Talking too much and constantly interrupting is not helpful. Learn to concentrate on that person's words. Look right into their eyes. Touching can be very important when they are in pain emotionally or physically. Thinking, "What I have to say is more important" or "I'm too busy right now" are not the ways of active listening. A true listener will be loving, tender, and receptive of the other person's thoughts and words. The true listener will show kindness and love, revealing thoughts of "You are very important to me" or "What you are saying is very important to me". The more attentive listener will see their many different relationships improve.

Positive Thoughts are Important

Everything that we endure as we travel through our life on earth can be positive. Even losing our loved ones can turn into a positive situation. Things that we experience can become helpful to ourselves and to others. Challenges in our lives can be beneficial and can be perceived as positive growth. Let go of the illusions that we are the victim of a situation.

We may be able to help others due to our past experiences. We can learn through assisting others that we are able to take charge of future challenges we find our own selves in. View each challenge as a stepping stone to a better you.

When faced with a loved one dying, remember that only God has all of the answers. We can do all we can for this person, but only God holds the future. Sometimes life can seem so unfair. It is very hard to remain positive all of the time, but trying to do so will help us get through the situation easier.

Apply What You Learn

Throughout many years of being with patients and families who are fighting dreaded diseases I assisted them whenever I was needed. I have tried to listen very carefully to the patients, family members, and friends. What I learned from each of them, I have remembered and shared the same words, thoughts, and feelings to others in similar situations. They have taught me to understand more about what they are experiencing. I do believe, however, that until a person is actually going through or has gone through the same situations, they cannot fully understand the emotional strain hanging over them. What we can do is be there for them when they need us. Sometimes words are not needed. Just our presence means a great deal to them. If they need to talk to you, try to listen attentively to every word.

Dealing with Patients
Who are Children

Over the years I have learned many things that assist me when talking to the patients and families. One of the main things that the parents and family members need to do is keep their hope alive for the survival of their child. The child needs that extra support. When I have seen the parents give up even before the child is terminal, that child will die sooner. That child will not develop a will to survive. Without the will to survive, the disease will take over the body quickly.

Children who are diagnosed with a life threatening illness (even the very young children) have a greater chance of surviving if their attitude is positive. Parents need to stop fighting among themselves and with everyone around them and learn to think only positive thoughts. Their sick child knows when the parents are fighting even when it being hidden from them. The child's intuition is very great especially with the ones they love. Parents need to get their priorities straight and work at learning to love and forgive one another and be strong for their child that so desperately needs them.

When your family's whole world turns upside down due to an illness in the family it is easy to become a negative person with negative thoughts. To help you, your family, and the patient you need to think before you speak or act. Try to remember to share loving thoughts and actions. It will surprise you to see how much better this will be for everyone. The sick child is depending on your support to help them to recover.

The one thing that I have witnessed over and over again is when the family has positive attitudes and hope for a total recovery; I have seen miracles happen right before our eyes. Even when the physicians have given up and said that the child will not live through the night, not only did they make it through the night, but they improved, eventually had a total recovery, and went back to living a normal life again.

I believe that when God has decided that our purpose on earth has been fulfilled only then will He take us home. No one knows for sure when that day will come. I believe that only God has those answers.

I do believe that each of us have a purpose for being on this earth. When I have sat with patients and watched them take their last breath, I have tried to comfort the family members. I feel that my purpose for being here is to help these families to get through the most difficult times in their lives. I will never go to the families unless they request my presence. When I meet them I let them know that if I am needed I will be there. When they are ready to talk, share their concerns, or just need a friend I am just a phone call away.

It is not easy to be me. I cry a lot! I have also learned that it is okay to cry. Sometimes the parents and I cry together and share our emotions openly. It is good to show that we are not robots. We are humans who have deep feelings and emotions. This creates a bond between us. Showing them that I care helps them to know that they are not alone and someone will be there if I am needed.

On Death

One of our biggest fears is death. Death is an inevitable part of everyone's life. No one has a guarantee of long life on earth. Understanding that death is a part of life will help you live a more meaningful life.

All over the country things are changing. More people are talking openly about death. Questions that were once improper to ask can now be discussed more freely. Therefore, we learn to assist one another by communicating our thoughts and fears.

Those who are faced with a fast approaching death need to express their feelings, angers, and emotions. Take that extra time to listen to them. They need to feel close to the ones that they love, the ones who really matter in their lives. They need to talk openly about their illness and to tell their loved ones good-bye. Families need to forget about disputes among themselves and learn to keep that line of communication open.

Children are often excluded from the family discussions or kept away from the person who is ill. We must remember that they are going through this trying period, too. They have the right to be included and have a need to share their feelings, thoughts, and fears. No two people have the same exact thoughts, feelings, and experiences. These trying times are not easy for anyone in the family or for the friends. Families should learn to band together and be there for one another.

The Normal Grieving Process

For us as Christians, we find comfort in believing that our deceased loved ones are in a far better place.

Grieving is an essential process in recovering from the death of someone close. Sadly, no two family members seem to grieve at the same time. It is common for one family member to be very distraught and their spouse to be coping very well on the same day. The following day it is not uncommon for these roles to be reversed. Everyone is different, with different needs, feelings, and emotions.

According to most professionals; during the first phase of grieving is the denial of your loved one's death. The griever even sometimes believe that they see their loved one sitting in their favorite chair, walking across the room, or even holding conversations with them. Painful thoughts and dreams may occur during this phase.

After some time has passed you may not be able to remember anything at all about your loved one. This is only temporary and is not unusual. This phase will quickly pass. Usually this occurs when you have accepted the death. Memories will return and the process of letting go will begin.

Months may go by and the crying worsens. This is when you realize that your loved one will never return, but you are stronger and can face reality better by this time. Crying more is perfectly natural. Anger sets in to replace those feelings. It is normal to feel anger about your loss. Guilt will soon follow because of the anger. Fearing loss again may make you afraid of showing your love to others.

Sometimes the family members will get angry with one another because they somehow have justified (in their minds) that the good one was the one who died. What is happening is they are remembering only the good about the deceased, making a picture of this person as a faultless dream character. During this phase it is helpful to try to remember that no one is perfect. We are all human beings with our own different faults. Everyone is special in their own way.

Learn to respect each other and give each other room for grieving. Receiving counseling may be necessary to recover from the grieving process. Seek Christian counseling. Feelings of relief will begin to occur. Time does heal all. Soon life starts to return with more stability. This experience (no matter how harsh) will strengthen you. We enter a new phase of life. Now we need the presence of others in our lives. Hopefully through the process of grieving, the understanding of other people's needs will be seen more easily. Getting involved with assisting those in need will heal you faster and make you feel better about yourself and about others.

To hope is to risk failure, but to not try at all is sure failure. The person who risks nothing, gains nothing, and becomes nothing. I believe that giving and receiving are the same. You only receive what you give.

Memories Both Good and Bad Need to be Remembered

Memories live forever, even if your loved one is not here to share them with you. Remembering the good and precious moments are essential in keeping their memories alive. After the death of a loved one letting go does not mean you should forget them. Letting them go means that you are allowing them to go on to a better place where they will never again have pain and suffering.

Remember the good times and the bad times. It is okay to feel your true feelings. They are your feelings. Also remember that other family members and friends have their own private feelings. It is good to go through photo albums and remember how it was when your loved one was healthy. Try to remember that they are now whole again.

PART 2

**The Ups and Downs
of having a
family member
diagnosed with a
life threatening illness
do not just
affect the patient.
It affects
everyone
around them!**

Chapter I.

You can slip into the lives of some of these families and friends as you read the following stories. The parents, siblings, friends, and even the patients have shared their deepest feelings as the dramas unfold. Here you will see how different each person views the same situations from his or her own perspectives.

MARY BETH (Dream—To go to Disney World)
By Charles, Father of Mary Beth

Marybeth with Mickey Mouse at Disney World

On May 24, 1976, our family was blessed with a newly found joy Mary Beth. For the first 3 years of her life, she did everything that a normal toddler would do.

On February 15, 1980, when Mary Beth was only four, one of our local pediatricians gave us the news that would forever change our lives. He diagnosed her with Acute Lymphocyntic Leukemia (ALL) with a "null cell". That same Sunday afternoon we were sent to a children's hospital. Mary Beth underwent the normal routine treatment for this type of leukemia. Fortunately, the disease was caught in the very earliest stage, and she had no problems with the treatments. At this point, Mary Beth had "beat" the disease.

For the next several years, Mary Beth participated in numerous everyday events with other children her age. She was a cheerleader for her grade school football team. She played soccer at our local youth center, and for two years she played on a softball team. She attended school just like all children her age. We later found out that some of the problems that Mary Beth was experiencing were related to the medication that she had taken as part of her ongoing treatment.

In the summer of 1987, at age 11 Mary Beth began to drop things that she was holding in her right hand. Shortly thereafter, when she began a new school term, teachers noticed that she was having problems in school. In the later part of September of 1987, she was diagnosed with a malignant brain tumor. We were advised that she should have immediate brain surgery and we consented to it promptly. We will never forget the day that Mary Beth had that surgery! After she awoke from the anesthesia, the first thing that she asked for was fried chicken. The nurses saw to it that she got her fried chicken that very night. She began her recovery from the surgery and was placed on a chemotherapy program.

Finally the day came when we went home from the hospital. Our phone rang and that new voice became a positive part of our lives. That young lady soon became very dear to Mary Beth, my wife, and me.

Someone had referred Mary Beth to a dream-making group and our new friend was a volunteer of that statewide organization. She told us about the organization and asked if Mary Beth knew what she would like for a special wish. Mary Beth's long time dream was to go to Disney.

In January of 1988, Mary Beth got her wish. I will always remember Mary Beth's excitement as we boarded the plane for Florida. The next day, her excitement multiplied as we rode the ferry across the lagoon and entered into "Mary Beth's Dream...Fantasy Land". All that day, we walked through the park and rode the rides.

Later that evening, we were privileged to ride in the Parade of Americas representing our own state. You could see the joy and happiness gleaming through Mary Beth's eyes and face and hear it in her voice. During the plane ride home, the pilot announced her name over the intercom as an honored guest on the flight. After we landed, he allowed her to go into the cockpit and sit in his seat. Thanks to our newfound friend and the organization, we will have those very important days of Mary Beth's precious dream to remember forever.

The following Sunday, our church had the privilege of hearing Mary Beth sing a solo during the morning service. She loved our church very much, and the church expressed their love for Mary Beth on a continuing basis. There will always be a love in our hearts for the kindness our church showed for our daughter, her mother, and me throughout her illness.

Later that spring, we were invited to an air show along with many other patients through the dream-making group. We were allowed to sit in a designated area just for our group, closest to the action. We got to meet the Air Force Precision Flying Team which consisted of nine very talented men who were known as "The Thunderbirds". They were so very kind to all of the patients and family members, allowing us to look at the planes up close and giving us a personal tour. Mary Beth loved that wonderful day!

When softball season rolled around, Mary Beth was unable to play, but her team allowed her to dress out in uniform and sit with them in the dugout for several games. That same summer, she got to go to a three week camp for children diagnosed with cancer. This would be her second summer to attend. She looked forward to the following summer so she could return again.

In October of 1988, the founder of the dream-making group made some surprise arrangements for Mary Beth. They had invited her to go to the airport to catch a glimpse of President Ronald Reagan. He was flying into our state to campaign for George Bush, Sr. for President. The entire state showed up at the airport to see President Reagan. We were privileged to be ahead of the entire crowd in the very front beyond the roped off areas. All of the television, radio, and newspaper reporters were 50 feet behind us! We were in front of the podium among the Secret Service and the President's personal staff.

Accompanying Mary Beth was her mother and I, an RN carrying the IV bag and monitoring the medications, the ambulance driver, and founder of the dream-making group. Mary Beth was so excited to be there that she could hardly contain her emotions. She was smiling from ear to ear.

One of the Secret Service agents approached the founder of the dream-making group with a note and stuck it in her jacket pocket. The note was from a newspaper reporter which read, "To my Dearest Friend, Vicki—Could you please come get my camera and take a photo of President Reagan because you are much closer than we can get?" She shared the note with us and we all laughed out loud. She sent an agent to retrieve the camera and then took several photos of the President. The following day, her photos were the ones that ended up on the front page of the newspaper! Also, photos of Mary Beth she took showed up in the newspaper, too.

After President Reagan's speech ended, released into the air were thousands of red, white, and blue balloons filled with helium. The music played, "Hail To The Chief" as the crowd roared. We could hear the enthusiasm of the crowd as they cheered. What a wonderful sight to see and experience!

The President was leaving to board Air Force One as the Secret Service surrounded him. All at once, a Secret Service agent appeared and handed Mary Beth a large piece of paper and smiled as he walked away. She looked down to read the note as the President walked toward Air Force One. The note from the President read, "Best Wishes to Mary Beth" and signed "President Ronald Reagan". Before boarding the jet, President Reagan turned, looked our way, smiled and waved. Mary Beth cherished that note for the remainder of her life. That small gesture meant everything to Mary Beth and to our family.

How could we ever thank those people who were responsible for bringing this joy to my little girl? Now was the time that Mary Beth needed her strength and this exciting event gave her the energy and the will to keep fighting her disease.

That very afternoon, Mary Beth underwent a new procedure in another hospital where catheters were placed into her brain. Radium beads were inserted into these catheters in an attempt to shrink the tumor. She had to have this heavy metal halo attached to her head. She was the youngest patient to ever have this done, and she also received the most radium implanted of any patient who ever had this treatment. No one was allowed to be close to her because of the dangers of the radium beads planted in her head.

Now I know how horrible this may sound, but we felt that we had to allow this procedure because this could mean her life if we didn't try. Special arrangements were made to have us (her parents) in a room next to hers. A camera, speakers and a monitor were installed so we could communicate with her. The founder of the dream-making group made all of these expensive arrangements possible. She worked with the hospital and found the companies to donate the use of this equipment for our unique set of circumstances. The media covered the entire procedure from beginning to end since this procedure was unknown to the outside world. The founder of the dream-making group took charge of the media, setting up the interviews with the hospital staff, doctors and our family. This coverage turned into a week long series on the early and evening news. We knew that everything being done was for the sake of Mary Beth, and we greatly appreciated it. In telling our story we may be able to help someone else.

Then it was home again. By this time, Mary Beth's favorite thing to do was to go over to our newly found friend's house to play with her daughter. Mary Beth would go over to her house on Wednesday nights while my wife and I attended choir practice. Our new friend and her husband were loving people who cared deeply for our little girl. They would always make Mary Beth's favorite dish—macaroni and cheese. As a matter of fact, it got to the point that Mary Beth would refer to them as "Momma and Daddy #2"! That family was a blessing to us.

All throughout Mary Beth's illness, she kept a positive attitude. She had positive people around to help her, talk with her, listen to her, and love her. When a reporter from a local newspaper inter- viewed her he asked her what advice she had for other children who had been diagnosed with cancer. Her reply was simply said, "Don't ever give up and you will always win."

On May 1, 1989, Mary Beth had to be hospitalized due to a seizure which she experienced in the early morning hours. That same week, I was diagnosed with a malignancy and had to have surgery. Due to the kindness of the staff at the hospital, I was placed in the pediatrics ward so that Mary Beth and I could be together.

Still hospitalized on May 24, Mary Beth had her 13th birthday. Although she could not see or talk, we felt very sure that she knew what was going on around her. That morning, a nurse came in and put lipstick and rouge on her. A little later on, the minister of youth from our church and other members of the youth choir came by to sing a Happy Birthday song for her. We were not certain of the depth of Mary Beth's awareness, but we did detect a slight smile on her face as the children sang. The following Saturday morning, I went in to see Mary Beth and told her that she "fought a good fight" and that she had suffered long enough. I told her that she had permission from her mother and me to go and be with Jesus.

In the early hours of the following morning, Mary Beth "lost the battle, but she had won the war" when she fully realized her "Victory in Jesus" as she went home to be with Him. Finally, I can fully visualize Mary Beth no longer being crippled or unable to speak. Instead, she is there singing in that wonderful heavenly choir.

My wife and I would like to dedicate this story to our beautiful daughter, Carol. Secondly, we dedicate it to all of our many friends who stuck by us through it all and whose names I dare not try to mention for fear of omitting even one. We thank you and Mary Beth thanks you.

By Charles, Father of Mary Beth

MARY BETH (Dream—To go to Disney World)
By Vicki Kelly, a Friend and a Volunteer

I am a volunteer of a dream-making organization. I first met Mary Beth in October of 1987. Mary Beth was 11 years old when she was diagnosed with a brain tumor. She was referred to our dream-making organization by a physician from a local children's hospital. Her dream was to go to Disney World. In January of 1988, her dream became a reality. With her parents and her sister, they boarded a 727 airplane headed for a five-night, six-day fun filled vacation to Florida. This was a special trip that she and her family would always remember and cherish. To this day, I can still see that special smile on her face as she talked about her dream trip.

Mary Beth and her parents became active volunteers in our dream-making group, helping us to raise money for other patients like Mary Beth. She attended our organization's monthly meetings, as long as her health permitted. She loved helping others. Even years after her death, her parents were still active in the organization. Her father became the Chaplain of the dream-making organization.

My family and I spent a lot of time with Mary Beth. We became her second family. She taught us about life, love, strength, and so much more. We will always treasure the time that God gave us with her. There is a special place in our hearts that will always be hers. She is gone but her smile, love, laughter, and memories will always be present. We had many wonderful days with her. Sometimes we would go to the park or sometimes to the mall where she managed to always find those wild earrings that she so loved to wear! For the last several months of Mary Beth's life, she was confined to her bed. Even though she had lost her speech, she still stayed in touch with those beautiful blue eyes and contagious smile.

Mary Beth was determined to become a teenager and she turned 13 on May 24, 1989. We (her family and friends) gathered in her hospital room with Happy Birthday banners, balloons, and gifts of love to celebrate her last birthday. Although she was in a comatose state, we know that she was aware of her birthday party and of everyone there on that special day. We think that we even detected a faint smile on her face as we sang Happy Birthday to her.

Mary Beth's favorite song was "Victory in Jesus". I know in my heart she found that victory with Jesus. Not everyone knows who his or her personal guardian angel is by name, but I know mine is Mary Beth. She is with me everyday.

By Vicki Kelly, a Friend and a Volunteer

Vicki Kelly

SHELLY (Dream—To go to Washington D. C.)
By Shelly, Patient at Age 20

In January of 1984, at age 12 I was diagnosed with Hodgkin's disease, a form of cancer of the lymph (the watery, colorless fluid that travels through the lymphatic system in the vertebrates).

It almost seems as if now it were a blur when I try to remember everything. I do wish that it could have only been a bad dream, but it wasn't. It was real and so are all of the other things that go along with the six-letter-word "cancer"!

It hit every member of my family as hard as it hit me. I can remember the expression on my parents' faces when the oncologist told them that I had a form of cancer. As I look back to that moment, I can still remember that weak uneasy feeling that I got when the doctor was telling us about the disease. Even today, when I go into that children's hospital as I walk down those halls and think back on that day, I get the same frightening feelings all over again. The news that we received on that first day could not have been more devastating to me or to my family.

It seemed like days and weeks went by as I battled with the same question, "Why me?" I couldn't figure it out. My thoughts and feelings were building up inside of me. My emotions of anger, fear, and frustration all turned to bitter thoughts and actions. I felt as if I was enclosed in a glass wall and couldn't get out! My two weeks in the hospital seemed like an eternity. I built up many bitter thoughts and feelings during those first two weeks. I caught myself dwelling on my disease and feeling sorry for myself. I felt so alone not understanding any of my emotions and wondering, "Who could understand them?" It didn't take too long to figure out that feeling sorry for myself didn't get me anywhere. My bitter feelings only caused me more frustration and a lack of patience. I soon learned that "patience" was very important when dealing with a disease such as cancer.

My very first day of chemotherapy was hard and scary, but on that day I realized that in the word "Team" there is no "I". My family was there when I needed them the most and I knew that we were all going to have to work together as a team to get me well. Chemotherapy and radiation became my way of life. This was something that I faced daily with my family's help.

Many prayers from friends helped us tremendously. Without the Lord's help and guidance, we would have never been able to make it. The Lord was the "coach of our team" and it was because of Him that we overcame this battle against cancer. After almost a year of chemotherapy and a solid month of radiation, my therapy was over. I was now in remission.

As I look back on all of the hard times that we went through during that first year of my illness, I can remember each individual person that touched my life in a special way. I will always remember the special dream that was granted for me. My school had elected me to go to a special legislative conference in Washington, D. C., but my family could not afford the expensive trip. My heart was broken until I got a call from the founder of the statewide dream-making organization who "heard through the grapevine" about my need to go to Washington, D. C. She offered to assist me by making all the arrangements and paying for the trip. This was truly a dream come true for me! As I learned through experience, positive relationships and thoughts are very important in surviving an illness. This trip uplifted my spirits and encouraged me to keep fighting to stay in remission.

Before this dream was granted to me, I had known the founder of the group for many years. I had never had a dream granted—not because I wasn't asked, but because I just never needed to have anything special that my family could not handle. I knew her because of my illness, because I was a cancer patient. She and her many volunteers arranged the Christmas parties for all of the survivors of life threatening illnesses from around our state. I had attended many Christmas parties in the past.

Any patient lucky enough to meet her was soon invited to the next Christmas party. The volunteers spent months preparing for this special day talking to the parent to find out exactly what each child wanted for Christmas and then finding people to purchase the gifts. I remember how excited each child was, waiting for their name to be called next. I know that for many of these children this would be the only Christmas presents that they would get. Many wonderful caring people were involved with the founder of the dream-making group because they could see that what they did made a difference in the lives of these families.

When I turned 18 and graduated from high school, I wanted to work with this lady at least for a little while. I needed to feel good about myself by helping others. I ended up working in her office for six months. It was hard work, but well worth the experience. I saw some terrible situations and even some children who died quickly after they had their dreams granted. I saw the good that came from assisting others in need. I felt that what I did was important and needed. I had seen first hand how important it is to make the patients feel loved.

The work that I contributed to the daily grind in the office was a need that I could fulfill when families would come into the office. It was hard meeting the patients and their families, but I learned how to cope with the emotions. Wanting to be an RN was my goal and this experience motivated me to get into nursing school.

Through that rough time in my life, I met new people, learned new things, developed many inward qualities, and watched a very special bond grow within our family. I have also been left with a strong desire to help sick children. I am now attending nursing school and hope to soon be a registered nurse. I thank God every day for bringing my family and me through those hard times.

By Shelly, Patient at Age 20

DAVID (Dream — To have a Nintendo, Games & TV)
"The Life of David As Seen Through the Eyes of His Father"
By Mike, Father of David

David & Mom

David was born on February 19, 1978. He was my first child, and his birth was one of the happiest times of my life. David was an average boy in most things however; he enjoyed being around adults the most. David was very inquisitive wanting to know all that he could about how things worked and what made them tick. David was more interested in helping others than with playing with his playmates.

In January of 1990, David started suffering earaches. We took him to the doctor three times in three weeks, but they found nothing wrong. On February 22, my wife was called to school because David was sick. When she brought him home, I could tell that he was in a lot of pain. We proceeded to the doctor's office at once. David was dehydrating, so the doctor advised us to take him to the hospital for more tests.

After being admitted, the doctor did a spinal tap and found blood in the spinal fluid which made them suspect a blood clot. After running a brain scan, they discovered a brain tumor. Immediate surgery was recommended. David was in surgery for ten hours. The doctors informed us that they had found a malignant tumor and they could not remove all of it. At the time, I remember thinking, "Which kind of tumor is cancerous, malignant or benign?" The next day, the doctor informed us a follow-up scan showed no signs of growth in the remaining tumor or bleeding. This was great news, but I was still in shock and unable to grasp what this news meant. I wanted to know more and expected the doctors to tell me something. Getting information from them was like "pulling teeth". I felt like I wanted to know it all, but didn't know what questions to ask.

After three days in ICU, David moved to a room where we were able to be with him. He had some paralysis to overcome; his left side was useless, having a loss of sensitivity. His sight was also impaired. In the coming days, with physical therapy, his abilities returned. David began radiation a week after surgery to kill any remains of the tumor. Because of David's age (12), I remember wondering if we should tell him that he had cancer. All we told him was that he had a tumor and it was removed.

As the days passed, David's condition improved and two weeks after his surgery we were able to take him home. By the time radiation was over, (which was every day for six weeks) David's physical ability had improved to the point that he was able to do just about as he pleased. However, the doctor suggested that he remain home from school.

A month after radiation the doctor recommended chemotherapy, so we felt that he knew best. It was at this time that we told David that the tumor was cancerous and the treatments could keep it from coming back. We started a six-month treatment program. After many trips to the hospital and talking to many different people, I was still unsure of what the future might bring. I remember asking a social worker about what we should expect and her response was, "Take it one day at a time and enjoy each day to its fullest". I remember asking myself, "Is she trying to tell me something indirectly?"

For several months David was as normal as possible, and I was feeling great about his progress and his future. Then during his fifth treatment, things began to go wrong. His tumor had returned and the doctor recommended a bone marrow transplant. We were informed of the many complications that could occur, and we discussed them with David. He knew there was a possibility that he would not make it.

David was a strong young man. He chose to inform his class-mates of his condition and asked for their prayers. He talked to his two brothers and told them he may die and that he loved them. He actually divided up his toys and told his brothers which ones were for them. He gave me his "Pound Puppy" (a stuffed toy) and told me to call it "David" so he would always be with me.

David went through the transplant program without too many complications, but as each day passed I was on constant edge hoping nothing would go wrong. When his condition began to improve again, I became more at ease. After the transplant, we were informed that the tumor appeared to be only half of its original size. This was good news; however, it did not last long.

In the following weeks David did not improve much. The doctor said it was hard to tell if the tumor was alive or dead, and we would have to "wait and see". After several weeks of no improvement, they said his tumor must still be growing, and they did not know or would not tell me how much time David had. I remember asking this question several times and getting the same answer. (It was not until after his death as I was reading some of the doctor's reports that he had classified David as terminal 45 days before his death.) Once again, I guess they were trying to tell me David's condition was terminal by saying that they did not know how much time he had left. But since they never used the word "terminal" I did not think that his death was near.

It was around this time in November of 1990 that one of the nurses informed us of the statewide dream-making group that grants dreams for patients diagnosed with life threatening illnesses. Through the physicians, we submitted a "wish list" of items David had made. The following day David received his dream—a color TV, a Nintendo System, and games while he was hospitalized.

Even though he was very excited about receiving these items, in the days to come he was not able to enjoy them much because he was getting weaker. Even though he was not able to enjoy these gifts for very long, his brothers surely have. The Nintendo System became a blessing for us at this time because it kept our two younger sons pleasantly occupied and gave us more time to spend with David. David would be very pleased to know that the last thing that he was able to do was pass on these gifts to his brothers for them to enjoy and remember him by each time they played, and I believed they did.

We lost David on February 7, 1991, almost one year after his diagnosis. He is always on my mind. What makes his death a little easier to bear is remembering the courageous attitude he had throughout his illness. He never thought it would get him, but if it did, he was prepared for that, too.

By Mike, Father of David

DAVID (Dream — To have a Nintendo, Games & TV)
"What Is A Lumerax?"
By Paul, David's Younger Brother at Age 11

My brother David was admitted into the hospital a few days after his 12th birthday. Later, he had brain surgery and started talking in his sleep. He kept saying, "Lord, what is a lumerax?" which means "a good ending".

On February 2, 1991, I got my first dog. Then five days later my brother died. Even though my brother never got to see my dog because he was so sick and always lying in his bed, I will always remember my brother when I see my dog and her puppies.

My uncle lives in St. Louis and now has cancer in his brain. Last fall, he gave me a St. Louis Cardinals' cap. Whenever I see that cap, I will think of him.

My grandmother also died of cancer when I was two and a half years old. Soon after that my little brother Mark was born. I have nothing to remember my grandmother by, though I wish that I did. It is good to have things to remember loved ones who have passed on. Whenever you see these things you will think of the happy times with them.

When my brother David was dying, he said, "I can't wait to see my grandmother and grandfather in heaven". I found out that my brother's "lumerax" was in his dying because he will have no more pain, and he will get to meet our grandparents again.

By Paul, David's Younger Brother at Age 11

DAVID (Dream—To have a Nintendo, Games & TV)
"Journey in Love"
By Jerri, Mother of David

When our son's doctor first said the words "malignant brain tumor", I was in total shock! These were not words that I could associate with a 12-year-old boy who had always been so full of life. It all seemed like a bad dream. The emergency trip to the hospital, a frightening night spent in an ICU waiting room, an almost unbearable 10-hour surgery to sit through the following day, then only to find out that we were facing such a formidable enemy as "cancer" was too much to take.

I felt as if the bottom had dropped out of my world. As I grasped for something to hold onto, my faith became my anchor. I remember silently reciting the 23rd Psalm over and over for days, until slowly the shock and fear began to subside and reality sank in. And the reality was that our son David was about to engage the enemy in a fierce battle!

When David was born, my husband and I were deciding upon his name. I remembered thinking about the Bible story of David and Goliath being one of my favorites. Later, while filling in his baby book, I immediately completed the section titled "named for" with "David, the giant-killer". As David grew, he began to live up to his name. He was never afraid to undertake any big project, whether it be hauling trash cans out to the curb in his little red wagon when he was five, building his own playhouse in the backyard at age seven, or helping his dad roof his grandparents' house when he was ten.

He always began with great enthusiasm and would not quit until the job was done. So, when David was diagnosed with cancer, I began to believe that like his namesake, our David would beat the odds stacked against him. It was this belief in David that gave me strength and courage to face the battle with him.

In the beginning of his illness, David was frightened. He could not understand how the tumor had gotten inside his head, and he kept asking us if he was going to die. Telling him that no one knew how the tumor got there did little to console him, but when I told him that he was not going to die, I truly believed it. My faith had taken over. We prayed together every time David felt worried. Our parish priest who visited regularly made sure David knew his classmates were praying for him, too. This helped to put David's mind at ease. Slowly, he became less frightened and became more trusting of the doctors, their procedures, and treatments.

In the weeks and months that followed surgery, David's spirits soared. Even having to endure physical therapy three times per week and daily radiation did not get him down. His joyful attitude prevailed. He became great friends with every one of his caregivers, whether it was a doctor, nurse, therapist, or just an orderly who happened to be pushing his wheelchair. He called everyone by name and always seemed happy to see him or her. Once, while seeing a doctor who entered the examining room with a greeting of, "Hi, David!" our son immediately responded with a joyous, "Hi, David!" (That was the doctor's first name, also.) I'll never forget the broad smile that broke out on that doctor's normally stoic face.

It seems strange now when I think about it how at such a traumatic time in his life, David was able to show such amazing joyfulness. Even David's teachers remarked at the time how "neat" David was to be around as if his attitude was contagious. The only explanation that seems to make sense is that David's joy was a divine gift brought about by all of the prayers being sent heavenward in his behalf. As a result, David's smile gave us all the strength and hope that we needed to face each day.

After radiation, the neurosurgeon referred David to an oncologist to consider chemotherapy. It was in the oncologist's office that David heard the word "cancer" for the first time. For the previous three months, we had only referred to "it" as a tumor. My husband and I could not bring ourselves to use that word when we talked to David. Maybe we didn't think that David could handle knowing. After all, he had been improving so fast and feeling so well. Maybe we thought that knowing would jeopardize his recovery. Though we worried about not telling David the whole truth, we just could not face telling him.

Of course David was shocked to know that the tumor had been cancerous, but when the doctor talked with such confidence about the recent scan showing no tumor re-growth, we were all encouraged. I remember feeling relieved that David finally knew the truth about his tumor, but I also remember feeling very scared about chemotherapy itself. As I sat there listening to the schedule of treatments and possible side effects, I wondered if I looked as frightened as I felt. On the outside I was trying to appear brave and optimistic, but on the inside I felt like screaming and running from the room.

The first chemotherapy treatment was frightening because we didn't know exactly what to expect. Even though the doctor had informed us ahead of time which drugs would be used and what their possible side effects were, we had to experience it one time in order to know exactly how David's system would react. Once I knew which drugs caused mild reactions and which ones caused violent reactions, I felt better prepared emotionally to handle things. So the treatments became somewhat less frightening as the months went by, but I never stopped praying for the strength to get through each one. To David those were a-once-a-month nuisance that he had to plan his life around. I remember him being especially annoyed when his fourth treatment was scheduled on the first day of a new school year.

Then during the fifth chemotherapy treatment, something went wrong. David started having a seizure. The doctor ordered a C.A.T. scan which showed the tumor had grown. We were devastated. David had been through so much pain during these months of chemotherapy, only to find out that the treatments had not done him any good. David had fought hard and done everything that was asked of him. David had "played by the rules" and the tumor hadn't. It was not fair. I felt like I was losing control.

The following day, the doctor informed us of the only remaining option—a bone marrow transplant. This was a risky procedure without any guarantee for success. The risks were explained in great detail to all of us, including David. The doctor felt that he was old enough to weigh the facts and help decide whether or not to undergo the transplant. We were told to think about it for a few days before making our final decision.

My husband was ready to tell the doctor "yes" immediately. He could not bear to just "give up" and stop fighting. He was afraid that David might say no to the transplant. I needed time to think and to pray. I also thought that David should have time to consider exactly what this procedure would put him through. For one, it would mean another surgery or aspiration had to be done in order to retrieve some of his healthy bone marrow before massive doses of chemotherapy were given which would completely destroy his immune system and hopefully the tumor. Then his healthy marrow would be re-injected so that his system could begin functioning again. After much discussion, thought, and prayer (my answer came from Proverbs 3:27), we all believed that David should have the transplant.

With the decision behind him David rallied. Somehow he drew upon his inner strength and found a source of courage. He talked to his classmates and teachers to inform them about the procedure. He asked them for their prayers. He told his younger brothers that he might not live through the transplant. He wanted them to know he loved them, and they could have his toys if they agreed to share them.

On October 11, 1990, David entered the hospital to prepare for the procedure. One week later the bone marrow aspiration was done and a central line was placed within his chest; whereby David could receive nourishment and I. V. medications for the duration of the transplant period. We had previously been told that the aspiration might require as many as five or six "sticks" in each hip in order to remove enough healthy bone marrow from David. However, after the surgery the doctor's nurse informed us that they only had to make two "sticks" in each hip. I was overjoyed at this news because it was the answer to a specific prayer of mine in David's behalf.

As we waited for David to come out of recovery, a woman whose child was currently in the transplant isolation unit visited us in the

waiting room. Her four year old son had undergone this same procedure a couple of weeks ago. She wanted to tell us what to expect in
the weeks ahead and to let us know that the whole experience had
not been as difficult as she had expected. As I listened to her my
heart filled with hope, and I marveled at this stranger who had taken
her time to console and encourage someone whom she had never
met before. But this had been the case throughout David's illness.
Almost everyone with whom we came into contact with was very
giving, understanding, and compassionate. We may not have liked
the situation that we found ourselves in, but caring people such as
these were always there to help us feel that we were not alone.

While the transplant ordeal was not a picnic, my anticipation of
it had been worse than it actually was. The four and a half weeks
spent in the isolation unit with David passed by rather quickly. The
procedures that were done and David's physical reactions to them
basically went according to what we had been told beforehand.

However, one morning at the end of the fourth week of isolation
David began having a seizure. We had been warned that seizures
might occur. When the tumor tissue begins to die and become
absorbed within the brain swelling can occur; thereby causing a
seizure. This is what we had hoped was happening. Of course, we
were already aware that tumor "re-growth" also caused seizures.
While another C. A. T. scan revealed much swelling, the doctor also
thought the tumor appeared smaller than before. From this point on
all there was to do was to wait and see. I tried to remain optimistic.
I was getting used to living one day at a time.

The day finally came for David to leave the hospital. I was filled
with mixed emotions. While I was glad we were going home to be
reunited with our family again, I was also nervous. David's weakened immune system left him very vulnerable to infections of any
kind. I worried about what might happen and whether I would be
able to handle it.

David's homecoming did not last long. Within three days of
his discharge, he was readmitted into the hospital. He was having
trouble keeping food down, and there was concern that he would
become dehydrated. Once we were back in the hospital I felt somewhat relieved as a soldier might feel when relieved from sentry duty,

but I was beginning to grow weary of this emotional roller coaster that I found myself on. I have never liked roller coasters, and I was ready for this ride to be over!

It was at this time that one of David's nurses told my husband about the statewide organization that grants dreams for children diagnosed with life threatening illnesses. Since it was almost Thanksgiving, she said that David should make out a Christmas list and submit it to the organization. The nurse talked to David's physician who then contacted the nonprofit organization. The nurse also gave my husband their phone number to call.

A couple of days later, I called and spoke directly with the founder of the organization. She was so friendly and good-spirited that I felt as if I was talking to an old friend.

Although I had felt somewhat uneasy about contacting this organization, the founder's sincere interest in my son gave my heart a lift and left me feeling very glad that I had called. When I informed her of David's wish for a color TV, Nintendo System, and games, she also asked me if my family had received an invitation to the upcoming annual Christmas party held on the second weekend of December. When I told her that we had not, she immediately invited our whole family to attend and gave me details of the event.

The dream-making organization invites state-wide patients who have been diagnosed with life threatening illnesses. She asked me to give them a list of Christmas gifts for David totaling $100.00. The organization then finds sponsors who will purchase the gifts to be given to the patients during the party. She also wanted a list from David's two brothers and explained that "Santa" calls each one up to the front and gives them presents, also.

That Christmas party was the highlight of David's year! David has always been the first person in our family to get the "Christmas Spirit" each year. He loved anything to do with the Christmas season. So at this Christmas party he felt right in his element and loved it! Each year the Christmas Party had activities for the entire family to participate in. This year's family activity of constructing a Gingerbread House couldn't have been more appropriate. I felt that it was tailor-made for David who had always been interested in building things. David sat there with his "Gingerbread Construction

Crew", hardhat on, and became the foreman for the project. Under David's supervision, our whole family worked together to complete the house that became a beautiful centerpiece for our holiday table.

When Santa called each child up to give them their gifts, David's younger brothers were surprised and thrilled to be included. They still talk about what fun they had that day. In a year that was filled with confusion, anxiety and necessary separation, we can look back on that Christmas party as an especially happy family time. We will carry these fond memories with us and cherish them for a lifetime. Many thanks go to the sensitive and caring people that make up that wonderful dream-making organization.

A couple of weeks later, David received his dream of the color TV, Nintendo System and games. I was overwhelmed! I felt that the Christmas party itself had been such a wonderful gift for David, that I was not expecting anything more. After all, at the party David received a very expensive remote control racecar that was one of the items on his "wish list". We were content that the organization had done their part granting his dream. We did not realize that they would give him everything on the list.

It was at this time that David became concerned that his younger brothers might be jealous of all of the attention that he was receiving. So he decided that the Nintendo System should be a gift from "Santa" to the whole family. David took great pleasure in personally wrapping the Nintendo System and games. He took everything out of the box and wrapped the parts individually in smaller boxes so as to mislead his curious brothers. I can still remember the smile on David's face, that Christmas morning, as he watched his brothers unwrap each part, one at a time. The joy that David received from that act of giving was miraculous. As it turned out, that was the only joy David was able to derive from the Nintendo. The day after Christmas David became sick again. We hoped that it was just a stomach virus that was "going around" at the time, but headaches and vomiting increased until he had to be hospitalized on December 28, 1990.

Although he spent only three days in the hospital, he was barely home a week before he had to be readmitted. Since he was unable to keep food on his stomach, David could not keep medicine down either; therefore, he began experiencing small seizures. As long as he was in the hospital on I.V. fluids and medications he was fine. So the decision was made to contact a home nursing group who would teach my husband and me how to administer the I. V. medications that David needed. That way David could stay home which proved to be a blessing to our family.

Although it was initially frightening to deal with strange medical equipment and procedures, we had such a wonderful support system in the home nursing group. The benefits of having David at home by far outweighed our fears. We were so thankful for these home health care professionals who would visit on a regular basis or come anytime we called with a problem or concern.

In the three weeks that followed, we began to feel comfortable with the I. V. equipment and procedures. Once the medicines were on a regular schedule, the daily tasks became routine. By now, David was sleeping most of the time. We were told that this was a result of the medications being given to keep him comfortable.

David's doctor referred a Hospice team to come to our home. When they visited our home for the first time, I did not want to accept what they were telling us — that the end was near. Although they were kind caring individuals who gave us helpful literature to read and outlined a schedule of their visits, I did not want them to be there. Maybe I was not being realistic and rational, but I still could not give up hope that David would live. Through my faith in God I still believed a miracle could happen that would turn this situation around, and I was going to hold out for that miracle, in spite of all the signs telling me otherwise.

Then on Sunday February 3, 1991, David's condition took a turn for the worse. His kidneys failed and he had to be catheterized. Later that night, he developed congestion and had difficulty breathing. My husband and I were afraid that David would not live through the night. At 11:30 p. m., as David struggled for every breath, I knelt beside his bed to pray. I knew that the Lord was there with us when David's breathing immediately eased as I placed my hands on his head. We all slept peacefully for the rest of the night.

During the next three days, I cannot remember much of what happened. All I know is that a feeling of peaceful acceptance was beginning to take over within me. I began to realize that there were things far worse than death. Also I knew that no matter what happened, we were not alone.

On Thursday morning February 7, my husband took our two younger sons to school. The house was quiet, so I picked up my Bible and began to read. The scripture passage that I read was Hebrews: chapter 12, verses 18-24. As I read, I felt that Jesus was speaking directly to me. He was telling me not to be afraid — death was not the end. I knew that it was time to let go. I got up from my chair and went to sit at David's bedside.

When my husband returned home, he came into the bedroom and saw me sitting, holding David's hand. I could not speak, but when he looked at me I think that he sensed that it was time to say "good-bye". Within a few moments, David peacefully drew his last breath.

Today when I think back on that year I'm reminded of the story entitled Footprints about the man who dreamed that he saw two sets of footprints in the sand representing his journey through life. He realized that the second set of footprints had to be those of Jesus walking along with him. But what the man did not realize was that during his most difficult times when he saw only one set of footprints, that was when Jesus was carrying him.

Now I know that the miracle that I was waiting for and praying for was happening all along the way. Through the constant prayers of our loving family and friends, we felt the presence of our friend Jesus walking beside us. Through their thoughtful expressions of concern, we felt the loving arms of Jesus uplifting us. And through the kindness and caring of the many medical professionals with whom we dealt, we felt the strong and certain support of Jesus carrying us through to the end. Thank God for the miracle of love!

By Jerri, Mother of David

PART 3

Out of all of the dreams
that were granted over
the 14 years,
every one of them
was equally important.
The following stories are
about the wishes
that were granted
that have stood out
above all of the others.
Most of these stories
were gathered from
memories and notes
that were taken
over the years.

Chapter II.

Around 5% of the 833 wishes that were granted by our organization were requests to meet the idol of their dreams. Most of those wishes went very well without any problems, although not all of them worked out exactly as planned. Not only are these stories interesting, but they can be helpful to show how God intervenes to make our futures easier. Only a few of these stories were chosen to share with you.

SHAWN (Dream—To meet Lt. Col. Oliver North)
"Lt. Col. Oliver North Is Shawn's Miracle"
By V. O'C. Davis, a Volunteer and a Friend

Shawn meets Lt. Col. Oliver North

Early on a Monday morning in July of 1987, a physician from the oncology department (at a local children's hospital) contacted me by phone. I was asked to come and visit a patient who was not responding to treatments. At that time, I was the Founder and

Executive Director of a non-profit organization that granted wishes of children diagnosed with life threatening illnesses. It was said that I had the gift of teaching patients how to help themselves. I was often contacted when all else had failed.

The physician told me about a child named Shawn who was once a football star on his high school team and weighed 164 lbs before his illness. Since his diagnosis of bone cancer eight months earlier, he dropped down to 80 lbs. and was refusing all treatments. He told everyone that he was tired and "just wanted to be left alone!" He was also refusing to eat any food brought to him. The day that I was contacted, he was no longer even speaking to anyone. The doctor told me that Shawn was 16 years old today. Because his family could not be there due to family problems only added more negative reactions from Shawn.

I was already at the hospital when I was contacted. You see, my own eleven year old son Patrick had a serious accident and had been through four surgeries in seven days on his leg. My son's hospital room was only a few doors away from Shawn's room.

That same morning, I made a visit to Shawn. He first ignored my presence and stared at the television set. (I had been told that he watched the Iran-Contra hearings 24 hours a day.) I let him know that I was not a doctor, nurse, or even associated with the hospital in any way. I told him about my own child who was in the hospital just down the hall. When Shawn finally realized I was not going to leave any time soon, he started talking to me.

We talked about today being his birthday. I asked him what he wanted for his birthday. He said he wanted a cassette player, certain tapes and magazines, and a red hat to cover up his balding head. He felt ashamed to go anywhere or have anyone see him because he could not deal with his hair loss.

I said that I would come back later, but right now I had to get back to my own child's room. Outside in the hall were two nurses waiting to see if he responded to me. I asked them to get together enough money for a birthday cake and have it brought up here this afternoon. I went back to my child's room and began making phone calls to get volunteers to purchase the requested gifts, wrap them, and bring them to the hospital by 3:00 p. m.

My son was very excited about being involved in helping another child. That afternoon after the cake and gifts arrived I put my son in a wheelchair, piled the gifts on his lap, rounded up nine nurses and the cake, and rolled him down to Shawn's room. With lit birthday candles on the cake, we burst into his room singing "Happy Birthday". Shawn did not even smile. I asked him to blow out the candles, and he told me to let my son do it for him. I put the gifts on Shawn's bed and asked him to open the largest one first. He said, "No, maybe later." I said, "Shawn, it was not easy getting these presents for you. The least you could do is open this big one. Then we'll leave you alone if that's what you really want." He acted as if he could hardly even raise a finger to break the wrapping paper. He very slowly and unenthusiastically ripped off a small strip. He could see the words "cassette player" on the side of the box. He sat straight up in the bed and began tearing into the package, and then he unwrapped the other gifts. Everything that he wanted for his birthday was there. He loved all of his presents!

That day was the first day the nurses had ever seen him smile. That evening his family came up for a visit. No one had forgotten his birthday after all!

The next morning I went back to Shawn for a visit. He was watching the Iran-Contra hearings again. After a brief silence I asked him why he was watching this station since there are 32 channels to choose from. He looked up at the TV and said, "Do you see that man? That is Lt. Col. Oliver North. He is a very strong person. I wish I could learn to be just like him." I said, "Shawn, why do you feel that you are not already like him? What would it take to help you learn to be stronger? Would you like for me to try to help you?" Shawn asked, "Do you think that you could talk to Lt. Col. North and ask him to come see me?" I stumbled around for the right words to gently let him down. I knew that getting this very busy gentleman away from the hearings would be next to impossible.

I said a small prayer to myself and then thought, "How could I possibly accomplish this? There is no way to find Lt. Col. North! Anyway, even if I did, he is in the middle of these hearings." I finally told Shawn that I would attempt to reach Lt. Col. North, but I could not make any promises, only that I would do my very best.

After briefly saying goodbye to my son, I left the hospital and went to my office to get caught up on the daily operations of the dream-making organization. Our organization was strictly an all-volunteer organization. No one was paid a salary — not even me! I had been a volunteer for the last four years and worked an average of 60 to 70 hours per week. I was currently working on arrangements for five children and their families to travel to Florida to meet Mickey Mouse. They would all be riding on the same plane to Florida together. "What a simple request going to Disney World seemed to me." I thought, after reminding myself of what task was ahead of me for Shawn.

I had not slept much in the last week due to my own son's illness, trying to tend to the needs of my other two sons and my husband at home, and my many responsibilities with the nonprofit agency. Around 10:00 a.m. at my office, I collapsed. I had internal bleeding. By 12:00 noon, I had been admitted into the hospital. It wasn't even the same hospital that my own child was in!

After completing all of the medical tests I was sent back to my room. Even though I was lying in my own hospital bed, I couldn't get Shawn out of my mind. He was so very sick. I knew he would not live too much longer and I had to try to help him quickly. I prayed for an answer for a long time. I asked God to help find a way for me to reach Lt. Col. Oliver North for Shawn's sake.

Suddenly it came to me. I remembered a man I had recently met from Atlanta, Georgia. I thought that he said he worked for the C.I.A. out of Washington, D. C., but I couldn't remember for sure. I requested to have a phone installed in my room. Around 4:00 p. m., it finally came. I called this man in Atlanta. In my eagerness, I said "Hello, Ron. This is Vicki O'Connor from Little Rock. Didn't you tell me that you worked for the C.I.A.?" He remarked, "No, Vicki, I work for the E.P.A.! There's a big difference!" We both broke out into laughter.

I explained the situation I was faced with and asked for any suggestions. I even said, "If I could just get my hands on anyone's phone number inside the Pentagon, I could talk my way around until I found someone who knew Lt. Col. Oliver North. Surely, I could find a connection if only I had a starting place." He remembered an article from the week before about an older man living in Atlanta who had a son who works at the Pentagon. He promised to call the newspaper and find out what he could.

About ten minutes later, he called me back. He said, "Now here's the name and number of his son at the Navy Annex, in Washington D. C. I failed to ask the father what his son's job is, but maybe he will help you get Lt. Col. North's private phone number." I thanked him and immediately dialed that number.

A very kind voice answered the other end. I explained that he did not know me, but I had gotten his number by way of the Atlanta newspaper. I told him about the child who needed a special wish granted. I was desperate to find a way to reach Lt. Col. North. Not thinking that this man even knew him, I said, "I know that you probably don't know Lt. Col. North, but for the sake of this child, couldn't you please help me find the right phone number or even the name of anyone who might know him?" He surprised me when he chuckled and said, "Well, Ollie's not in right now, but if you'll leave your phone number, he will be back in about 20 minutes." I could not believe my ears! I questioned him with amazement, "Do you really know him?" "Of course, I do. We work together in the same office. You called Ollie's office." I must have thanked him at least ten times before I gave him my number, but I failed to tell him that I was in the hospital.

About 20 minutes later, Lt. Col. North called back. I was in a semi-private room. My roommate answered and then gave me the phone. He and I talked for a while. I told him about Shawn. (Remember, this is only Tuesday, one day after I met Shawn for the first time.) Lt. Col. North asked, "Will Friday morning be soon enough for me to come to meet Shawn? I will only ask one thing of you. You must not tell anyone about my visit. This must be kept very private. This meeting must take place with only the fewest number of people involved." I readily agreed.

Then Lt. Col. North said, "Two Naval Security Agents will be flying in on Thursday to make arrangements. They will help you set up what is necessary." Though I had not known it when I first called him, Lt. Col. North and his family were guarded around the clock because of threats from Middle Eastern terrorists. I assured him I would meet his people at the airport and assist them in whatever way was needed.

During one of the phone calls that Lt. Col. North made to me on Tuesday evening, my hospital roommate had answered the phone for me. He asked, "Is your secretary still working this late?" I laughed and finally remembered to tell him that I was in the hospital. I told him that I believed God had put this task on my shoulders because this was His plan for all of us. I was only doing what I thought God wanted me to be doing. Lt. Col. North stated, "Nothing will keep me from coming to Little Rock on Friday. I am looking forward to meeting such a dedicated person."

Wow! I had to get my son home from the children's hospital and then get myself released from the hospital so I could get started quickly. I didn't have much time.

When my physician came into my room, I told him I couldn't stay in the hospital. My tests would have to wait until the following week. I had a very important job that had to be done now. Even though the doctor was quite angry with me, I couldn't tell him why I had to check out. He was a Christian, so I knew that after the meeting took place, I could explain it all to him and he would understand.

The following day I got back on the right path. Everything flowed very smoothly. Both hospitals released us with no problems. Now I could devote my time to assisting Shawn.

I was so very excited for him! He needed this man's encouragement, and now he was actually going to meet Lt. Col. North. I knew that this was in God's hands. Things had happened so quickly that only God could have put the right people and things in my pathway. He was answering my prayers. God had taken charge!

Over the next 24 hours, Lt. Col. North and I spoke many times to set up the meeting and to discuss Shawn's expectations. We both knew that this was not going to be easy on him. This child was expecting a miracle to happen and Lt. Col. North was the key to make that miracle happen. I would not want to be in his shoes!

On Thursday morning, I met with two very nice men who worked for the Naval Intelligence. Together, we went to the children's hospital to meet with the administrator to ask permission to allow Lt. Col. North to enter the premises. I had invited the child's primary oncologist to attend the meeting. This physician was the head oncology specialist for the children's hospital. He was very kind, gentle, and intelligent. He and I had a good relationship because we both cared very much for the children. I had worked with him constantly for the past four years because 80% of the children who requested dreams through our organization were cancer patients.

The hospital administrator refused to allow Lt. Col. Oliver North to enter the grounds. The physician and I looked at each other with dismay. The doctor tried to explain the entire situation to him. He told him that Shawn was much too ill to be moved anywhere else for the visit to take place, but the administrator would not back down. He just said, "No way!" and showed no emotion at all when we pleaded with him.

Finally, I asked the doctor if I could be responsible for moving Shawn out of the hospital into a hotel room for the day. I said that I knew of a treatment center that would gladly loan us an ambulance and driver. The doctor thought for a moment and said, "Vicki that is a good idea. I think that if we take all of the necessary precautions, everything will be fine. I will help you." We stood up and walked out of the administrator's office while the administrator was still objecting.

As we walked down the hall to the front lobby of the hospital, we planned the schedule for tomorrow. The two government agents and I split up. They were headed to the Little Rock Police Department to make arrangements for Lt. Col. North's visit. I went to the Capitol Hotel to meet with the manager so I could beg for rooms to set this up. Shawn was so ill that he had to be lying down at all times. Also Lt. Col. North would need a room to freshen up and change clothes.

Unlike the hospital administrator, the hotel manager was very receptive to the idea of Lt. Col. Oliver North visiting Shawn in the Capitol Hotel. He even volunteered to donate the use of the Presidential Suite, a large adjoining sitting room, and another adjoining hotel room. What a blessing he was! This restored my faith in human beings, especially after having to deal with that hospital administrator.

Later that evening, I met the two Naval Intelligence Agents to go over any last minute changes. Since I had left my own hospital before any medication could be given to me, I was feeling miserable and still hemorrhaging inside, but the excitement kept me going. Anyway, I thought that I could always take care of myself after this very important event took place.

The next morning arrived quickly. I had not slept all night. Shawn's doctor had taken care of getting Shawn to the hotel using my contacts for the transportation. The federal agents had picked up Lt. Col. North at the airport. I met Shawn, his mother, and his doctor at the hotel and checked him in. The hotel manager had everything set up for us. I talked to Shawn and his mother while we waited for the others to arrive. Shawn was so excited! He still had a hard time believing that this was reality. He kept saying, "Am I dreaming?"

In walked one of the Naval Intelligence Agents. He approached me and said, "Lt. Col. Oliver North is in the Presidential Suite putting on his uniform. He has requested to meet you first. Will you please follow me?" I was in shock. I had not expected to actually meet him in private. For some reason, I had imagined only seeing him after he had visited with Shawn. As I followed the agent down the hall, my heart felt as if it were in my throat. I thought, "What will I say to him?" I began praying for the right words.

As we were introduced, we shook hands. He said that he would like to spend a few minutes with me to find out what Shawn was expecting from him. He remarked, "How will I ever find the right words to help this child? I have prayed that God would give me the strength to go into that room next door and face this child. What if I say or do the wrong things?"

I talked to him from my heart. I said, "God will give you all of the right words to say. This child is depending on you to teach him to find a way to deal with his fast approaching death and the pain of leaving behind a family to suffer his loss. He has lost almost all communication with his family because he is afraid.

Shawn is looking for the right words to say to them. He told me that he loves them very much, but he doesn't know how to tell them. He said he had not told them that he loved them since the day he was diagnosed. You can help him find a way to talk to them. If you have prayed for help, God will give you all of the right words for Shawn. God will not fail you or Shawn. This task is much too important."

I knew that Lt. Col. North was a man of God. Now I understood what so many others already had known. This man who was greatly admired by thousands of people was a man of high quality and a Christian above all. The presence of God was radiating through his every word and in his mannerisms. I knew that he already knew all of these things that I had said, but I also knew that it sometimes helped to hear them again. I told him that I had been praying for Shawn, constantly, since I had met him. I said with assurance, "God will not let anything but good happen from this meeting." We talked together for about 20 minutes.

Lt. Col. North asked that I call him "Ollie", but I found that difficult to do because I developed such a high regard for him especially after meeting him in person. Before that day, I had never even thought about having an opinion of him or his involvement in the Iran-Contra affair. Of course, I had watched some of the hearings and saw how honest he behaved. Now that I had met him, I saw inside his heart. I knew that this wonderful caring and honorable man had taken time out of his busy schedule to come to Little Rock to help a dying child.

Lt. Col. North even paid for his own flight! Each of the six Federal Agents had also contributed to make this visit to a dying boy in Little Rock a success. I offered to allow the organization to pay for the expenses, but none of them would even discuss it with me. They just said, "Take whatever money you would have spent here and help another child who needs it."

One of the Federal Agents and I had many discussions over the past two days. He was very nice and very polite. I told him that I knew that he was a Christian by the way he conducted himself. He said, "All of us working close to Ollie are Christians. When we first started working for Ollie, if we were not Christians before we met him, we became one after being around Ollie and learning from him." He had a great admiration for Lt. Col. Oliver North. Years later, he still worked with him on a daily basis. To me, that says a lot for Lt. Col. North.

It was finally time to let Shawn meet Lt. Col. Oliver North. I took Lt. Col. North into Shawn's room and introduced Shawn and his mother to him. Lt. Col. North had a Bible clutched in one hand.

Lt. Col. North turned to us and said, "I would like to spend this time alone with Shawn." Shawn's mother and I went into the sitting room where the security men and others had gathered. I was quite amazed to see a huge serving table with food and drinks, enough to feed an army! (No pun intended.)

We waited for one and a half hours before Lt. Col. North emerged from Shawn's room. He asked for Shawn's mother to come in. Again we waited impatiently pacing the floors hoping that everything was fine. After 30 more minutes had passed, she and Lt. Col. North came out to talk to me.

I had many questions. As Lt. Col. North looked at me, he had tears in his eyes. He said, "I bought a Bible for Shawn. I have spent the past four days and nights reading it and marking scriptures for Shawn to read. I hope that I was able to help him." Then we went into the sitting room where the others were. I introduced him to each person. He stayed there for two more hours visiting with everyone. He was so kind.

As his departure time approached, we made our way to the hotel lobby where television and newspaper reporters yelled, asking questions and putting cameras and microphones up to us. I had been so careful about keeping this meeting very quiet. "How did they learn that we were here?"

When a reporter approached me I asked him how he knew we were there. He told me that the chef at the hotel had contacted them to brag about serving lunch to Lt. Col. North and guests. He also told me that while Lt. Col. North was flying in on the airplane this morning, the pilot called into the Little Rock Airport and said, "Guess who I have on board and who is getting off in Little Rock!" Someone at the airport had also contacted the media.

But when Lt. Col. North arrived, the Intelligence Agents outsmarted the media. When the plane landed and pulled up to the gate, the reporters were waiting for him inside the airport. The agents had a car waiting outside in the back of the plane. They departed the plane from the rear exit and drove him away while the reporters waited inside. The media was stumped. After losing him, they began combing the entire city for him. No one knew where he was all day until the chef told them.

Lt. Col. North would not give any interviews to the media. He was quickly swept away by the agents and dashed to the airport for a safe flight home.

After the end of this exciting day, Shawn's physician allowed Shawn to go home with his mother to be with his family. Later that evening, I received a phone call from his mother. She was crying. When I asked what was wrong, she began telling about the "new" Shawn.

This "new" Shawn was more like his old self. He was no longer afraid of anything. He spoke with his family openly, called all of his family together, and told each one of them how much he loved them. He talked about a place where he was going that would be so wonderful. He would never again be sick and the tremendous pain that he has endured all of these months would soon end. He did not feel ashamed of his hair loss anymore. He no longer feared his fast approaching death. He had learned how to not feel guilty about leaving his family behind to suffer his loss. God had a plan for him. All of this was "Shawn's Miracle".

Even though Shawn died only one and a half weeks later, his last days were much happier. His burdens had been lifted from him. His dream of finding the answers to his fears had been granted. All of this took place because of a man Shawn had only seen on television who in spite of terrorist threats on his own life had taken time out of a very busy schedule to come all this way just to see him. Lt. Col. Oliver North had listened to God. He did what was needed of him. I know that sometimes it is not easy to do the right things, but when you do, God will bless you for your endeavors. I am sure that God has blessed Lt. Col. North and his family for caring about young-sters like Shawn who have so little time left on this earth.

By V. O'C. Davis, a Volunteer and a Friend

ANGELA (Dream—To meet Brian Keith)
By a Volunteer and a Friend

Angela meets Brian Keith & Daniel Hugh Kelly

When I met Angela in the hospital, she was a seven year old patient diagnosed with a very rare and serious lung disease called cryogenics alveolitis. She had a very difficult time breathing on her own. Her parents told me that the pulmonary doctors had just left Angela's room. She had been through intensive testing for the last few days and the doctors sat both parents down to tell them that Angela needed to have a heart and lung transplant. They put her name on a waiting list. They would need to find a match for her but her chances were very slim of living long enough to even receive the transplant.

I was contacted by Angela's family to see about us granting a dream for her. I told them I would mail them the paperwork that needed to be filled out before I could proceed. Within days of mailing it to them, I was summoned to her room by an RN (on her floor) who told me that Angela was doing very badly. She thought that by having our organization grant a dream for her it might help her attitude to improve and help her think about something positive in her life. Angela's parents were exceptionally eager to talk to me about Angela meeting her favorite TV star. I came to the hospital with paperwork just in case they had not had time to look at the ones already mailed to them.

Her parents and I talked for hours in the upstairs lobby of the hospital. We bonded very quickly. There was something very special about both of her parents. I even invited them to stay at my home anytime Angela had to be hospitalized. They had a son that was the same age as one of my boys, so I told them he could stay with us when they had to be at the hospital with Angela. I had three young sons and one more wouldn't make a difference to me. They were all welcome anytime they needed a place to stay. I was very pleased when they took me up on my offer. Many times over the next few years they stayed at my home.

Later that same day, when I did speak with Angela, I told her what my job was and asked if there was anything that she really wanted to do. She said that she wanted to meet Brian Keith. I said, "Brian Keith?" "How do you even know who he is?" I knew she wasn't old enough to remember the TV series "Family Affair" where Brian Keith played the uncle of a pair of twins and their older sister. Angela said she watched a series on television faithfully called "Hardcastle and McCormick". (This was a series on TV every week and lasted only a couple of years.) She said she was in love with Brian because he was so smart and so nice and so good-looking! The character he portrayed was a coy and clever man who was almost always right.

I said I first needed to confirm travel with her doctors before I could even suggest a trip. It was totally up to her pulmonary doctors whether she could travel. Then I told her I could make no promises about Brian Keith either, but I would try to reach him and his agent to see if a meeting with him would even be possible. I would let her know as soon as I found out something.

I contacted the pulmonary physicians at the children's hospital, and they told me to come right up to their offices. When I got there, they told me that traveling to California would be fine for Angela but there were lots of arrangements that had to be made first. Angela needed an oxygen tank just in case she had a hard time breathing. Arrangements would need to be made with the airlines and a local oxygen company in California. She would need to stay on all of her meds and her parents would need to know everything about her needs before they left. (I believe that they already knew everything because they were very attentive with her.) The doctors said they would work with her parents to teach them everything they needed to know and would give them emergency phone numbers in case anything went wrong on their trip.

I went back to the office and looked up the information and called the Actor's Guild. Brian Keith's agent was with The William Morris Agency in Hollywood, California. I called the agent, and he was quite delighted that I had called. He thought there would be no problem as long as the girl and her parents could come to California. Mr. Keith was in the middle of taping his series. Then the agent said, "Hold on a minute." After I was on hold for a minute, he came back to the phone and said that he had Brian Keith on a three-way conference line with us.

Mr. Keith said he was very excited that anyone was asking to meet him. He said that this had never happened before; that no one had ever asked to meet him before now! He seemed elated. He laughed and carried on a conversation with both the agent and myself. I spoke of the arrangements for the trip and Mr. Keith suggested that Angela and her parents come on the set and watch the taping of one of the shows. He gave details of certain days of the shootings. I explained Angela's health problems and told them how very ill she was. I said I would get back with the agent when the travel and medical arrangements were finalized. We could set a date and time then. All agreed and we hung up.

I called and gave the parents the good news and began making airline, hotel, and limousine reservations. When I had the dates and reservations set, I called Mr. Keith's agent and gave him the days that Angela and her parents would be there, and we finalized the details of the meeting to take place.

Within two weeks, they were off to California. The parents called me from their hotel room to let me know they arrived safely and to say that they were set to go on the following day to the set of "Hardcastle and McCormick". The agent had left the details of the meeting at the hotel desk to be given to them upon arrival. I had dealt with other celebrity agents in the past, but none were ever as friendly or helpful as this agency! I was amazed and grateful because of the love and care that we were shown.

That following evening the parents called me again just as promised. I was expecting them to tell me about the wonderful day of happy events for Angela to forever cherish. Well, it happened, but not exactly that way and not without complications.

The mother said when they arrived (someone on the set was watching for them) they were approached and greeted and were taken to another set for filming. They were asked to stay there until Brian Keith came to meet them. Angela was on oxygen at that time, so of course she had her oxygen bottle with her and had an oxygen hose in her nostrils.

Mr. Keith arrived with a bang, swearing (using the "f" word) and throwing things. He was also smoking a cigarette. He told them to hurry up and get this over with and said to get the picture taken. Her parents brought Angela over to his chair, he smiled with that great smile of his and they took the picture. The parents didn't say anything but were horrified that he was so inconsiderate knowing that Angela was so ill and on oxygen. He left with the same bad attitude as he came in with. It was over in just minutes.

The family stayed there because they did not know what else to do or where else to go. The meeting was set for four hours which included watching the taping of the show. As they were waiting, a very nice handsome young Daniel Hugh Kelly came up to them and introduced himself to Angela. Oh, Angela already knew who he was! He was the other star of the series — the younger and better looking star!

Mr. Hugh Kelly was everything that Angela was looking for. Her parents were delighted that he had saved the day for her. She had experienced the worst behavior from a grown man who was selfish beyond anything imaginable by any of us. Now Mr. Hugh Kelly took over to salvage the day for her. Actually he did much more than that for her.

He spent time with her and even let them watch the entire day of taping. During the breaks of the taping, he would run over to her as if she was the center of attention. At one point before it was time for them to leave, he took off a ring from his finger and placed it on Angela's finger. He told her to always keep this ring with her to remember him. They traded addresses and phone numbers, too. She left there feeling like a queen!

The William Morris Agency was wonderful to us. Even when they found out what Brian Keith had done, they wanted to help make it up by setting up future meeting for other patients to meet other celebrities. We gladly allowed them to assist with many other patients and never had another bad incident again. We don't blame the agency for what Mr. Keith had done. They had no control over his actions, as we did not either. Only Mr. Keith must bear the guilt of what he did that day.

For the other three days of their trip, the family got to visit the Grauman's Chinese Theatre and walk among the Hollywood Stars of Fame and play at the beach. But nothing could top the time she had with Daniel Hugh Kelly!

Angela returned home but it was a short stay. She ended up going back in the hospital and really never recovered. She was very weak and just couldn't keep fighting the disease that was destroying her body. For the next few months, she was in and out of the hospital.

Mr. Hugh Kelly stayed in contact with her and her parents. She was never without that ring and had such fond memories of Daniel Hugh Kelly! We lost her shortly afterwards.

When she passed on she was only nine years old. She was buried with that ring on her finger. Daniel Hugh Kelly will forever be admired. What a wonderful person he was! When he met her he tried to make her day better and ended up becoming her best friend. It takes a very special person to be like him. His kindness and compassion will be greatly appreciated for the rest of our lives.

By a Volunteer and a Friend

ANGELA (Dream—To meet Brian Keith)
By Christy, Mother of Angela

I am sure most parents think their child is great. Our Angela <u>was</u> a wonderful child. She was a beautiful baby when she was born. She had a full head of dark hair and her skin had a darker tone. When she was one year old she had pneumonia, or at least the doctors thought it was.

Since birth, she had to be hospitalized twice a year for pneumonia. When she was four her regular doctor moved away, and we took her to a new one named Dr. Russell. He would remain her local doctor throughout her life.

The first time he saw her he thought something was not right with her. He performed a sweat test on her and determined that the diagnosis was some type of fibrosis. He immediately contacted Dr. Warren at the children's hospital and asked that he see Angela.

We then went to the children's hospital, 126 miles away. Dr. Warren did a sweat test again on her and then a lung biopsy. Just as our second doctor had determined, it was a type of fibrosis — cryptogenic fibrosing aviolitus.

I remember the day as if it were yesterday. The doctors called my husband Roy and I in to a small room with three other doctors where they very grimly told us the bad news. They said she only had two years to live. We were devastated.

Dr. Warren placed Angela on prednisone. After a few days, we returned home. Every night I would go into Angela's room and check to see if she was still breathing. It was almost unbearable to thing that this beautiful sweet child only had two years to live.

The prednisone swelled her up badly; she went from 18 pounds to 30 pounds in a matter of weeks. Roy and I both said we did not want her on the medicine any more. Angela could hardly walk, but you know she always had a smile for everyone.

Dr. Russell did take her off the prednisone slowly, but not slowly enough. She almost died. She had to be placed in the hospital. The doctor asked if we wanted to put her on a respirator if needed. She could not breathe on her own and was dying. These were unspeakable words to us. "Our daughter was dying?"

She was a strong little person though, and she pulled through. The doctors placed her on a smaller dosage of the prednisone. She was able to breathe better and did not gain so much weight. We went back and forth from home to the children's hospital. The trip was 126 miles in each direction. Dr. Warren had suggested a heart and lung transplant and contacted the Bethesda, Maryland hospital. Nothing happened with the transplant and the waiting game began.

Angela lived past the two year prognosis and was able to enter first grade on time. She loved going to school. Over these next years she was in and out of the hospital always with breathing difficulties and so much more!

The principal at her school told us about a dream-making organization and asked us to contact them. This is how I met Vicki. She was so wonderful to us. We became good friends. We even stayed at her house at different times when Angela was in the hospital, mostly. She had four boys living at home at that time. She had three small sons and an older step-son. Angela's brother Chris (age 5) was the same age as one of her sons. He loved playing with her children when we visited.

Vicki asked Angela what she wanted to do more than anything else in the whole world. Angela's dream was to meet Brian Keith. She said her favorite TV series was "Hardcastle and McCormick". This was a show she watched each week. The stars were Brian Keith and Daniel Hugh Kelly. So Vicki set up all of the arrangements for Angela to meet him.

I contacted Dr. Russell to see if it would be okay for Angela to fly and he said it would be fine but she needed to have an oxygen tank with her. Vicki contacted the airlines and explained that Angela would probably need oxygen on the flight and would have an oxygen tank waiting for us in the limousine. So off to Hollywood we went and Angela was so happy!

When we arrived in Hollywood, we were met at the airport with a limousine. How cool was that? The driver took us to Grauman's Chinese Theatre and we saw all the hand prints of the stars. Then we went to the hotel. Everything was wonderful so far.

The next day we were taken to the set of "Hardcastle and McCormack". This is where they were filming the series. We were instructed to sit in a room where they were going to do some of the filming. After a while Brian Keith came in. He came in cursing and smoking. He stated "Let's get this picture over with!" We did not know what to think. We lead Angela to the chair Brian was sitting in and he smiled real big and they took the picture. He stood up and started cursing again and left. We were devastated for Angela.

After a few minutes, Daniel Hugh Kelly came in. He was wonderful. He sat beside Angela and we took several pictures. He said that he had to go back to the filming and asked Angela did she want to sit in his chair. Of course it had his name on it, and she was thrilled.

Later, he came back and asked her if she wanted to meet some of the other stars of the show and she said, "Yes". The entire cast signed her autograph book. One of them was from Arkansas which was really neat.

After the autographs, Daniel asked if Angela wanted to wear the ring he was wearing during the scenes. Angela said sure she did with a big smile on her face. Daniel spent all of his time between tapings with Angela. He had to borrow the ring back because he had to wear it in one of the scenes, but he gave it back to her to keep after that taping.

We never saw Brian Keith again. After a while we went back to the hotel to get ready for the trip back home. The next day the limousine driver took us by the ocean where we took several pictures. Then we were off to the airport.

On the plane traveling back home, I could tell Angela needed oxygen but she did not want to use it because she didn't want everyone to know that she was ill. She was such a strong child.

When the plane landed, we were back in Little Rock. On the drive back to our hometown we stopped and purchased a small three-wheeler for Angela. In our neighborhood, all the children rode around on their bicycles and Angela could not. She could not breathe well enough to do that. Most of the time, her friends would go to other friends' houses to play. When we got Angela the three-wheeler she could go where all of the other kids went. Now she didn't feel so left out. She even built a ramp to jump with her three-wheeler.

It was so wonderful to see her so happy. Not long after that she became very ill. I remember her coming to me and saying she did not feel well. It was in the spring and was still cool outside. We placed a blanket on the floor and turned the heater fan on and lay down on the floor to keep her warm. She struggled to breathe all night long.

Daniel Hugh Kelly had given Angela his personal telephone number so I called him to tell him she was in the hospital. The night before she died the scene that we saw Brian Keith and Daniel filming was on TV. We all watched. We also noticed the scene where Daniel's ring was missing from his finger. It made Angela smile that he cared so much to give her that ring.

I took her to the doctor the next morning and the outlook was bleak, but the doctor said she could go home with us. That night she became too ill to recover and we knew the end was near.

I called Daniel and left a message about Angela being very ill. She died the following day. Daniel returned my call the day of Angela's funeral. We talked for an hour. He was such a wonderful man. I thanked him for being so kind and caring.

The Bethesda, Maryland hospital finally called on the day of her funeral to talk to me about Angela's heart and lung transplant. I was too upset to even talk to them. I thanked them kindly, but told them it was too late. She had died.

Angela was buried with the ring Daniel Hugh Kelly placed on her finger.

By Christy, Mother of Angela

JIMMY (Dream — To meet David Hassellhoff)
By V. O'C. Davis

Jimmy meets his favorite actor
David Hassellhoff

Like many times in the past, on this day, I was visiting with the parents and a patient who had already had a dream granted. As I walked down the hallway at the local children's hospital, the head of the oncology unit caught up with me and pulled me over to the side and said that we needed to talk. He came to me with a request for another child to have a dream granted. He told me about a little boy, five years old who was diagnosed with ALL (a type of leukemia), and he was not doing well. The treatments of chemotherapy and radiation were not working as well as they thought it would. He was very ill and was not bouncing back after the last treatments. They were afraid they were losing him. The oncologist thought that this child needed a boost to help with his attitude.

We both believed that having a positive attitude was the key to getting better even if it is only for a little while. Maybe we were buying the patients just a little more time to spend with their families and sometimes even a new start free from illness. Over the years, there were many patients the doctors had almost given up on. Then the patient miraculously would go into remission after a dream was granted for them.

The oncologist told me what room Jimmy was in. He had already told the parents that he would talk to me about Jimmy getting a dream. When my business was finished with the current patient I was visiting, I went down to Jimmy's room and knocked on the door. Both of Jimmy's parents were there. I asked them to please come down to the lobby on that same floor where we could talk openly.

I explained to the parents that Jimmy's oncologist had contacted me about a dream for Jimmy. I asked if they knew what Jimmy would ask for. They immediately told me that he idolized David Hassellhoff from the TV series of "The Knight Rider". My stomach turned upside down! It had not been but a couple of months ago when Brian Keith had been so horrible to a dream child.

As I told them the normal procedures of granting a dream, I gave them the legal papers to be signed. I asked that they sit down with Jimmy's doctors for a discussion on this matter and have the doctors sign the physician's portion. They had no problems with signing the paperwork and knew that since the doctor recommended our organization, he would probably have no problem signing it either.

I commented that when a patient asked to meet a celebrity, we could not make promises that involved claiming what a celebrity will do. In fact, we have recently learned that we <u>do not</u> have control over what another person will or will not do. Sometimes celebrities might agree to meet a child and then when the meeting is happening, they might be having a bad day and not be so nice. All I could do was try to see if Mr. Hassellhoff would be available and was willing to meet Jimmy. What happened during the meeting was completely out of our control. We will usually only ask for them to meet the child for a few minutes. What they do after that is totally up to the celebrity.

If the family was willing to go forward with such a meeting, it would be their own decision. We then went in to talk to Jimmy. I asked him, "Jimmy, if you could have anything that you wanted, more than anything else what would that be?" He did not blink an eye! He sat up in his hospital bed and blurted out, "I want to go see The Knight Rider and his car!" I basically told him the same as I had told his parents, I would try to see what I could do but I could not make any promises. Just the thought that this might be possible, Jimmy was already perking up.

The following day, I decided to make a call to The William Morris Agency first. It was only two months ago, when the agent had said, "I would like to try to make up for what Brian Keith did. We are not all like that! If you ever need a child to meet another celebrity, just call me and I will be happy to assist you! If we do not have them as a client, that is okay, too. We will do whatever is neces- sary to find the celebrity for you if it is possible." Now I was holding him to his every word. I just hoped that he remembered what he had said to me!

I can tell you that when I called him, he <u>did</u> remember and he was glad to assist us! He knew exactly where to find Mr. Hassellhoff and set up a phone call for me to talk to him directly. This agent was "heaven sent"! I was talking to David Hassellhoff on that same day. He said he was exceptionally pleased that a child wanted to meet him. He would be taping a show around the same time as Jimmy and his family could come. (The oncologist had given me a timetable that I could follow for Jimmy's hospitalization and treatments, his "protocol".) Okay, now everything was set up for two weeks from today. Mr. Hassellhoff was so gracious on the phone. I just hoped that he was the same when Jimmy got there!

I called the travel agency (that works with our organization) and set up the arrangements for the airlines, car rental, hotel, etc. By the following day, all arrangements were finalized. I called the family and gave them the good news and confirmed those dates. They were elated!

Those two weeks flew by very quickly. I met the family at the airport and made sure all last minute plans were being followed. Jimmy was so cute. He was so happy and so full of energy! He was wearing a t-shirt that had his name on it and it also said, "Knight Rider, Here I Come!" While we were waiting for the boarding to begin, around 30 people gathered around the family and were all wishing them well on their trip. Before they boarded, I asked that they please call me to tell me how things went with the meeting of David Hassellhoff.

I received that call the following evening. I was pleased that it was Jimmy that I spoke with first. He was so excited and just had to tell me every detail of the day's events. He was talking very fast because he had so much to say. I laughed because he was beyond happy! He almost talked my ear off! His mom got on the phone when he was finished talking and we laughed together at the excitement of her child.

She said that everything was great! Mr. Hasellhoff spent the entire afternoon with them in between tapings of the TV series. He also took Jimmy for a ride in the famous Knight Rider Car. Jimmy's parents even took photos of the two in the car and gave me one later on. Mr. Hassellhoff showed them all of the different things involved with the making of the series, the cameras, the "talking computer" in the car and basically everything that he thought Jimmy would be interested in. They were even invited to come back the next day to watch more of the taping. "Awesome!" I was so pleased that everything went so well.

They did other activities while they were in California and never had a single problem on the entire trip. I had been praying that no problems would occur on their trip and God had answered my prayers. They made it home safely without incident.

The family said that Mr. Hassellhoff was the same kind, thoughtful person that he portrayed on the series. Maybe even kinder than that! David Hassellhoff was so wonderful and went out of his way to be extra kind to them. He is so very much appreciated for his kindness and willingness to take time from his busy schedule to spend time with Jimmy and his family. That time meant more than he will ever know.

We will never forget the time spent and kindness of The William Morris Agency, either. After this dream was completed, they helped us out time and time again to find celebrities. Even when the clients belonged to other agencies, they still helped us. Never did they complain that I called too much, or that they were too busy to bother with us. Never did they utter one unkind word to us. Everything from them was on a positive note. What a pleasure it was to find such wonderful caring people in basically an unkind environment. I will never forget how kind they were and can never thank them enough for helping us grant the wishes of so many deserving children over the many years of our relationship.

When Jimmy came back home and got back into his normal routine, he did much better with his treatments. He was on a high that wouldn't end! He breezed through his treatments with great results and soon went into remission.

This was the ultimate goal of our organization. We wanted the patients' attitudes to improve so that their treatments would work better. Usually after the patients received something they were longing for, sometimes beyond the parents' reach, they would feel much better and work harder to survive their illnesses.

As we have said many times already, without the assistance of others, there would have been no organization nor would so many well deserving children have had their dreams granted. We want to thank each person who had a hand in granting these dreams, from the people who raised the funds to pay for these dreams, to the volunteers who worked so very hard to see these dreams become a reality, to the travel agencies who helped us get these children to their destinies, and to the celebrities and theme parks that saw these children and treated them like "Kings" and "Queens". We want to thank each and every one of you for helping to make the difference in these children's lives.

By V. O'C. Davis

DANIELLE (Dream — To meet "New Kids on the Block")
"What does it mean to have a normal life?"
By Kathy, Mother of Danielle

Danielle is a beautiful blonde haired, blue-eyed bundle of joy. When she was two years and two months old our world, as we knew it had turned upside down. I took her to our family doctor in our hometown because I thought she was breaking out with the measles. She was also very tired and cranky; her skin was pale and covered with bruises. The doctor took one look at her and ordered blood work. As we sat in his office, I knew something must be terribly wrong. He came back in the examining room and told me that he thought she had acute leukemia. I never suspected leukemia. That was the last thing I would have suspected. I was quite stunned. I still don't remember how I drove home that day. I felt as if I had just been run over by a Mac Truck.

Our local doctor told us not to wait but to get her to a specialist right away. He suggested we take her to a children's hospital located in our state. Danielle's hemoglobin was low, and she needed a blood transfusion quickly. My husband and I headed for the children's hospital about 5:00 p. m. late that same afternoon. What should have been a two and a half hour trip somehow actually took us four hours. I don't even remember why. We were both dazed and numb. All I could think about was this horrible thing we were facing. In our minds, it had to be a mistake. Our daughter was just a tiny two year old baby and could not possibly have cancer!

The date was April 12, 1989. We arrived at the hospital and were overwhelmed at the sight of the building. It was huge compared to our little hometown hospital. Upon our arrival, we were immediately whisked away to a room and the tests began. I don't think I slept all night. I felt like I was having a bad dream.

The next morning we met the main hematology and oncology doctors. Much was happening all at once. The conferences, the talks, the language was all so foreign. We were told that Danielle's chances were good. The cancer had not invaded her spinal fluid. They put a port in her chest and started chemotherapy. Everything was supposed to be fine except that about two weeks before, Danielle had been exposed to the chicken pox. They explained that this made the situation life threatening. After the first treatment we prepared to go home for a short while, but something suddenly went wrong. Danielle broke out! Our worst fear was now a reality.

The doctors started her on antibiotics but that night her health deteriorated. Before we could blink an eye, doctors and nurses were everywhere. She started bleeding internally and couldn't get a breath. I don't even know what all was wrong with her. They ended up moving her to ICU. She was somewhat comatose for days. I am still haunted by the sounds of all of the machines that she was hooked up to. I kept thinking, "This was not supposed to happen!" All I could think about was Danielle. Those next two weeks were all a blur. Danielle somehow found the strength to pull through and became stronger. She would continue to amaze and astonish her caregivers with her will to live.

Danielle spent many nights and days at that hospital — too many to count! Some days we were out of our minds with worry. Danielle was at death's door more than just that once. We had missed holidays and other special events during that long period. I didn't get angry though. That seems to be such a small price to pay for the life of my precious child.

We were in the hospital during her third birthday. Danielle was surprised by the party that the nurses gave her and especially by one nurse's gift. As the present was given to Danielle, her face lit up.

It was a videotape of the singing group "New Kids on the Block". The nurse saw her excitement at the sheer mention of this new rock group and watched Danielle as she viewed the tape. Because of the reaction Danielle had toward the rock group, the nurse had a great idea. She left Danielle's room and called a dream-making group to see if it was possible to get Danielle to meet the rock group. "New Kids on the Block" was coming to town in a matter of a few days and maybe Danielle could get a chance to see them at the concert.

Only a few days passed and all arrangements were set up not only for Danielle to meet the group, but there were back stage passes for her and her dad. She was going to meet each one of them! Danielle was so thrilled! Another female cancer patient who was 15 years old was being treated at the same hospital. Her family was in contact with the same dream-making group, and she was set to go meet "New Kids on the Block" at the same time.

That exciting day finally came. Danielle acted like a teenager, so excited! Her goal was to get a kiss from Donny Wahlberg. Before the concert even began, each one of the band members of "New Kids on the Block" visited with both girls. Each member of the group was so very polite and seemed so genuinely caring. The visit went well and the two girls even got their photos made with the group. Danielle even got a photo of Donny kissing her! WOW!! Afterward, the girls and their families were seated outside for the concert.

Even though Danielle was just three years old at the time, she will always remember that night. She still loves to show her "New Kids on the Block" photos to anyone who will sit still and look at them. Though she didn't understand why she was so privileged to have this event take place, she will cherish it for life as long or short as hers may be.

The months that followed were a blur of infections and other serious problems, such as low blood counts, antibiotics, and trips to the hospital. Danielle's chemotherapy was altered and she was proving once again that she was not a normal kid with cancer. She was still fighting for life and trying to enjoy being a kid. Though she doesn't understand why her mom sometimes won't let her play outside with other children or let her go to McDonald's and "eat inside", she still loves life and acts quite normal for her circumstances.

Four years have passed and she finished her chemotherapy. People say to us, "And now what?" Many people have asked us, "Do you now resume a normal life?" and "Will the nightmare finally be over?" All I can say is that we are doing very well right now "today", and that is what matters. For a while, I thought that a normal life for us would mean "cancer". This word forever forged into our brains and in our memories.

No, we won't ever have the normal life the way that most people think; the life "before cancer", but we are having one now. We are enjoying every minute with our daughter and loving life just as she does. This is our normal life and we are thankful for every day.

By Kathy, Mother of Danielle

CANDACE (Dream—To meet "New Kids on the Block")
By Karen, Mother of Candace

Candace meets "New Kids on the Block"

Our story begins around the time of Candy's 15th birthday. For several weeks prior to this, she had been saying that her abdomen hurt. She was not "sick", and the pain was not severe, and she was able to do all of the normal activities. At the point of her running a slight fever, we took her to the local doctor. She diagnosed and treated Candy for a bladder infection. After all of the prescribed medications were finished the fever disappeared, and the pain subsided but her abdomen still seemed to be swollen. Within a few weeks, she told me that she could barely button her jeans. She asked me to feel of her abdomen. When I reached down and felt how hard it was, I immediately thought that she had a tumor. We took her back to the same doctor the following day.

After an exam, the doctor told us that Candy had a pelvic mass that seemed to be coming from her ovary. The doctor ordered an ultrasound from our local hospital. However, this was Friday, and we had to wait until Monday for the test to be taken.

On Monday, it was Candy's 15th birthday. She had a birthday celebration with some friends on Saturday night and family members on Sunday night. Still, our weekend was very tense.

After the tests were done on Monday, the results came back and showed that the mass was solid. The doctor told us that a solid tumor is usually malignant. At that point I didn't think we had heard her correctly, but I am sure that I saw tears in her eyes as she spoke. She referred us to a specialist at the university hospital who saw Candy the following day.

The specialist examined Candy and told us that there was a 75% chance that this was a malignant tumor. My husband and I were there with Candy and the specialist at the time. I am not sure what I would have done if my husband had not been there by my side throughout this day. We were still just newlyweds trying to adjust to being a "step-family".

While we were at the hospital, more tests were done including another ultrasound and an MRI. The specialist came back and had us admit Candy into the hospital. They scheduled her for surgery the next morning. It was very hard to leave her in that hospital and go home for the night. We lived two hours away. Responsibilities took us home for the night as we had much to rearrange to prepare for the upcoming days. Our lives were about to change drastically.

The next morning was very hard for everyone. None of us had ever dealt with surgeries of any kind before now. When the doctors tried to prepare us for what lay ahead of us, it was very frightening. We knew that we had to put our trust and faith in God.

It seemed to have taken forever for the surgery to be over. We waited for about five hours. The doctors came out and gave us the bad news that the tumor was malignant. I guess that we already knew this, but it was so hard to hear it out loud. I thought that I had prepared myself for this. He said the tumor was the size of a football, and he had removed a couple of lymph nodes, as well. He said he removed her right ovary and fallopian tube. The left ovary, fallopian tube, and uterus were all okay, and the tumor had not yet reached them. He explained that since the tumor had invaded a few lymph nodes, follow up chemotherapy was recommended.

Having to tell Candy that she had cancer was so stressful and frightful. I really didn't know how I should tell her. She was too groggy that night to comprehend anything, so I waited until the next morning. Here is another night that I must leave her all alone in the hospital and go home. It was even harder for me to leave tonight than it was the night before. I cried all the way home and then cried myself to sleep.

The next morning, I was standing over Candy when she asked me if it was cancer. I told her that it was. Telling her was not as hard as I had made it out to be. She was so brave with no tears and no hysterics. When she asked if she would lose her hair from the chemotherapy, I said "Probably". She just calmly said that if it made her better then it would be okay with her.

Since she is so young, strong and healthy, she recovered quickly from the surgery. She went back to school as soon as the doctors said she could. We live in a small town and her school was just wonderful throughout all of this! The teachers and students were so helpful. Candy was not supposed to lift anything heavy for a while, so the teacher's had extra books for Candy at school. We also had a set at home. A couple of strong young men volunteered to be her bodyguards in the halls at school to prevent any accidental harm.

Candy was scheduled to start chemotherapy treatments several weeks after the surgery. The protocol was for her to receive chemo over a period of the next five months, five days at a time, three weeks in between treatments. We had to take her to a children's hospital for the chemo treatments in the same city as the university (teaching) hospital two hours from our hometown. Her first week of chemo seemed to go pretty well. She did get sick and very weak, but by the end of that first week she came out of it feeling okay.

By the weekend, things changed. She started vomiting constantly and having much pain. At first, the doctors, my husband, and I thought that it was the chemotherapy making her sick, but she wasn't getting better. We had to take her to the hospital through the emergency room. She was immediately admitted. They quickly discovered that Candy had a bowel obstruction caused from scar tissue related to the recent surgery. It had only been one month since her surgery, and here we are again. "What could possibly happen next?" we thought. We barely get over one hurtle, and there is another one waiting to be dealt with.

With everything that Candy should be thinking about, there was only the one thought in the forefront of her mind. Here she was sick again, and she was going to miss the "New Kids on the Block" concert coming to town! She had bought the tickets months in advance, and now she was going to miss them!

She had to have emergency surgery to correct the blockage. Her surgery was successful and quick compared to the last one. The concert was coming up in one week and her doctors did not think it was wise to allow her to go. This is when I called the dream-making group for help. Sure enough, they talked Candy's doctors into letting her go, arranged for back stage passes, and great seats for the concert!

It was right about now when she started losing her hair. While she was still in the hospital, we had to quickly rush around and find a scarf and a hat for her to wear to the concert. We had to work fast! Only days remained before her visit with the rock group. I do not think that anything could have stopped her from going to that concert, and getting to actually meet them was beyond her comprehension.

Only three days before the main event, Candy was released from the hospital. She had to have been the happiest girl on the face of this earth! To see her excitement before and during the night of the event was something we will never forget. To look at her now, you would have never guessed that she had two surgeries and just walked out of the hospital. She got to meet several of the members of "New Kids on the Block" while she was backstage and got to take photos, too. To top off the night of her life, she got to meet the very one she wanted to meet....Jordan!

To be able to have this dream at this time was probably the highest point of her young life. After this, she had a wonderful and positive attitude for the rest of her cancer treatments.

Now it has been more than four years since Candy's last chemo-therapy and she is doing very well, leading a busy life of an 11th grader. She is very active in school, taking difficult subjects and getting excellent grades. She also plays basketball and takes dancing lessons. Every time we go back to the doctor for a check up and hear the good news that she is still doing well, I just want to shout it from the rooftops!!

By Karen, Mother of Candace

TIMMY (Dream—Wanted a Telephone Call from Jerry Lewis / Then a Flight in a Helicopter)
By a Longtime Volunteer

A phone call came into our office from Timothy's mother. She had read about our organization in the statewide newspaper. We had just granted 17 children with their dreams in the last 28 days. And we were trying to raise enough money to grant another dream of a cancer patient who needed to leave on his trip within the next four days.

Timothy's mom told us that her nine year old son had a devastating form of muscular dystrophy, was hospitalized, and was not doing very well. I made an appointment to meet with her and her son for the following morning. Meanwhile, I spoke with Timmy's physician, and he confirmed Timmy's diagnosis and prognosis which was not good.

The following morning, I arrived to meet with Timmy and his mom. Timmy was very ill and was not able to move around very much due to the tremendous pain he was having. When I asked him what he wanted to do for his dream, he already had one in mind. He dreamed of talking to Jerry Lewis some day because he said that was his favorite movie star of all times. Timmy bragged he was "one of Jerry's kids" to everyone he met. His mom said Timmy has always made sure that everyone knew he was very proud to be one of Jerry's kids. He would say that Jerry loved all of his special kids, and Jerry loved him, too! Timmy told me every year he watched Jerry Lewis on the telethon that raised money for all of "his kids" with muscular dystrophy. Timmy's doctors had already told his mother that travel was out of the question. Timmy thought since he couldn't actually go to meet Jerry Lewis, the next best thing was to get a phone call from him.

That seemed like such a simple request to me. I had his mother fill out the paperwork, go down to the doctor's office, and get him to sign the papers, too. By the time she came back to the room, Timmy and I seemed like old friends. He was a talker! He was a pleasant child but I could see he was hiding the amount of pain that he was having. The nurses on that floor said he was a "real trooper" when it came to his therapy. He did not complain. He just smiled and talked to everyone.

I returned to my office and began making phone calls to try to run down the information on Jerry Lewis. I found Mr. Lewis' agent, but he said Jerry was unreachable, and he could not assist me any further. I called someone who owed me a favor. They helped me reach another person who told me that the way to find Jerry Lewis was through his best friend, Ed McMahon. (Mr. McMahon was on television every weeknight on the Tonight Show with Johnny Carson.) I was given his home phone number and location, so I called him.

Mr. McMahon answered his own phone! I first apologized for calling him at home and then began to explain my situation. I told him what had happened up to this point and asked for his assistance in locating Mr. Lewis. He was so very kind to me. It didn't even seem to bother him that I had called him at home. He told me Jerry had just gotten married two weeks ago and was now in France. I pleaded with him to call Mr. Lewis and see if it was possible for him to call this child. Mr. Lewis would only have to talk to him for just a few minutes. I would be happy to pay for the phone call. Mr. McMahon said he thought Mr. Lewis would oblige with no problem. I gave Mr. McMahon my phone number to call me after he had spoken with Mr. Lewis. I had also given him the phone number to Timmy's hospital room just in case Mr. Lewis wanted to call right away.

About 45 minutes later, Mr. McMahon called me back. He was sorry to have to tell me Mr. Lewis said "No". He did not wish to be disturbed while he was away. I understood that Mr. Lewis was on his honeymoon and did not want to be bothered by anyone. On the other hand, he could have tried to make another date to call the child when he returned. Mr. McMahon regretted that Mr. Lewis had not been very kind about the situation. I asked for Mr. McMahon to please notify me when Mr. Lewis was back in the country, and we would try again then. He agreed to call me then.

I called Timmy's mom and asked her to meet me in Timmy's room. When we entered his room, I told Timmy Mr. Lewis was out of the country because he had just gotten married and was on his honeymoon with his new wife. We did not know how long he would be gone. I asked him if he wanted to wait for Mr. Lewis to come back in the country or was there anything else he would like as a dream to replace the call. He definitely wanted to wait. He didn't care how long it would take. This is really all he has ever wanted since the first time he saw Jerry Lewis on a telethon. After all, he said, "I am Jerry's kid!" It was about one month later when Mr. McMahon called me. Jerry Lewis was back, and now was a good time for me to call Mr. Lewis' agent to see about setting up a call to this child. When I reached the agent, he told me that Mr. Lewis was not going to ever make a call to any child. He said that I could quit calling because it was over. He said, "The answer is no!"

I made one last call to Mr. McMahon thanking him for his kindness and apologized for bring him into this. In return, he said if I ever needed help finding any other famous people, to please call him again. I was pleasantly surprised and most grateful. What a wonderful person he was to offer his assistance! Mr. Ed McMahon was a perfect gentleman and I will always hold a deep respect for him. I could tell he cared very strongly about helping others. I wish everyone could have that special quality in his or her personalities. The world would surely be a brighter and more peaceful place.

Now I had to go back to this child and tell him what had happened. I met his mother outside of the hospital room and told her what had taken place. She was furious! She said she would have to tell her son Jerry really did not care about him. Mr. Lewis was too wrapped up in his own life to take time out to even place a call to a very ill child. She said she was going to tell Timmy to stop calling himself "Jerry's kid". I talked her into letting us tell Timmy gently. I didn't want this to affect his therapy or his attitude. I asked her to let me talk to him and see if there was anything else that he might want for a dream other than getting that phone call.

When Timmy heard that Jerry could not talk to him on the phone, he said, "Let me call his agent and I will ask him to get in touch with Jerry. If he knows that one of "his kids" is calling, he will do it!" I tried to tell him as kindly as I could that Jerry has refused to talk to anyone. Timmy started crying.

I felt so bad for him. Even though I could understand why Mr. Lewis did not want to have an intrusion while he was on his honeymoon, I could not understand why he could not make plans for later to pick up the phone and just call Timmy to say hello. The longer that I watched Timmy cry the angrier I got with Jerry Lewis! I wish he could see how hurt Timmy was. Timmy did not even know Mr. Lewis was not nice about the situation. How much trouble could a phone call be? If he really cared about these kids as he claimed, he would have been happy to call and just say hello.

That experience 21 years ago broke me from ever watching that telethon again. I just could not take looking at him acting as if he cared about those children. Later, I found out that he was being paid approximately one million each year to do the telethon. Most people thought he was doing this as a volunteer. People need to know the truth sometimes, even if it hurts.

It took a couple of weeks for Timmy to calm down and get back into his routine of therapy. I again visited him and asked him to think about doing something else for a dream. His doctor talked with him a lot during those two weeks. I finally received a call from Timmy's mom and she said he was ready to ask for something else. I dropped everything I was doing at the time and went up to talk to him.

Well, he decided he would like to fly in a helicopter! When he told me, I was worried about where we were going to find one. I knew that one of the TV stations had one and the police department had two, but the liability was going to be a problem. I called them anyway just to check. Both said, "No way!" for the reasons that I just stated. The police department gave me a person to call at the airbase located just outside of town.

When I called the airbase, I went into the whole story of Timmy and Jerry Lewis, the TV station and the police department rejections, and told them that they were pretty much our last hope. By the time I had finished telling them everything, they agreed to help us get Timmy airborne. We made all of the arrangements with the physicians, the hospital, and the airbase. Finally Timmy got to go up in the helicopter. They took him a long way — all over the center of the state, showing him the mountains, the river, the lakes, the city, and the airbase. He was thrilled! He finally got a wish granted!

The gracious people at the airbase were so wonderful to Timmy. How were we ever going to thank them? This meant everything to Timmy and his mother. Later, Timmy told me that going up in the helicopter was "way more fun" that getting a phone call, but deep down inside I could still see the pain from the rejection.

For most of Timmy's remaining life, he spent at the hospital. We lost him about ten months after our initial request for that phone call. Timmy was a very special and unique child. I will always remember him for his laughter and his amazing smile.

By a Longtime Volunteer

Chapter III.

As you will see, many of these families live from one crisis to another. Most of the time, they will finally get a break and their lives turn around. Others will never get any better until they change the way they live. This chapter is devoted to documenting the interesting and unusual events surrounding some of these patients and their families.

RAY (Dream—To go to Disney World in Florida)
By a Friend and a Volunteer

Our organization was swamped with 28 requests for dreams all at once. All of the requests came within a two week period from around the entire state. Ray was number 18 (of those 28 children) at the time. Since his case was an emergency, we had to move him up to the head of the list. While we were working on his dream, we did not forget the others. It sometimes took weeks to make the arrangements for most non-emergency trips, and we could work within the time frame that the patients' doctors gave us to use.

Ray was 12 years old and was diagnosed with a cancerous brain tumor. His neurologists gave us a window of four days to have him on his way to Florida. That did not give us much time to find the money to send him on a dream, but we set it up quickly and promised the travel agency we would pay them as soon as the money came in from donations.

Our funds had been depleted. We were desperate to find the funds needed for all of these dreams, but especially for Ray's dream first. At times, this job could be very stressful from the fear of letting a sick child down. But just like this time, we had to learn to take those challenges one at a time and have faith that God would see us through. He always would come through by sending us a donor or donors just in the nick of time. As for the 28 pending dreams; every one of them was helped in a timely manner. The funds seemed to always come in right when it was time to pay. In the end, though, everything always worked out for us with His help. I believe that God touched the right people at the right times to take care of these very needy children.

In all of the years that I was a volunteer, there was never a child turned down. No matter how many dream requests came in, the money would soon follow just in time to pay for what we had already charged to our credit cards or ordered through the travel agencies. I had approximately 12 to 15 speaking engagements per month which kept us fresh in the minds of all who listened. We also had TV and radio PSAs (commercials) that also reminded the public that money was always needed for dreams. Throughout our state, we had over 400 volunteers out there raising money for these dreams. I do not think we could have made it without their assistance. I believe that God blessed each of them for their efforts and their support. We are all instruments in God's plans for these children and their families.

Like clockwork, Ray and his mother were on their way to Florida on time. While they were there they visited Disney World, Sea World, the Epcot Center, and went to see the ocean. They had a wonderful trip to remember the "good times," because for Ray, his mother and his older sister, the next several years of their lives would become a nightmare that seemed to never end.

Just to give you some of the background of their lives to this point, Ray's mother and father had divorced several years before. The dad actually left them (Ray's mom, Ray and his older sister) to marry another woman. He only moved to the next town, but he had three more children with his new wife. He was not paying child support for his first family even though Ray's life consisted of doctors, hospitals, surgeries, and even worse things to come. Ray's mom struggled to work at a job and take care of Ray and his sister. The dad was not even visiting or calling Ray during this life crisis.

As soon as Ray returned from his trip, he went back into the hospital because the tumor was growing again. Many complications arose from the new growth. It soon became necessary to have the surgical procedure to cut away some of the tumor. The surgeons were not able to remove the entire tumor for fear of accidentally hitting his spinal cord and causing permanent paralysis.

By the time Ray was 13 years old, he had been in and out of the hospital for over a year. He had dropped out of school and had to adjust to a whole new life. Not having his father around just made things worse for him. This was the time when he needed his father the most. It was hard enough just being a teenager. Ray had to endure so much more pain mentally and physically, since his father would have nothing to do with him. My family became very close to them; we hoped that our love and assistance would ease some of their pain from the many trials yet to come.

Ray and his mom spent much of their time in our home, and we spent a lot of time in their home, as well. His mother was so wonderful to him. She helped him in every way possible. She had to be mom and dad and still had to bring in an income for them to survive. Even his older sister went to a job after school to help with the bills.

Since entering his teen years, Ray decided that he wanted to become more involved in making decisions that pertained to his illness. The neurologists finally had to sit him and his mom down and tell them it was time to decide whether Ray was going to go through with another surgery. The tumor was still growing and the radiation was not doing any good. The draw back was they could possibly hit the spinal cord while removing it. This was a huge decision that had to be made quickly.

Ray and his mom talked about it for a week, and he said this was his decision to make since it was his life. Ray was ready to commit to the surgery. I remember visiting them the day before he went back to the hospital for the surgery. He was determined to go through with it because if they got the entire tumor, he could be cancer free and could then move on with his life. He was ready for this to be "over". His mother was not 100% sure she wanted him to go through with the surgery, but he wouldn't listen to anything she had to say on the matter. This was overwhelming to both of them. While I was visiting before his surgery, Ray didn't even want to discuss it any more. He had made up his mind. It was going to happen and he was ready.

The surgery took around five hours. We rotated waiting in the surgery waiting room and walking around outside. Finally the neurosurgeon came out to talk to us. The worst thing that could happen

<u>did</u> happen! The tumor was wrapped around the spinal cord at the base of his skull. They wouldn't know for sure if it damaged the spinal cord until after Ray woke up.

After Ray was recovering, they took him back to his hospital room. The doctor came in and examined him. Ray was unable to move anything but his head. He would be paralyzed from his neck down for the remaining years of his life. What a low blow! It was hard to focus on the future for them right now. Their entire lives would be turned upside down yet again! There is not much anyone can say or do during situations like this. The best one can do is to be there for support, listen to them, be a friend, and pray for them.

Over the next few years, Ray and his mom could not agree on anything. Remember that Ray was still a teenager! He went through a couple of years telling his mother that all of this was her fault. He would say it was because of her genes that he got cancer, and it was her fault that he had the surgery that made him paralyzed. He said very deep, hurtful things to her almost daily. He was so angry and felt as if he had to blame someone. She was the one who caught most of the flack. How could he blame his dad when his dad was never around?

I deeply admired his mom for all she endured through those years. I just don't think I could have been as strong as her. She would have to fight SSI for Ray's every need, and it was still never enough to take care of him. He had to have therapy three times a week and a wheelchair to be mobile, depending on his mom to push him around. She had to hand feed him, lift him in and out of the wheelchair, and bathe him with no outside assistance. Ray had become quite heavy during his illness and was virtually helpless without her.

She still managed to get him whatever he needed medically and physically, but there was always more that was needed. Still, she wasn't getting child support which would have taken some of the burden off of her. I told her many times to get a lawyer and sue him for child support and back support, but she would just say, "Well, if his dad ever decided to start seeing Ray, I don't want to rock the boat and make him mad." I don't know how she was able to keep going as she did. I knew she was exhausted from lack of sleep. She managed to stay strong-willed, but she struggled every step of the way. I do know that she had a very strong faith in God and believed in prayer. I think that was the only thing that kept her going.

There were many times that his mom would call me and say that she needed help talking to Ray. He just would not listen to reason coming from her. I would go over there and do my best to talk to him. Some days I could get through to him and other days no one could get through to him. My family would visit them often and we tried to help out whenever possible. She always thanked us and I know she appreciated us. She and I became very good friends.

When Ray was around 16, he decided that he would like to have a computer. We helped him find someone who would get it for him. We had to special order pieces to go on it to help him to move the mouse without his hands. We bought him games to play on the computer first. After a while, he became excellent with it. Later on, through therapy he was able to barely move a couple of fingers on his right side. We got him another type of mouse that made it easier for him to use.

Finally, I had talked her into going after Ray's dad for support. Her lawyer filed, and it wasn't long until dear ole dad had to start paying for Ray's child support and arrearages. She was finally able to do more for Ray.

Things around the house started leveling off and running smoother for them. Ray and his mom became closer. Hallelujah! It was about time that Ray straightened up. The fruits of his mom's endurance and efforts were now blooming into a more fulfilling life for both of them.

Within one year, Ray turned 17. He decided that he could use the computer for finishing high school. This was when his life started turning around for him. He took all of the courses over a couple years and got his diploma. We were all so proud of him!

His mother had not really had a life of her own over the last five years because she was consumed in Ray's well being. Now she finally started trying to have a life of her own. She started dating a wonderful man. She dated him for over a year before they decided to take that next step of marriage. Ray and his mother seemed to be very happy with the new arrangements of bringing a new person into their lives, and this man seemed genuinely interested in sharing their lives together. I was very happy for them.

After the marriage was only six months old, her husband was driving home from work and had an accident that almost took his life. He was driving behind a logging truck that had a huge load of logs. As they came upon an underpass, the truck driver did not see the height limit. He kept going under the bridge without stopping. The logs that were on the very top of the load hit the side of the overhead bridge, knocking them backwards, right through her husband's windshield. One of the logs hit him square in the face and head almost completely removed his face. It was a miracle that he was alive! He was hospitalized for months and had to undergo several surgeries to repair the damage to his face. Now she had Ray and her new husband to care for. She just didn't seem to get a break from the hard times.

Her husband came home from the hospital, and they retained an attorney for the lawsuit against the logging company. Months and months went by. As far as she knew, the marriage was doing fine and her husband seemed as normal as possible after the surgeries. Finally, it was time for their day in court. They walked out of the courthouse knowing that the logging company would pay them a hefty settlement; enough to pay all of the medical bills and leave them comfortable for a long time. They could finally have a home of their own and not have to pay rent anymore! She could finally get rid of her 14 year old car and get a decent one. After what they had been through, this seemed to be a blessing for all of them.

The day came when her husband had to go down to the attorney's office to pick up the check from the settlement. She waited and waited, but he did not come home. She called the attorney's office only to learn that her husband had already picked up the check and left hours ago. He did not come home at all that night. The following day, he came in and told her that he was packing and moving out. There was no fighting before hand and no warning that he was even thinking of leaving. He gave her no reason for moving out and he would not even talk to her about it.

Two weeks had gone by before I heard from her. She was crying as she told me what had happened. She said that he cleaned out what money was in the joint banking accounts. He did not even leave her money for food, rent, or anything! I went to the grocery store and then on over to their house. I tried to pick up food that they could live on at least for a little while. I tried to comfort them as much as I could. I thought surely he would at least come by and give her some money until she could find a job, but he never ever came back to help out. He just disappeared with every bit of money that they had. What a greedy soul!

How selfish can one person be? It just never ceases to amaze me what some people will do when it comes to greed! It is beyond belief that a person could stoop so low. This man cared nothing about Ray or his mother. It did not seem to even bother him that he left them without food, knowing that Ray was completely depending on them for everything. It was some months later that Ray's mom heard from her husband. He wanted a divorce and he gave no explanations of his past actions.

By this time, Ray had completed his GED and had decided to go on to college. He did not let anyone sidetrack him. There was a college right there in the city, but he was unable to get from class to class without assistance. His mother was so devoted to Ray that she agreed to wheel him around campus in and out of classes. They signed Ray up right before the semester began.

After a few weeks of classes, his mom said that if she had to be with him during classes to assist him with his papers, books, wheelchair, etc., she might as well sign up and take the same classes and get credit for it. She had to be there anyway!

Both of them went to college for the next four years, putting everything else in their lives on hold. Their faith had brought them a long way and the trials and hardships were mostly behind them. The day came when they graduated from college together. When the President of the college called their names to walk up to receive their diplomas, Ray's mom pushed Ray in the wheelchair across the stage as the entire stadium crowd stood up and clapped for them. The TV stations even covered that wonderful moment and broadcast it over and over.

Everyone who knew them was so very proud of them. What they had gone through to get to this point was such a great struggle. She said when they crossed that stage it felt as if they were walking into another life. Doors would be opening for both of them above and beyond anything that they could have ever dreamed.

Ray soon started his own internet company and is becoming quite a lucrative businessman. He is now 32 years old and has never had a reoccurrence of cancer. He now has 65% use both hands, but is still unable to walk. He is a brilliant young man and I am so proud of him.

His mom got a new job and still had time to help Ray. Through her church, she met and married a wonderful man who also had a very strong faith in God. After three years of marriage they took a giant step and moved to another state. I have received two letters from them and all is well. She deserves everything good that life can give because for her entire life, everyone else had always come first. For the first time in 20 years, she now has someone willing to take care of her and love her. I am so very happy for her. No one deserves it more!

By a Friend and a Volunteer

JOHNNY (Dream—To go to Disney World)
By Terry, Mother of Johnny

Johnny & Mom on their way to Florida

Family life as we knew it would change forever starting on October 27, 1983. My husband had left us without warning. My brother, my eight year old son Johnny, and I were traveling from one state to another to start a new life when we had a car accident. Our car flipped end over end five times before coming to a stop. I was not wearing my seat belt and was thrown from the car while Johnny and his uncle remained inside the car. Johnny's face was injured and he was bleeding from around his mouth. His face was black and blue immediately after the impact, but with no major injuries. Luckily, my brother was uninjured. I remained in a coma for the next four months while Johnny moved from family member to family member until I was able to recover enough to go home.

Johnny and I tried to make the best of things as we struggled through these hard times. I still needed rehabilitation to become more mobile, and Johnny was my rock during this time. We had to move into an apartment far away from our old home. Johnny started back to school, and we tried to resume as normal a life as possible.

One day a few months later, Johnny's school called me when he became very nauseated. Since I was still unable to drive, I called a friend who drove to the school to pick him up for me. I treated him with meds from over the counter because it seemed to be some type of stomach virus. Four days into the illness, he still had no fever and no other symptoms. Two more days later, he was no better, so my friend took us to the emergency room. The emergency room doctor said it was only a virus, and it would pass. Poor Johnny was weak and dehydrated but was sent home anyway.

By the time we had reached our apartment, I had a gut feeling that something was very wrong with him. He was never sick! I asked a friend to take us to another hospital. As soon as five doctors at once looked him over, Johnny was immediately admitted for tests. His vision was dull, and he had pressure behind his eyes. Weeks went by, and he was still in the hospital slowly losing his sight. I stayed with him for three days at a time only leaving when friends drove me home for a break.

After one of my trips back and forth, Johnny had a seizure. The doctors decided to transfer him to a children's hospital by ambulance.

The children's hospital put him into a room where there was a bed for me, too. Tests were done immediately, and the results were that my precious son had a brain tumor called Astrocytoma. The doctors said that he had only three to five years to live. With this type of slow growing tumor, Johnny was probably born with it. The car accident had nothing to do with it. Until now, there had been no reason to suspect anything was abnormal with his health.

Inside I felt like falling to pieces. I cried and believed deep down inside I must have done something in my life to cause this illness on my only son. Here I am not completely over the ordeal of the car crash and now this. Johnny is and will be my only child, and now they are telling me he will not even live to see his teenage years. I began to say, "What have I done to deserve this? This is not fair! How could Johnny live nine whole years and not have any signs of this terrible growth in his head?" Of course, there are no answers to my questions.

In came a neurosurgeon who explained Johnny needed to have surgery in the morning. Exploratory surgery would allow them to remove as much of the tumor as possible, and at least give him back his eyesight for now.

Details of the surgery were explained including the incision that would start above one ear, across his forehead, and down to the other ear. My son and I discussed how much hair he wanted to have shaved off. He decided to have it all off at once so it could grow back evenly. The following morning, they shaved his head, collected it into a plastic bag, and gave it to me. To this day, I still have that bag of hair!

Johnny's father and grandpa lived in another state and had no contact with us until now. I made the decision to contact them and inform them of the illness and trauma that would follow. To my surprise they flew here for the surgery the following morning.

For the next five hours we waited in the surgery waiting room. The waiting room would fill up with other patients' family members and then empty out. Again it would fill up with other people and empty out. "Where were those doctors? Why hadn't they come out to explain what is going on? What if something went terribly wrong and they did not want to face us?" Horrible thoughts were going through my head.

Finally they came out and said Johnny had made it through the surgery. They had several problems not yet resolved. The tumor was connected to his brain and to his nerves going to his eyes. They could not remove the entire tumor because too much of the brain would have to be removed to rid him of the tumor. Johnny could not live a normal life without that part of the brain. If I could change places with him, I would gladly give my life for his.

I could only visit with him for a minute in recovery. As I watched him, I could see that for the first time in months, he was totally free from pain. How hard this had been on him! At one point, he opened his eyes and looked at me. His head was bandaged so I told him that he looked like a mummy. He chuckled. I needed to hear that laugh from him. His father saw him and then left to go back to where the grandfather lives.

After a couple of days of recovery, it was time to start chemo-therapy. Also Johnny would start radiation treatments. They marked plus signs all over his head with a black magic marker. We were told not to wash them off until all 21 treatments were finished. Every morning I wheeled him over for radiation treatments and he did very well. They told him to expect to be ill from the treatments, but he never once became sick!

One year had passed since the car accident. So much had happened during that year. The hospital finally released him when I promised to get him back on time for his treatments. Here it is almost Thanksgiving, and we had so much to be thankful for! By Thanksgiving Day, he and I were finally home and together as a family should be.

The home visit was short lived, only three days, when Johnny began sleeping so sound that I couldn't wake him up. Back to the hospital we went. Too much pressure from fluids on his brain was the problem.

The neurosurgeon came back to talk to us again. He explained there are three ventricles in the head. One was on the left side, one on the right side, and one at the base of the skull at the neck. Johnny's tumor was blocking one of them and needed a shunt put in to relieve the pressure from the fluid building up in his brain. The doctor said a shunt is a tube they would put down the neck and connect to the stomach. Johnny had only one major question for the doctor. "Was he going to lose the little bit of hair that was finally growing back?"

After this surgery, Johnny came out with only a small portion of his hair shaved.

Then the doctor came out to talk to us. It was not exactly what I wanted to hear. They had found a cyst growing in his neck, and they could not remove it. The shunt was placed beside it with the hopes that the tumor would not grow and disrupt the shunt's location.

Another set of doctors made their entrance. Endocrine doctors introduced themselves and gave us a cup in which to measure every-thing that went into Johnny's mouth. We had to document everything he ate and drank. They started him on steroids and said he would eat better while taking them. Now it was Christmastime! How nice it would be to be able to take him home for the holidays! And he did get to go home on December 23.

This home visit lasted 30 glorious days! Then things started going wrong. His memory was going downhill. I started counting how many times that he asked me the same question. It was six times in 30 minutes and this was not good news! I called the hospital, and they said to bring him back.

The cyst was growing and pushed aside the shunt in his neck. The surgeon gave me an ultimatum; we could either leave it alone and Johnny would just sleep his life away or we could allow them to go in and try to remove the cyst with the possibility that he may be paralyzed from the neck down for his remaining time. I allowed Johnny to make the final decision. Yes, he wanted them try to remove the cyst.

The surgery took eight hours. I thought they would never come out to talk to me! Finally, the doctor returned and said there was no way of knowing if Johnny would ever walk again until he wakes up, but they were able to remove most of the cyst. Of course it was a possibility that it would start growing again, but at this time this was our only option. When he awoke, he could feel and move his legs. We were so thankful!

Soon Johnny was released and life at home became a struggle to get back into a routine. Soon I asked him, "Remember school?" Johnny needed to get back in school. He had lost an entire year and had to have a tutor to catch up to his classmates.

As life began to calm down, I had thoughts of moving. I thought Johnny was stable enough to move and I felt that we needed a new start. He agreed. Ever since we first came to Texas, we had bad things happening and I couldn't bear the thought that Johnny might be buried in this horrid dust ridden state. Off we went to find a new life in another state!

We took all of Johnny's medical files with us. We moved near a city that had an excellent children's hospital. As soon as we settled into our new home, we checked into the children's hospital to fill out the paperwork. He had to go through all of the tests needed for the new doctors and everything looked fine.

Life was great and Johnny even loved his new school. Once again, we were becoming a normal everyday family. Many years had passed and all was well. We had a special bond because we had been through so much together.

One day when Johnny was 14, he was looking at me and talking. I noticed that one eye turned inward. He said, "What's wrong?" I guess I had a funny look on my face. I called for an appointment at the children's hospital, and they wanted him in there as soon as possible. Surgery was recommended to correct the eye problem. All of the old demons woke up inside of me and I was afraid that this was the end.

My fears were quickly diminished after the surgery because it went very well. This was done as an outpatient, and there were no scars and no complications. The doctor told us that because we had gone through such hard times, he thought Johnny needed to boost his morale. The doctor said he had all of the right answers for Johnny. He suggested that I contact the dream-making organization right here in town. Johnny had said that someday he would like to go to Disney World in Florida, but he knew we could never have enough money to do this. This might be just the thing he needed! I talked to him and he agreed that we needed to call these people.

He could not stop smiling, not even for one minute. We both had the giggles. I called the organization and arrangements were made immediately. It was hard to believe that we were really going to Florida only days away.

We meet the representative of the organization, and she explained all of the details of the trip to come. She told us that many people donated the money to pay our way. Johnny was so amazed and could not believe that people he had never met cared enough to help him.

The trip was far more than we ever expected. We went to the Magic Kingdom, Epcot Center, Sea World, and the Arabian Nights Supper Club. We got to swim in the ocean and look for shells. Johnny even got to go fishing and actually caught some fish! We played miniature golf, had breakfast with the Disney characters, and even found time to share our excitement with each other. We could never have done any of this without help from the organization.

The sheer thought that others cared enough to see Johnny get a break and take time to enjoy life was overwhelming to him. When we returned home, he called to thank them and asked if they could use toys that he had and never played with. He gathered up all he could find, and we took them to the organization. He wanted to help other children just like him. Those toys were given to many of the patients associated with the dream-makers. Johnny was so proud that he could share with other children like him.

Now it has been six years after our ordeal first began. We have kept in touch with the founder of the dream-making group. She has made a great impact on our lives and has become a very good friend. Johnny is still doing wonderful! Things are all back to normal thanks to all of the wonderful caring people who took the time to keep up his spirits.

It means a great deal to us that others can be so unselfish and giving. They bring happiness into the lives of children and families like ours, especially when it is needed the most.

By Terry, Mother of Johnny

STACY (Dream—To go to Disney World and to the Beach)
By a Volunteer and a Friend

One day, while working in the office, I got a call from a lady named Sue, who lived about 65 miles south of the city. Sue began to tell me the story of her daughter and granddaughter's struggles up to the present date. She said that she would like to see her granddaughter, Stacy, and daughter, Tina, go to Florida for a vacation. Without someone's assistance, they could never afford such an extravagant vacation. Their lives had been riddled by tragedies, one after another.

Her accounting of their lives was so tragic that it was hard for me to understand how they could even still be alive. After I verified the medical history (which took days), I decided to meet Tina and Stacy to discuss a dream for the little girl. Upon the first meeting with Sue, Tina, and Stacy, I very much liked them and we became fast friends. As time went on I witnessed even more deadly events that struck them. I deeply admired the strength that each of them showed as they were pushed to a point that was almost beyond belief. Their faith in God was their strength. Each of them was a kind, warm, and loving individual, and I could not help but care deeply for all of them.

The story starts out as Tina dated and then married her high school sweetheart at the early age of 17. She became pregnant shortly thereafter. Everything seemed to be fine with the marriage until a near fatal car accident.

When Tina was eight months pregnant, she was in a car accident that put her in the hospital in a coma. She had severe injuries to her entire body and many broken bones. While pregnant and in a coma, the doctors decided to go ahead and try to save the baby. They took the newborn from her and found that the baby had several injuries as well. While Tina lay in the hospital, the doctors did several surgeries to try to correct her injuries. In the meanwhile, Grandmother Sue and Granddad Tom were caring for the newborn between hospital visits.

The newborn could not stay in the same hospital because her injuries required them to take her to a children's hospital 65 miles away. For six months, Tina remained comatose. Stacy, the new baby, had undergone several surgeries by this point.

To everyone's amazement, the new mom woke up after Stacy was six months old. The doctors were ecstatic! They had saved the mother and her child! They told Tina about her new baby girl, so the grandparents brought the baby to her in the hospital.

Tina asked to see her husband. But to add to her horror, the grandparents had to explain how her husband had picked up his things and had left two weeks after the accident. No one even knew where he was and no one had heard anything from him since the day that he left. He never even called to see if his wife and baby were all right.

Through much therapy, Tina was finally able to go home. Their new home was now with Tina's parents. They lived with them for several years. When Stacy was less than one year old they noticed that she was having trouble hearing. The doctors soon told them that Stacy was completely deaf in both ears and the damage was irreversible. The entire family and Stacy would need assistance from The School for the Deaf, located 65 miles away. This school would teach the family to communicate with Stacy since she was old enough to start learning sign language. The entire family drove back and forth to take the courses.

Over the next six and a half years, Stacy was in and out of the hospital due to injuries she received from the crash while still in her mother's womb. Tina was unable to walk without the assistance of crutches and a wheelchair for the rest of her life. This was going to be as good as it gets for both of them, health wise. All of the surgeries had already been done to try to correct Tina's crushed hip and legs; no therapy could correct the problems that she had. Tina still had internal injuries that flared up sometimes. She would have to be hospitalized back and forth, just like her daughter. During all of this time, Tina's parents took care of them.

When Stacy turned seven years old, she began to have sharp pains in her abdomen. It was back to the hospital for her for more testing. They soon learned that Stacy was diagnosed with cirrhosis of the liver. She needed to be living closer to the hospital. With Tina's health problems, this was going to be a challenge for her to keep going for her daughter's sake. Through government-assisted programs, Stacy and her mom were able to move on into the city, on their own. Even though it would be tough living by themselves, living close to both hospitals would be better for them. Stacy's mom was a very strong willed and determined young lady. She loved her little girl and took very good care of her. Tina tried to find her husband, but had no luck. Of course, he was not paying child support either! She had to depend on SSI for herself and her daughter, which was not much money to live on. They were forced to live in a small trailer in a trailer park just outside of the city limits.

When I came into the picture, Stacy was seven years old and her mother was 25 years old. The grandmother, who contacted me, wanted us to try to bring some joy into their lives because the entire life of the little girl had been a struggle of survival. I met the entire family and received all of the signed forms from them. Stacy did confirm that she wanted to go to Florida to see the ocean and to visit Disney World. Her doctors agreed to let them both go, but the grandparents were needed on the trip, too. Both Tina and Stacy where unable to walk without assistance. The trip was set up and they soon went to Florida for a whirlwind vacation. They very much enjoyed their stay in Florida and had a peaceful few months after their return. No one had to be admitted into the hospital for a while which was rare.

I had kept in contact with Tina off and on to be assured they were okay. Also, I would call Tina's mom once in a while to check with them to see if they were doing all right. Some days, I would make a run to their trailer to do odd jobs and such for them when I had the spare time. They were so grateful and so loving that I just could not help wanting to do for them when I saw the need. They never asked me for anything; I just saw that things were needed and did them or found others willing to help.

A few weeks had lapsed with no contact between us when Grandmother Sue called. Tina had fallen down the steps of the trailer trying to carry a load of laundry to the car, heading for the laundry mat. She was back in the hospital again. Her hip was injured in the fall. While she was away, I went to talk with the owner of the trailer park where they lived. I asked if it was possible for us to put a washer and dryer in the trailer. They agreed that we could as long as it did not cost the owners anything.

I had to find an electrician who was willing to work for free and a donor for the washer and dryer. I prayed about it, and the very next day, God sent me this very nice man who was a retired electrician. I just ran into him at the hardware store and we struck up a conversation. On finding out that he was an electrician; I told him that he was sent to me to help this family. He stammered, "What?" After telling him the story, he was hooked. He then told me that he could do the plumbing as well. He gladly put in the connections for the electricity and the plumbing to hook up the washer and dryer at no charge.

All we needed was an electric washer and dryer. I prayed for days before I got an answer. As I had just finished seeing a family off at the airport for a dream vacation, a big man approached me. He had a shiny shirt on with the shirt opened half way down, showing his very hairy chest. He had gold chains hanging from his neck and gold rings on every finger. He came up to me and said, "Hi. I'm a Christian." and then shook my hand. Then he told me his name. He said that he knew who I was because he had seen me many times on news stories helping children. He had two gentlemen with him and introduced them to me, also. I asked him how I could help him and he said, "No, How can I help you?" Boy, he did not know what he opened himself up to!

First of all, I did not trust him right away because he thought he had to tell me that he was a Christian, even before he told me his name. I have always believed that if you are a Christian, you should not have to announce it. It should be known not by your mouth, but by your actions. If someone thinks that they have to tell another person that he or she is a Christian, then I feel that something is really wrong with this picture!

"Okay", I thought. God sent him to me, so I am going to use him. I told him, in front of his friends, that I did need his help. I needed him to purchase an electric washer and dryer for a family that I was working with. There was a good sign — he didn't run away! He asked for more information, and I gladly gave him whatever he needed to know.

He promised me that he could find a donor or buy them himself within a week and he could "guarantee" that the appliances would be brought to her trailer by the following Friday. I told him okay and I will meet him there. We exchanged information and I left. I really was not going to depend on him actually following through with his promises, so I knew I still needed to look for someone else to help. I really did not even believe that the information that he gave to me was legitimate, but I hung on to it anyway.

During that following week, I called him several times but there was never an answer nor did he have an answering machine to leave a message. But the phone line was at least connected! I had not found another person to donate the appliances and there were only two days left before that Friday, when I got a break.

On Wednesday, this same man drove right passed me in his older model white Cadillac convertible (with the top down) going down one of the main streets in town. I just got behind him and followed him. He never spotted me behind him because he was too busy primping in the mirror at every stoplight. He came to a stop and parked in front of a building that just happened to be the building where my lawyers' offices were. I pulled up beside him and got out of my car and said, "What a coincidence! Are you here to see my lawyer?" "Have you made the plans to get the washer and dryer for Friday, yet?" He nodded a "no" at me and said how busy he had been. I said, "Why don't you let me go with you to buy them today?"

He was trapped. I had caught him off guard and he was at a loss for words. He agreed to go with me to buy the items after his meeting from inside this building. So I said I would just go inside and visit with my attorney while I waited for him to finish up his business.

When he finished his meeting, we went together (but in separate cars) to the department store, just blocks away. He purchased the items by putting them on his credit card and then we made arrangements for the delivery on Friday. I could be there to let them in. I also asked for him to pay for the installation of the washer and dryer and he did, reluctantly. I thanked him and went on my way.

It just so happened that I knew the salesman who sold the washer and dryer to us. His name was Gene. I called him later to tell him the story about this family needing help and this man asking if he could help us. I thanked him for getting the manager of the store to give us a break on the cost of the items.

To my surprise I received a phone call from Gene on the following day, on Thursday. That man had called to cancel the sale and wanted credit back on his credit card! The salesman told him he would get back to him later that day. Then the salesman called me and said, "What do you want me to do?" I was shocked at the would-be donor, but deep down, I was really expecting something bad from this guy. I asked Gene what my options were. He said that he had a plan but decided not to tell me about it until afterwards. He told me not to worry because the items would still go out on Friday for installation, just as we had planned. I was very concerned, but he assured me that everything would turn out just fine.

Friday came and so did the washer and dryer! I had them install the appliances and make sure everything was in working order before they left. It was done. The next day, Stacy and her mother came home from the hospital. When they arrived, they had a great surprise! I told them that a very nice gentleman had purchased these items for them. I also told them about a very nice retired electrician who worked hard to get the electricity and plumbing ready for the appliances. Now she wouldn't have to carry out laundry to a laundry mat any longer. I signed to Stacy what just happened and Stacy was just as excited as her mom!

By the following Monday, I was busy in the office when I received another phone call from Gene. He told me what he had done. He called the donor and told him that they had already installed the appliances and couldn't give him credit for them unless he went out and retrieved the appliances himself. Gene knew that he wouldn't have the gall to do that. I wasn't so sure, but just in case, I called Stacy's mom and gave her the heads up on this guy. Nothing ever happened. He did not dare try to get the appliances back nor did he even call me to ask.

Normally, I would never become involved with a character like him but at the time I just felt that maybe he needed a lesson. I believe that God sent him to me to teach him what a real commitment was all about. A couple of years later, I ran into him at a restaurant and he was as sweet as pie! He also had people with him to impress. He introduced them to me, bragging about how he had helped a very needy family. I just smiled and let him talk. After all, he did help them in the end.

I wish I could say that this is the end of the story of Stacy and her mom, Tina, but there is more. Around six months later, I was watching the 6:00 evening news and to my disbelief, there was their trailer in a ball of flames. Some drunk had run off of the paved road straight up toward their trailer and hit the main natural gas meter going to the trailer park. Tina's rented trailer just happened to be beside the main gas line.

The car and the trailer blew up. The drunk had gotten out of his car completely uninjured while Stacy and her mother were trapped inside the trailer. Remember that Stacy is deaf and Tina cannot walk without assistance. A courageous neighbor had heard the impact and ran out to help. He jumped over the flames to enter their trailer through the only exit/entrance to the trailer — the front door. He managed to pull both of them out, one at a time. Stacy and her mom were saved from harm. They were not burned at all, even though the neighbor carried them through the open flames to safety. The neighbor ended up with only slight burns to his arms. What a wonderful person to risk his own life to save Stacy and Tina. If he had not been there, both would have surely perished in that fire. All three of them had to be taken to the hospital due to smoke inhalation but were released shortly.

Of course, Tina had no insurance to cover their losses and the drunk did not have any insurance, either. Everything that they owned was in that trailer, including the new washer and dryer. The trailer was a total loss. Nothing could be salvaged. The media covered the event and asked for others to donate anything that they could to help them. People came from everywhere to help this family. Some bought them clothes, others got them new furniture, food, etc. They got another trailer close to this one and people helped them move into it. I was glad to see that so many people were there to help. It restored my faith in mankind! There are good people out there! You just need to know where to find them.

A short time later Stacy had surgery on her spleen. Soon she became too weak to recover, and we lost her. I know that her mom was only hanging on to life for Stacy. Within a few months, we lost Stacy's mother, too. I felt so sorry for the family members who were left behind to grieve for their losses. I miss them, too. Even though this has been about 20 years ago, I still miss the grandparents, also. I used to talk to them periodically, but eventually we lost touch all together. I do miss them in my life, but I do not know how to find them.

By a Volunteer and a Friend

JEANNIE (Dream—To go to Disney World in Florida)
By a Volunteer and a Friend

Most of the dreams we granted over the years went just as planned without any problems. But there were some dreams granted where problems had developed for one reason or another. This is one of those stories where we were totally blindsided to the lifestyle of the family because it was hidden so well from us until it was too late to change the plans.

Jeannie was 12 years old when I met her. Her mother, Joan, had called me after learning that our organization granted wishes for children diagnosed with life threatening illnesses. Her daughter was recently diagnosed with a brain tumor and was undergoing chemo-therapy and radiation treatments. The tumor was shrinking, but the physicians said that surgery would be necessary at a later time for the removal of the rest of the tumor.

Jeannie wanted to go to Disney World in Florida. In the past few days, we had requests from two other patients who also wanted to go to Disney World and to visit the beaches in Florida. After receiving all of the paperwork necessary for the patients to visit Florida, it was time to start setting up the three trips. An article was already in the process of being written in the statewide newspaper about our organization, so I asked them to add the information on the three present patients' requests and ask the public for assistance in paying for the trips. The day the article was published, I received a call from a national computer company based locally in our city. I was offered the company jet and pilot to fly all three families down there at the same time. Then six days later they would fly them back. This was such a blessing because our organization was always running low on funds. This would save us money due to the normally high cost of airline fares.

I informed all three families that it would be possible for them to fly on the private corporate jet and all agreed that they could go at the same time. I began making the final arrangements when Jeannie's mother contacted me with a problem. Jeannie's mom, Joan, was having some health problems and would need extra help while on the trip. She suggested that since Jeannie's father was nowhere to be found, she would like for her sister, Sarah, to go with them for an extra pair of hands. Jeannie could walk for short distances but needed the wheelchair for the long days at Disney World, the Epcot Center, Universal Studios, and Sea World. Because of Jeannie's condition, we agreed to allow the aunt to go. The aunt came in and signed the legal paperwork and she was ready for the trip.

All three families arrived in a timely manner and boarded the private plane at 6:00 a.m. Several of the organization's board members were there to see the families off on their trip. Since I had made the reservations for all three families to stay at the same place, their hotel rooms were all close together. Two of the families had a car waiting for them at the Orlando Airport at the car rental booth. Jeannie's mother did not have a valid driver's license and was not able to have a car rental. I had made arrangements for them to be carried back and forth by a cab service. This turned out to be a blessing for us but at the time, we were not aware of any of the problems yet to come.

Each day was carefully planned out for each of the families. They were each given an itinerary to follow along with the entry tickets to each dinner theater and theme park. Their trip would be for five nights and six days. I did plan for each of the families to be on their own, away from the other families. This was because it was important for the families to spend this special time as a family and hopefully create a bond together to share these precious moments for a "happy time" during their current life of chaos.

On the second night of their trip, in the a.m., I received a terrible phone call. One of the other families, the Hayes family, called me to tell me a horror story about Jeannie's mother and aunt. The police came to Jeannie's hotel room and arrested her mom and aunt for creating a disturbance at a local bar earlier that evening. After they had left the bar, they returned to their hotel suite. Evidently they had told someone at the bar where they were staying. The police knew right where to go to get them.

Mr. Hayes had gone over there while the police were there. He then found out that Jeannie had missed the Epcot Center and Disney World on the first two days of the trip. He offered for Jeannie to stay with them (the Hayes family) in their suite that night and go on the following day to Sea World with them. Jeannie's mother and the police agreed to let her. Mr. Hayes explained that there were three families all down there for a wish for each of their sick children. He asked the police officer to please come to their suite so he could tell me what was happening in Florida. He thought it was important for me to be notified. Then two of the police officers followed Mr. Hayes back to the suite and phoned me.

A police officer got on the phone with me and told me that he could have added more charges, but declined due to Jeannie having other adults willing to take care of her. He said that he could have charged Joan and Sarah for public drunk, disorderly conduct, and abandonment of Jeannie for the past two days and nights. Jeannie had been left alone in the hotel and had missed two days of her vacation. She had missed going to the two theme parks because her mom and aunt were hanging out with some local men they had met at a bar. They were doing drugs and drinking for both of those days and nights. Jeannie was left alone in the hotel room and did not even have any food.

This was a first for us. I could not believe that a parent could care so little for her own daughter. I thought, "What was wrong with these people? Jeannie has a brain tumor and her mom and her aunt went down there and spent all of the money on alcohol and drugs in the first two days?" They did not even have enough to buy food for them for the remaining days of the trip! Any time we send a family on a trip, we gave them an allowance to pay for food, souvenirs and other extras that might come up. That is the money that they spent!

The Hayes family called me every day after that to keep me abreast of the day's events. They were a very close and loving family. They had adopted a daughter that was having the dream granted. Their daughter, Joyce, had recently been diagnosed with cancer and was undergoing chemotherapy. I found out later that they also had five other children who were also adopted.

I thanked God every day for the wonderful family that was willing to assist Jeannie. If they had not been there, I would have had to fly down there to get Jeannie and bring her back. That loving family had brought extra money with them and used it on Jeannie. I told them to keep all of the receipts and I would reimburse them when they returned. At least Jeannie got to go to Sea World and Universal Studios and to visit the beaches at the Gulf of Mexico, thanks to the Hayes family.

I called Jeannie's neurologist and told him what her mom and aunt had pulled. He wasn't surprised. He told me that Jeannie had missed more than half of her treatments because the mother just couldn't get out of bed to bring her 50 miles to the hospital. He had suspicions that she was a heavy drinker but did not know for sure. I asked him why he didn't tell me what I was in for and he said, "I thought her mother would behave on a special trip like this. I just did not see this coming!"

I could not wait to get my hands on that mother and aunt! I had already spoken to our attorneys and discovered what options were available in dealing with them. They could have been charged with perpetrating a fraud upon a nonprofit agency, which could become a federal offense if we pushed it.

When it was time to come back home on the same private company jet, guess who did not show up. An hour had passed and the pilot decided to call me to tell me that Jeannie's mom and aunt still had not arrived. He wanted to know what he should do. Since the two "problem children" did not show up, I told him that Jeannie's mother and aunt would not be flying back with them. They did not need to wait for them any longer. At least Jeannie was in good hands with the Hayes family. She flew home with the other two families. I met the plane when it arrived and picked Jeannie up and brought her to my home. Here she would remain with us until we found a way to get her mom and aunt home later.

While the jet was in route home, I got a phone call from Jeannie's mother. She was at the hospital because her sister started having seizures on the way to the airport. The cab took them to the main hospital in Orlando. Her sister was moved to ICU and was listed in critical condition. Of course, she said she did not know what went wrong. I told her, "It was probably all of the drugs you both had taken!" She acted like she didn't know what I was talking about. I told her that I had spoken with the arresting officer and he relayed the information to me. She actually asked me for more money to buy food. I just told her that she was on her own. If she did not have money for food, she should have thought about that before she spent it all and ruined her daughter's trip.

Well, I did have a dilemma. How would I get them home? Since we took them down there, it was our responsibility to get them back. I talked to our attorneys and they suggested that I pay for the return trip and then deal with the repercussions later. I called the hospital and ran down what floor Joan's sister's room was on and called the nurses station. A nurse went to the hospital room and brought back Joan to talk to me. I said that when her sister is well enough to get on a plane, she needed to call me and I would see that they both had tickets for the plane ride home.

Now, in the mean time, Jeannie is staying at my house. Jeannie is a "wild child", partially because of her family and partially because she was not thinking right due to the pressure from the brain tumor. She had about five to seven seizures a day and she needed to be watched constantly. Anyway, I had three boys of my own. Their ages were 10, 12, and 13. I could not leave Jeannie alone in my home, not because I did not trust my children, but because I could not trust Jeannie.

She was boy crazy and she was only 12 years old! I made her sleep in my bedroom every night so I could watch her. In the daytime I had meetings to go to, speaking engagements planned and other dreams to grant. I took Jeannie everywhere I went and I made her behave. As it turned out, she loved going with me and was eager to please me because I was paying her all of this attention. She was wearing my clothes, jewelry, and shoes. She was having a great time!

I was a single mom and had a date on a couple of those evenings with my future husband. I thought this was a great way to break him in. He would either run away or he would go with the flow. We took her with us out to dinner and to see a movie. She thought that going on a date with my boyfriend and I was the greatest thing of all. He just went along with whatever we had to do for Jeannie. He didn't seem to mind that she tagged along. Actually, he was very good around her and she adored him. I was happy to see that this did not frighten him away from me. I knew that Jeannie was not going to be the last sick child at my home. On many occasions, as a favor to the parents to give them a break, I babysat several different patients in my home in the evenings.

I did not know how long I was going to have to keep Jeannie in my home because her mother was still not calling me back to keep me informed. I called Jeannie's doctor to catch him up on the situation and he said to bring Jeannie up there for an examination while I had her in my possession. She had missed her last three appointments and he was concerned. I took her up there that very day. He told me that she needed to have surgery sometime soon. I said I would talk to her mom but I could not promise she would do anything she was supposed to do.

It was nine days before I heard from her mother, again. She had called me collect and told me she had been staying in her sister's hospital room and eating the hospital food meant for her sister. At this point, nothing else that she could have said or done would surprise me. She said that her sister was getting out of the hospital in the morning and they would be ready to fly back home. I told her that she needed to call me after 10:00 a.m. and I could give her the information on what flight and time they would need to be at the airport.

The following morning I had the arrangements ready to bring them back. At 10:00, she called me and I told her that the tickets would be waiting on them at a certain airlines ticket counter and they had better be on that flight. I told her, "I am not playing games with you. You had better be on that flight or I am going to have you

155

arrested." She believed me, so they did catch the right flight and left on time.

When their plane arrived here, I met them at the airport with Jeannie in hand, and told them that I wasn't sure what I was going to do with them yet, but I had many different options. I said that if she missed any more of Jeannie's appointments with the hospital for treatments or the doctors' appointments, that I would follow up and charge her with committing fraud against a non-profit organization and sue her for the extra expenses that she had caused us. I told her that I could turn her in to the Social Services for abandoning her child and I could probably come up with many more things that I could do if I just thought about it.

I think that I had put some fear into her, but I wasn't sure how long it would last. Later, Jeannie's doctors praised me because Joan actually kept the appointments. That worked for about the next two years. Jeannie even had her surgery during that time. The neuro-surgeon who did the surgery told me he was able to get the entire tumor, but Jeannie would always be slow and would continue to have seizures for an unknown period of time.

After Jeannie's 16th birthday, her mother called me one day to ask if I knew where Jeannie was. I had not seen nor heard from either of them in two years. Jeannie's mom did not bring Jeannie to the annual Christmas parties after that trip. I guess that was too much trouble for her mom.

Her mom told me that she thought Jeannie might have run off with an older man who was 35 years old! I asked her what Jeannie would even be doing around a man that old. She told me that he was a "friend of the family". I don't really know what happened after that.

Around the time of Jeannie's 18th birthday, another patient who lives in the same town told me that Jeannie was moving around from one man to another. They said she was so wild that they were worried that she was probably on drugs, too. I wish we could have a happy ending to tell you but I never found out any more about her. I have often thought about her and said a prayer for her. She should be about 27 years old right now if she did not have a reoccurrence of cancer.

If you have time, it would be nice if you could stop just for a moment and say a prayer for her. I am sure that she is in need of prayers right now. She has been through a lot in her life and I know that she has not had the proper guidance, but I am hoping that she has found her way to the Lord.

By a Volunteer and a Friend

CINDY (Dream—To Have a Bedroom Suite of Her Own)
By a Volunteer and a Friend

While traveling through the northern part of the state one morning, I passed through the outskirts of a small town about 80 miles away from the city. I noticed a little girl with a big sign at the end of her driveway. The sign was obviously written by her without the help of an adult, on a large piece of brown cardboard. The sign read, "Rocks for Sell".

When I had reached my destination about 15 more miles ahead, I was still thinking about that little girl standing out there with her torn dress and tattered look. I was on my way to meet a large group of businessmen at a luncheon. I was the guest speaker and my purpose was to try to talk them into helping with our organization in any way that was possible through fundraising or volunteering.

This was a good day indeed for our organization. The men collected several hundred dollars for us and handed the money to me before I left the meeting. There were promises of more funds to come from them. One of the local men, Richard, came up to talk to me after the meeting had adjourned. He was interested in working with me and wanted to volunteer his time to raise funds and become actively involved with any dreams that were granted in that area. It sounded wonderful to me! I was very grateful for his interest.

Before he and I left the building, I told him about the little girl selling rocks in front of her house. He not only knew about her but he knew the family. He told me her father was killed in an automobile accident two years ago and she lived with her mother who wasn't well. Then he said, "You know something, I think the little girl is ill, also." I gave him his first assignment as a volunteer. I asked him to find out about her mother's sickness and the little girl's illness and get back with me. He agreed to do this quickly, and we parted ways. I had to rush back to the city for a late afternoon meeting. On the way back I slowed down to see the little girl, but she was not there. I guess she had gone in the house so I went on by.

The following day, Richard was right on top of things. He called me and gave me the information on the little girl. Not only had he called around to ask questions, but he opened up the morning paper and there she was! The local paper had put an article in the newspaper about her selling rocks to buy a bicycle. She was running a lucrative business at rock selling! She had already received two bicycles and $72.00 by in the end of the day! Most of the people who stopped to give her money allowed her to keep the rocks and resell them again.

Also, in the newspaper article, it said that her mother was quite ill and had been for several years. The little girl, Cindy, age 11, had been recently diagnosed with two forms of leukemia and also had a rare bone deformation since birth. She was also being treated for a type of diabetes. Richard's information was nearly identical to the newspaper article with one exception. Someone had told him that she was being treated in the same city that I lived in.

It was not hard to track down her oncologist. When I found him, we discussed her condition and I asked who her main physician was since she had multiple problems. He said that he was the one who had overseen all of her treatments and kept in close contact with all of her doctors. I was glad to hear this, since this oncologist and I were good friends. He gave me her information and said that he thought a dream might be good for her, especially right now.

The oncologist said that Cindy could not travel anywhere. So if she asked for a trip somewhere, he would not allow her to go. That was fine with me because I would never do anything that the patients' physicians were against. We were there to help, not hurt, the patients.

The next day, I decided to give Cindy's mom a call. She was not well, so she could not talk to me for very long. I told her who I was and why I was calling. I asked if I could come meet with them to see if Cindy would like to have anything special. Her mom said that was fine, so I set up a date and time to come to see them.

The day that I arrived at their home, I talked with both the mother and Cindy. Cindy was sleeping on the couch every night because she had no bed. Her mother had the only bed in the house. I could see that they were living with just the bare minimum essentials and were barely getting by from month to month.

I asked, "Cindy, if you could have anything you wanted in the whole wide world, what would it be?" (I clinched my teeth and held my breath hoping that she would not say a trip to somewhere.) And to my surprise, she did not! She wanted a big bed "to have all to herself" and a matching chest of drawers and a vanity with a mirror and stool. That seemed so very simple. Now all I needed was a furniture company willing to work with our organization and the money to pay for the difference.

I had her mother sign the paperwork so we could proceed with the dream. I would take on the responsibility of getting Cindy's doctor to sign his part. I had the impression that if I left this for Cindy's mom to do, it would probably never make it to the doctor nor would I ever see it again.

I felt very sorry for Cindy. It seemed to me that Cindy was not the first one thought of in that household. My feelings were not that way because they were poor, but because I kept hearing the word "me" when her mom spoke. She really did not even sound too enthused about Cindy getting a dream. (Later, when I phoned Cindy's doctor, he had come to the same conclusions that I had about her mother.) Now, maybe we were wrong about that and maybe the mom was this way because she was so very ill. Maybe she just was not thinking too clearly at the time. I wanted to give her the benefit of the doubt.

I phoned my new friend and volunteer, Richard, before I left their town. He was eager to assist me and asked that I come straight to his office. When I got there, he called one of the men from the group (that I had spoken to). This gentleman owned a furniture company right there in their town! The furniture dealer was happy to work with us, so we hopped into Richard's car and went right over to meet the man at his store. When we got there we looked around until we found the furniture that Cindy had described.

Wasn't it amazing that he had <u>exactly</u> what we were looking for right there in his store? I thought so. My friends and I call that "a God thing". Sometimes God will just drop things right into our laps even before we have had time to ask for it. This happened quite frequently when I was in the process of granting a wish. I believe that many times God will put people and things right in front of us when we ask for His help. I found this to be true, especially when we were asking for assistance to help these very sick children.

Everything was happening so quickly! I called to see if Cindy's mom could bring Cindy to the furniture company to see the furniture for her approval before I actually paid for it. The mother said, "Today is not a good day for me." I said, "What?" "I was just there an hour ago." "What could have happened just since I left your house?" I offered to come get them and bring them to the furniture company, but she said no.

I lived 80 miles away and could not come back and forth just any time she decided to pick up the phone and call me to say, "You can come to get us now." I tried to explain to the mom that I was here in town today only. She said, "No, I'm not feeling well and I just can't deal with this right now!" I asked if we could come get Cindy to take her to the furniture store and she said, "No!" I thought, "Well now what am I going to do?"

I have always had to have order in my life. Everything has a time and a place. I couldn't just drop everything at once and come back up there without setting up a time first. I was almost booked solid for the next few weeks with granting other children's wishes, going to speaking engagements and overseeing fundraisers. My schedule was always tight. I worked an average of 60 to 70 hours every week, and I was still just a volunteer. I paid for my own gas and all of the expenses incurred while working with the organization. I wanted <u>all</u> of the funds raised for dreams to go directly to pay for the dreams.

I turned to Richard and asked if he would be willing to keep in touch with Cindy's mother, and when she was able to ride in the car, would he please drive to get them and take them to see the furniture?

Of course, he said that he would be happy to do so. I could tell, already, that this wonderful man was going to be a blessing for our organization! I thanked God for sending him to us.

Another two weeks had passed before I heard anything from Richard or Cindy's mother. I know that Cindy must have been wondering if this dream would ever become a reality. But deep down, I felt sure that she knew why it was taking so long! Cindy was only 11 years old, but she was very smart for her age.

Finally, I received that phone call that I had been waiting on. Richard had taken the mom and Cindy to the furniture store. The furniture that we had picked out for her was exactly what she wanted! I thought that it might be just right for her.

Great! Now we can move on to the next step. The furniture company would be willing to deliver it for free, but we had to have the cooperation of Cindy's mother. I called the mom to try to set up a time for the furniture to be delivered but here we go again!

She just could not think of a good time. "It is going to be so much more work for me to have to deal with bedroom furniture!" she said. I was about ready to start pulling my hair out! I took a deep breath and asked God to help me through this conversation without being ugly. I finally said, "What would you suggest for us to do? What do we need to do to get a time set where you will be home? You will not have to do anything but tell the men where to set up the furniture. I am sure that Cindy will be more that happy to put the sheets and bedspread on her own new bed without your help." (We had bought sheets, pillows and a beautiful bedspread for her.) "Let me talk to Cindy for a minute, please." She put Cindy on the phone and Cindy promised not to ask her mother for any help putting the bed linens and spread on the bed.

"Now Cindy, please put your mom back on." "Did you hear Cindy? She promised that she would not bother you or ask for your help. When can we get this furniture delivered?" She asked for us to hold it for one week longer, and I agreed. I set up a time with the delivery person. The schedule should work out just fine.

On the evening of the delivery of the furniture, I said a small prayer and picked up the phone and called their house. Cindy answered the phone. I was glad it was Cindy and not her mom. She said that the men brought in the furniture and set it all up for her. She said that they even helped her get the bed clothing on! Wasn't that nice? She said that she did not even ask her mom for anything. Her mom had not even come into Cindy's bedroom to see the furniture yet. I just told Cindy not to let her mom get to her because I knew that her mom was not well and I was sure that she just couldn't think straight because of her pain. I told her that I knew her mom loved her and I felt sure things would get better for her sometime soon.

I could sympathize with her because my mother had been sick for as long as I could remember, and I knew a lot about what Cindy was going through. At times, my mother was just like hers. I asked her to not let her mother hold her back from being a good and honest person. I said that she needed to try to always do the right things and God would help her through the tough times. I said that He would put people in her pathway to help her along the way. She said that she goes to church because someone in the neighborhood picks her up for Sunday school every Sunday. I told her that I would be her friend and would be there to talk to if she ever needed me.

I got to see her at the Christmas parties that we had for our surviving patients every December for a couple of years in a row. I was so proud that someone in her community would bring her and her mother to the party every year. And I was happy to see that Cindy's mother did not keep Cindy from coming to the parties. That was a great achievement all by itself! I finally decided that Cindy's mother had as much fun at the parties as Cindy did.

About the third Christmas party after her dream was granted, I had mailed her mother the paper work to be filled out and it came back with her mother omitted and a set of foster parents in her place. I wondered what had happened so I looked on the signed paperwork and found their phone number. I called and talked with the foster mother about Cindy.

This couple had adopted Cindy because her mother had died. I was very sorry to hear the news but on the other hand, Cindy will now be in the care of someone who will tend to her needs. The foster parents may have even been kin to Cindy, but I do not remember. By talking to the foster mother, and later meeting both foster parents,

I concluded that they seemed genuinely sincere about giving Cindy the very best care and love.

Cindy seemed very happy living with her new family. Each year thereafter, they never missed the annual Christmas parties. I watched her grow up into a beautiful young woman. She was smiling all of the time. During the early years that I spent around Cindy, while she lived with her mother, the only time that I saw her smile was on the day that she got her furniture. The volunteers took pictures of her standing in front of her new bed. It wasn't the same smile that she now has. In the photo, she had a "Mona Lisa" type smile and she was very shy.

Now when she smiles, you can see all of her teeth, and she laughs out loud with ease. She is now in her mid 20s. I hear that she has never had a reoccurrence of either of the types of leukemia that she was diagnosed with and treated for in her younger years. I am so happy for her and only wish the best for her. I pray that she will never see any more sadness or pain in her life.

By a Volunteer and a Friend

Chapter IV.

These stories will briefly talk about the dreams granted. The emphasis is on the families' situations and hardships. These carefully written words will give you a glimpse into the world surrounding some of our patients' lives and/or deaths.

BOBBY (Dream—To have a Red "Hot Rod")
By Mary, Mother of Bobby

Bobby & two siblings on battery-powered Jeep

B obby was born, weighing five lbs and five oz. He was a very
happy and healthy baby, always smiling and winning every-

one's heart. He had the most beautiful whitish-blonde hair and blue eyes that twinkled when he smiled. He was so easy going, getting along with his brother and sister.

Just after he had turned three years old there was a virus going around and we thought he had caught it. He became ill, so I took him into a local doctor who told us Bobby had definitely come in contact with a flu type virus. Medication was given to him. We were home and Bobby steadily got worse over the next few days. He was vomiting, losing weight and then began having trouble keeping his balance. I called another doctor in a larger town 35 miles away from where we lived. They had me bring him straight in.

This doctor looked over the medications that were prescribed by the other doctor and commented that the dosage was much too strong for a small child. He said to immediately stop giving him all of the medicines. He said to take Bobby home and watch him over the next couple of days. If he worsened then Bobby would have to be hospitalized and get some tests scheduled.

I was driving Bobby back home and he started vomiting again. We finally made it home and waited until his father arrived from work. Bobby was getting sicker by the hour. Back in the car we went and drove him straight to the hospital, admitting him through the emergency room. It was now 8:00 p.m. They did a CT scan and MRI on him that very night. The technicians were getting Bobby ready for an EKG when the doctor appeared and asked them to stop. He needed to talk to us right now. I knew by the look on his face that this was not good!

I could feel the bottom drop out of my entire world when the doctor stated that the very worst thing they could have found just happened. It appeared that Bobby had a huge brain tumor. He recommended two different children's hospitals and told us it was our choice where to take Bobby. Furthermore, we had only about five hours to get him to either hospital by ambulance. We chose to take him to a children's hospital in our own state that was still 150 miles from our home.

Since we had our other children with us at the time, we had to quickly make snap decisions and find family members to come get the children. We had to get home 35 miles away and pack our things.

Bobby's great grandfather would follow the ambulance, with Bobby in it, and we would meet them at the children's hospital.

This was a frightening time for all of us. I remember crying over Bobby before he left and telling him that whatever happened, he would be all right. Even if he had to go be with Jesus, he would be all right. Leaving him at the hospital was very hard to do, but I had to take care of everyone else, also. All of our children were my responsibility. I let Bobby know that we were on our way to the children's hospital via our home, and we would meet him there.

Upon his arrival at the children's hospital, steroids were immediately given to him because the tumor was causing his brain to swell. Pressure was building in that precious baby's brain, and the pain was terrible for him. After two days, the swelling came down enough for the neurosurgeon to operate. The surgery took hours and hours. Other family members drove all the way down there to wait with us. We waited for nearly nine hours for someone to come out to tell us what was happening.

Finally, two doctors came out and explained that they had removed the tumor. They believed that they had gotten all of it and said how thrilled they were that the surgery went so well. We were all relieved and happy that the worst was over. It seemed as if all of our prayers were answered. Bobby recovered from the surgery, and we were home again, trying to get back to a normal life with our entire family.

Weeks down the road, we were to bring him back for radiation treatments. It was about then that Bobby was chasing a balloon and fell, bursting open the incision from the surgery. We drove him on the 150-mile trip back to the children's hospital. After repairing the incision, they carted him off to get his radiation.

After his first treatment, the doctors complemented how good Bobby seemed to be. He never caused any problems nor did he move around when they told him to be very still. I explained that Bobby was always good and helped me with his siblings at home. He was a wonderful and loving child.

The treatments continued for several weeks. During most of that time, Bobby and I stayed in the hospital. We spent a lot of time together. We shared a lot during those next few weeks. Sometimes during the afternoons, we were allowed to leave the hospital (between treatments) but still had to come back and spend the night in the hospital room. We got to spend this special time together going to the zoo, going shopping, playing in the playroom, and spending quality time together. Sometimes I look back on those precious few weeks and see that this was a gift from God to allow me to have time alone with him away from everyone else.

Oh, there were other days when his brother and sister came with us, on days when he was just in and out the same day. Those were good times, too. He so loved his brother and sister. But the times that I was alone with Bobby are my most wonderful memories of him. If we had been home more, there wouldn't have been that extra time to spend with him.

It was during this time between radiation treatments that I found a true friend. I picked up a brochure about a dream-making group in the lobby of the hospital. One of the things that I immediately thought about was that Bobby had been saving his pennies for a red "Hot Rod". What he called a "Hot Rod" was actually a battery-operated car for young children to actually drive.

I went directly to a phone and called the organization. The founder was the one I talked to. She seemed so nice and sincere. I explained Bobby's condition, and she came to the hospital right then! I filled out the paperwork as she talked with his doctors. My husband had to sign the papers before anything could be done, but since we were heading home in the morning, I would have him sign them then.

One week later, I had a call from the founder asking if we would be home today. Next thing we know, she pulled up into the driveway with the motorized "red" Power Wheels Jeep for Bobby. We ran out to greet her. She had not only brought the Jeep, but a swing set and toys for everyone. We all helped unload the equipment and gifts. She taught them how to start and stop the Jeep, and then they were off! She was right in the middle of the kids having a wonderful time playing with them. They were riding all over the front yard, laughing and squealing and having the greatest time! There were two seats and three children, so they were taking turns riding the Jeep.

This was a wonderful gift, since Bobby needed to have laughter and joy during this period of his life. These gifts were for him, but he wanted to share them with his brother and sister as his gift to them. Bobby and his siblings played with these gifts every chance that they could. He so loved his new red "Hot Rod!"

The founder of that dream-making group became more than just a dream come true for Bobby. She was there for me when times got even rougher for us. I will never be able to thank her enough for all of the times that she was with me as I cried my heart out. She stood by me all of the way. She became a true friend and is still there for me today.

After the radiation treatments ended, he went back for his check up. Cancer cells had gotten into his spinal column after the surgery. Chemotherapy was the only answer now. All we had was hope. The doctors said his chances were slim. Once chemotherapy began he was very ill, but throughout the chemotherapy treatments he got stronger.

There it was, one month before his fourth birthday and the doctors asked us to come back in for another check up. The chemo had ended. Surely he was cured by now! We were ready for "the good news".

When we arrived, the doctors sat us down with a social worker in the room, and explained that the chemo did not work. "What? How can this be? Hadn't we done everything right?" At that moment, I wanted to just pick Bobby up and run out the door but my senses were numb. I became numb all over. I could not move.

Everyone left me in the room alone with Bobby for a few minutes. He looked at me and gave me the prettiest smile! I jumped up and ran into the bathroom attached to the examining room. I felt as if I just could not take any of this any longer. I began to cry uncontrollably. From the examining room, I heard this small but sweet voice of Bobby, singing. I had never heard Bobby sing before. He was singing, "Mommy, I love you, la, la, la, de—da!" His voice sounded like an angel's voice. I quit crying and ran out of the bathroom, straight to Bobby. Even though I never heard him sing again, that was one of the saddest and happiest times we shared together. We lost Bobby seven days later, only 20 days before his fourth birthday.

During this long and trying seven month period of our lives, the family broke apart. The only time that Bobby's father ever came to the hospital was for the first surgery. After that, he just stayed home and went to work everyday. Other family members and friends helped with the children. I had no emotional support from him at all during this battle for Bobby's life. It was just Bobby, God and I.

My husband and I have been separated and back together many times since Bobby's death, but it has never worked out. We finally separated for good and things calmed down in the household. It has been over a year now since we separated, and things are looking better.

What I have learned throughout this whole process is that you have to be strong and fight every step of the way, and not worry about anything else you should be doing. When you have a sick child, that child needs you there at all times, fighting the battle with him. Only God knows how long you will have with your precious child. I believe that God does not give them to you, He just lets you borrow them for a while.

By Mary, Mother of Bobby

BUBBA (Dream—To go to Disney World)
By V. O'C. Davis

My own son, Patrick at age seven, was diagnosed with a rare kidney disorder and had internal bleeding. He had been in and out of the hospital many times in the recent months. One afternoon while I was waiting in the hematology lab for my son to have his blood work done; I met the cutest and sweetest little boy and his mother. He was waiting to have his blood taken, also.

The little boy's mother began to tell me about her son, Tony. "Bubba" was his nickname. She started telling me how he was first diagnosed at one and a half years old with Acute Lymphoblastic Leukemia (A.L.L.). He underwent all of the treatments for one entire year. By age two and a half, Bubba was in remission.

When we met, Bubba was eight years old. He had some bruises come up on his body recently. Now it was time to come back to the local children's hospital for his check-up. Patrick and Bubba began to talk and really liked one another. Later on, when Bubba was hospitalized, I even brought my three sons to play with him when he felt up to it.

I was the Executive Director of a statewide dream-making organization, but I said nothing to his mom about it. When it was my son's turn to enter the lab for the blood tests, I asked the head RN about Bubba. Of course, the RN, who knew me very well, decided to let the doctor talk to me about him. When the oncologist walked in, I asked him about Bubba. He promised to get back with me when Bubba's test results came in. There was no way to be sure the leukemia had come back until then, even though they suspected that it had. How terrible for that child and his parents! It must be very hard thinking the disease that they thought was gone reappeared nearly six years later!

A couple of days passed and the oncologist called me with the bad news. Bubba was no longer in remission and the outcome was not good. Bubba was very ill. The leukemia had come back with a vengeance. He was hospitalized immediately and they had begun the battle for his life by fighting the disease the only way they knew how. Chemotherapy followed by radiation treatments was on the agenda. There were new chemo drugs out there that might rid his body of the disease, but it would wreak havoc on his already weakened state. He was very small for his age, probably from the treatments of his early years.

I contacted the mother and father when the oncologist told me to do so. We set up a time and met. Both were very kind and so sincere about saving their child. My heart broke just talking to them, knowing that the road ahead for all of them was going to be the hardest thing they have ever had to face! Bubba was their only child.

I thought, "Why does this have to happen to good and honest people like them?" But then again, I would not wish this on my worst enemy! I have seen so many children die over the past 14 years, and I do not have the answers to why these precious children must suffer and die. One day, maybe God will reveal this to all of us. I know that when I see Him that will be one of my first questions.

The conversation the parents and I had together was about Bubba having a dream granted as soon as his oncologist approved whatever Bubba wanted. I felt his doctor would probably approve of anything as long as all precautions were taken. After all, he is the one who told me about him.

Well, Bubba had made up his mind very fast. He already had been dreaming about going to meet Mickey Mouse and to do everything in Disney World. The trip had to be put together fast, between his treatments. Arrangements were made, and the day came quickly for us to see them off on their trip.

After they returned, they told me they had a wonderful memorable vacation to always keep in their hearts. Bubba said he had the greatest time! I was happy I could be a part of this special time in their lives. They will be able to remember those days they spent together, having fun, riding the rides, meeting the Disney characters, just laughing out loud, and being carefree as some of the "good days" of little Bubba's life.

Soon after their return, Bubba was back in the hospital. His father called me late one evening and said Bubba was really doing badly and was asking for me. It was 8:30 p.m. and I knew it was going to be a long night ahead. I tucked my children into bed, and we said a prayer for Bubba. I told them I would let them know how Bubba was doing in the morning.

I arrived at the hospital and entered his room. Both mom and dad were there. Bubba was so frail and so weak. I knew he would not be with us much longer. He asked me to come over to him, so I did. He said, "I want to thank you for being my friend. And thank you for that trip to Florida." He hugged me. I fought back the tears and told him that I loved him. I turned to leave the room, but Bubba asked me to stay. Then his dad nodded for me to stay. I sat down in a chair at the end of his bed and remained silent.

Bubba began talking to all of us. He talked about having visits in his hospital room from his grandmother who died last year. She had come to see him, at his bedside, several times over the last few days. He told us he was going to go with her when she comes back for him and he didn't want his parents to be upset when he leaves. He said his grandmother was going to take care of him. He was only eight years old, but he had matured so fast!

Throughout his recent illness, he was constantly asking for mom to do this and mom to do that, even though his father was right there all of the time. That night, Bubba said, "Mom, I love you. And thank you for everything that you always do for me." And then he turned to his father and said, "Pick me up. I want to sit in your lap and have you rock me." His dad reached over and picked up his thin, frail and naked body and held him close and began to rock. Bubba then looked up into his father's eyes and spoke as a grown man would speak. He said, "Dad, you know that I always asked mom to do everything for me and I don't want you to think that I don't love you, because I do love you very much! I may not let you do a lot

175

for me but I always knew you were right there. And I love you for being there for me." By this time all of us had tears running down our cheeks. Bubba cuddled up with his father and they hugged and rocked in silence for about five minutes. Then his father looked up at us and said, "He is gone."

I left the room sobbing. I found the awaiting family members and nurses that had gathered in the hall, and I told them Bubba had died. A nurse ran in and I heard loud cries because the parents did not want to let go of him yet. Bubba's father came out to me. He and I hugged and cried together for a long while. Bubba's mother came out and joined us.

I can't tell you how much I loved these dear people. The whole family was wonderful. I am sorry for the pain and suffering they endured throughout Bubba's short life. Bubba was wise beyond his years. His way of equalizing his time between both parents was by spending his last breath cuddling and rocking in his father's arms.

When I finally got home, it was 4:00 a.m. Patrick, my seven year old son, met me at the front door. He could see I had been crying. He told me he waited up all night, because he was praying for Bubba and his parents. Before I could even start to tell him what had happened, he said, "Bubba died tonight, didn't he?" I told him, "Yes". We sat on the couch hugging and crying for a little while longer before going to bed.

I have tried to teach my sons that dying is part of living and all of us will die someday, and no one knows when his or her time will come. That is why we need to do right and follow the teaching of our Lord so we can all meet together in heaven. With the volunteer job that I have had, my three boys have had many friends (over the years) who have passed on to another life. I brought many patients and parents home with me to spend nights and even weeks with us. My children got along great with all of the patients and never treated any of them any differently than they would have treated anyone else. I am proud to have such sensitive and caring children. I hope they will carry this quality on into their adulthood.

By V. O'C. Davis

EMMA (Dream—To go to Disney World in Florida)
By V. O'C. Davis

Emma, her Grandmother, & actress Candice Early

I thank God for the opportunity to have met Emma and her entire family. They were a very close and loving family who treated everyone with kindness. When I met Freda, Emma's grandmother, we became instant friends. I loved that wonderful lady. God blessed me when He sent me this wonderful, faithful friend.

When I was introduced to Emma and her grandmother, she was only ten years old. That day, her physician called and asked if I could come to the hospital to meet this special family. She said that Emma had a malfunctioning liver and needed a transplant in the coming years. Her physician thought that Emma needed a break from the hospital and doctor visits and asked if I could help her go on a trip somewhere.

As I spoke with both Emma and Freda, they told me her grandmother was raising her. Her mother was always close by, but it was in the best interest of Emma if she resided with her grandmother Freda. She wanted the same dream as most of our patients requested—a trip to Disney World and to meet Mickey Mouse. Since her physician was close by, I went to talk to her to make sure she would approve of Emma flying to Florida. She said there should not be a problem. I had paperwork with me at the time of the visit and gave it to the family to sign. I then took it to the doctor for her comments and approval of the trip. This is always the first step before any dream begins. Now I could move on to start the process of working with the travel agency to set up the arrangements.

When I found some time to sit and go over the paperwork, I saw that Emma would be nine years old in two weeks. I called her grandmother and asked what the family was going to do for her birthday. She said they were planning a surprise party for Emma, and all of the family would be there. She asked me to please come and bring my three boys. I asked Freda what Emma wanted for her birthday. She told me just anything I chose would be fine. I asked again, "What does she really want?" Freda said with hesitation, "A small pink or purple bicycle with a basket on it, but we don't expect you to go buy that for her." She told me no one in the family would be able to buy something that costly, but Emma would be happy even if we didn't bring anything at all. She said the fellowship of all of her friends and family would be enough for Emma to have a happy birthday.

After our conversation, I began calling around looking for a pink or purple bike with a basket on it. I found one place that had a small bike that was pink but they didn't have a basket to go on it. I ran to get the bike and stopped by Wal-Mart on the way back. They had a pink and white basket for a girl's bike, so I purchased it. My neighbor Mark was kind enough to come over and put the basket on the bike for me. It fit like a glove!

On Emma's birthday, there must have been 30 people there! And there was so much good food! Everyone was so wonderful to my children and me. They treated us as if we were a part of their own family. When the presents were all given to her, I had one of her uncles go get the bike from the trunk of my car. Emma was so grateful and so excited. She jumped on the bike and rode up and down the long driveway. That day will always be a special day for me to remember. There was such joy on Emma's face!

Our organization had a fundraiser coming up in two weeks and I had to get busy and find a limo and drivers to pick up five soap opera stars at the airport. It just happened to be on the same day that Emma was leaving for Florida. I found a dealership that would loan us a limo at no cost, but they had no drivers. I asked my neighbor Mark and his friend Ronnie if they would play the role of limo drivers for the entire day. I told them to take these people anywhere they asked to go while they were in town. I knew they were licensed drivers because they worked at a local car dealership. They told me they were delighted to do this favor for me and said they would even wear their tuxedoes. Mark and Ronnie were thrilled to be a part of it. I knew that with their kind personalities, they would be ideal for the job.

I had to be on top of everything going on the day of the event. The five stars from "All of My Children" arrived at 8:30 a.m. at the airport. The stars were Richard Shoberg as Tom Cudahy, Candice Earley as Donna Beck Tyler Corlandt Sago, Stephen Cafferey as Andrew Corlandt, Darnell Williams as Jesse Hubbard, and Debbi Morgan as Angie Hubbard. They were here to play softball against the local TV and radio personalities. We named the event "Soaps Alive". We invited all of our surviving patients to come out and watch the game and to meet these wonderful stars who took time out of their busy schedules to come help us raise the money for more children to have their dreams granted. I was quite surprised that most of these patients knew who these five stars were! It was because they were hospitalized or home from school so much and had plenty of time to watch the soap operas during the day!

When the plane arrived, the soap opera stars filed out of the plane, one at a time, and were interviewed by the statewide media. I was there to greet them and thank them for coming. Then I had to bow out gracefully because I had to hurry on to meet Emma and Freda at another gate before her plane left. Emma's plane was taking off at 9:30 a.m. and I was holding their plane tickets and itinerary. Candice Earley asked where I was going in such a hurry and I told her, "To see a dream child off to Florida." She was so sweet! She asked if she could come with me to see them off. I was happy that she was so kind. We met Emma and her grandmother and took lots of photos with Candice and Emma. Emma even knew who Candice was! She was so excited that a celebrity took time to come to meet her. I believe that she was as excited about meeting Candice as she was about going to Florida!

The day's events went just as planned. The games were very exciting and loads of laughs. It was a fun time at the ball park, and we all were pleased to be a part of it. So many of our patients were able to be there and enjoy the limelight with the stars. Most of our organization's volunteers were also there. This was a great day for everyone involved.

Emma had a wonderful vacation. She got to go to Disney World, the Epcot Center, and Sea World, and loved every minute of the trip. I was glad that she took her grandmother to share this special time with. She came home in a dream state. Her grandmother said that Emma was on "a high" for weeks and weeks. I was so happy for her! She had been through so much pain and was barely surviving her illness.

It wasn't long until Emma's liver quit functioning all together. From that day on, she had to take more medication just to keep her alive. She was in and out of the hospital. Still she fought every day to live. That entire family had such strength, because their faith in God was invincible. Freda was a very spiritual person, and I believe she was strong enough for both of them.

Freda and I became very close over the next year. She was so dear to me. One day, I received a phone call. It was Freda. She had been diagnosed with a rare type of untreatable cancer. They told her she needed to make whatever plans were needed quickly because she didn't have but a few months left. I cried for weeks and weeks. When I spoke to her, I tried to stay strong and let her know I loved her. We talked at least twice a week until her death. When she was gone, I knew that God had blessed me by bringing us together. She had enriched my life by allowing me to be a part of hers. Even though Freda has been gone for 18 years, her spirit lives on through everyone she touched. Everyone who knew her loved her dearly. There just are not enough Fredas in this world! Life could be so much better if everyone had a Freda in his or her life. I feel privileged just to have been called her friend.

After she had passed on, I lost touch with her family. The last that I heard from Emma was just after her 20th birthday. She said that she had a liver donated for her when she was 12 years old. After the surgery, recovery was fast, but she will need to take a drug for the rest of her life. This drug will keep her body from rejecting the new liver. She told me she was doing fine, had a good job and was completely well again. I'm sure that her faith has been what has turned her health around. Freda had enough faith for all of us, and I am sure that is why Emma has "beaten the odds". She had a good teacher.

By V. O'C. Davis

ANN (Dream — To go to Knott's Berry Farm and Disneyland)
By a Volunteer and a Friend

Ann was around 12 years old when her mom phoned me saying her daughter wanted a trip to California. There were many relatives that Ann had never seen before. Even her mom's brother lived out there, and they have not seen each other in 17 years. Ann wanted to meet her uncle and aunt for the first time.

Ann was diagnosed with non-Hodgkin's Lymphoma, which is a type of cancer characterized by chronic enlargement of certain body tissues similar to lymph nodes. She was taking intravenous medication at the time and could not travel until she was finished with her protocol (treatment schedule). We were looking forward to arranging a trip for her and her family, scheduling it for two months away.

I met Ann and talked to her to find out exactly what she wanted to do on the trip. She told me that she loved Snoopy and wanted to have a picture taken of her and "the real Snoopy". Since she would be in California for an entire week, we made plans for the whole family to go to Disneyland and Knott's Berry Farm. She was very happy about getting to go to Disneyland, too.

When she had a break with the treatments, we sent them on their way to California. I heard from them around the second or third day of the trip just to say thanks and to tell me that everything was wonderful. Ann was getting to meet many relatives for the first time.

The family was excited that Ann could meet them because her future was uncertain.

After they returned, I talked to them at least every other week. Sometimes we would meet and catch up on the events taking place at both ends. They lived about 55 miles from us so when I was in their town, I would call and stop by to say hello.

Ann went into remission after that first year of treatments. Things were looking up for her. She had not missed that much school during the treatments so it wasn't hard for her to catch up with the rest of the class. Ann was a very bright girl and very mature for her age. She wasn't the typical "hardheaded" teenager like most other teens at that age. She seemed quite levelheaded.

Things at home and at school got back on an even keel over the next one and a half years. Then I received a phone call from Ann's mom. She told me the following; "Ann was having a normal day and everything seemed to be fine with her. She was standing at the kitchen sink washing dishes when she let out a loud scream and she fell to the floor clutching her side." Her mom said that she ran to her but Ann was already gone. Ann was dead by the time she had hit the floor.

She said, "How could this have happened? She hadn't had any treatments in one and a half years and it wasn't very long since her last examination by the oncologist. Everything seemed to be normal. She was only 14 years old! This is not fair!" Her mom cried to me and I cried with her.

An ambulance came and took her away even though she was already gone. The driver told Ann's family that he just couldn't leave her there, lying on the kitchen floor. Later, the coroner called and said that an autopsy would have to be performed to investigate the cause of death. The family was horrified to have to allow this, but it was the only way to get answers that they all needed for closure. Her funeral had to be put off until the coroner could finish his job.

In the mean time, Ann's mom had started going through Ann's bedroom to clean up and decide what to do with everything in there. As she lifted up the Bible that was sitting on the dressing table, a note fell out. Ann's mom reached down to pick it up off the floor when she noticed the title of the topic. It said, "When I die" and there was more, "My funeral". Ann's mom sat down and began reading this letter. Ann had written it only three weeks ago. How did she know she was going to die when she was doing so well and had even gotten a good report from the oncologist just weeks ago?

She read further, "When I am buried, I want to wear my pretty white dress. (The one that I wore to Sarah's wedding.) It is hanging in the right side of my closet. I want to wear my pearl earrings and necklace that I got for my birthday last year. You can find them in my jewelry box on the dresser. Please have them put my white sandals on me, too. Before they close the casket, put this Bible on my chest."

Ann's mom went straight to the phone and called me and told me what had just happened. She asked if I had ever heard of this happening to any other families. I had not. This was my first. I told her that she should call the oncologist and ask him. He would surely know. She did call him and he acknowledged that he had, indeed, seen others that knew that their deaths were near.

Within a week, Ann's mom called to tell me when the funeral would be and where. The results of the autopsy were back. Ann's pancreas had suddenly exploded without warning due to the medication that she had taken during her treatments for non-Hodgkin's Lymphoma. No one could have predicted that beforehand. There were no outward signs to follow up on. They could not explain how Ann knew her death was near.

Then she said that she had found more writings from Ann in her work notebook from school. Among the papers was a drawing that Ann drew of herself wearing these same items that she had revealed that she wanted to be buried in. There was a note on the same page that said, "This is what I want to look like in my coffin." She added a little note in the corner saying, "Tell my brother that I love him."

I cannot explain how Ann knew she was going to die soon. Maybe she had pains and did not reveal them to anyone else because she did not want to alarm them. Maybe she just had a premonition of her death and wanted to make sure that her funeral was how she wanted it to be. That is something that we will never know for sure.

I kept in touch with Ann's family over the next six years but eventually that time lapse grew larger and larger until I have lost touch with them completely. Now I do not know if they are even living in the same town anymore. I think of them often and sometimes say a special prayer for them. They were such wonderful people, and I do miss them in my life.

By a Volunteer and a Friend

KENNETH (Dream-To go to South Padre Island, Texas)
By a Volunteer and a Friend

Kenneth was 13 years old when he was diagnosed with a malignant brain tumor. I first met him when his mother requested that I visit with them at the local children's hospital. He just had surgery on his brain to try to remove the tumor but they were unable to get all of it because of its location. It was too close to the back of his neck, next to his spinal cord. If the surgeon had tried to remove it and had accidentally hit the spinal cord, Kenneth could become paralyzed from his neck down. The surgeons were not willing to take that chance.

After surgery, his options were slim. He had to start radiation therapy immediately. He had weeks of radiation and then started getting his strength back. He asked if he could go back to school, but first on his agenda he wanted to travel to South Padre Island in Texas. His physicians agreed he could travel and signed for him to have his dream vacation of seeing South Padre Island.

He lived with his mother and older sister. His beautiful mother's assets were calmness and strength. She had to be strong to deal with what was before her. Not only was her son very ill but also she had lost her husband in an accident recently. Kenneth and his sister leaned on her for support, too. I had told Kenneth that he should be very proud of his mother. She was the perfect picture of what all mothers should be.

Two years before, his father died in an automobile accident. Kenneth had been and still was angry with his father for leaving him. He desperately missed his father and needed him now. Kenneth said he could not forgive his father for leaving their family at a time when he was needed the most.

I asked Kenneth, "Why South Padre Island?" He told me his father once lived there and had talked about how wonderful and beautiful this place was. He wanted to see this place that he had dreamed of seeing for most of his life, and it was, to him, a connection to his father. In his mind, he needed to go where he thought he could talk with his father to make things right between them. Kenneth thought that if he could get to this same place, his father would meet him and make everything all right for the future.

I made all of the necessary arrangements. He and his mother would leave soon. Two days before it was time to go on their trip, I called Kenneth and asked if he would be home for a while. I wanted to bring him something. He said, "Yes and Mom is here, too." They didn't live very far away from my home, just to the next town. It was Easter morning and I had already been to church with my children. I wanted to surprise him with something very special.

When I drove into the driveway, he ran out to meet me. I asked him to go get his mother because I wanted her to see what I was about to do. He ran inside and brought her back out to my car. I got out and handed Kenneth an Easter basket full of surprises. Not only were there candies and a stuffed rabbit, but also there were plastic eggs of different sizes and colors and each contained something special.

As Kenneth began opening the plastic Easter eggs, he found airline tickets, hotel vouchers, car rental reservations and most of all — money in several eggs! This was the cash that they would need to eat, buy gas, buy souvenirs, etc. on their upcoming trip. I took photos of him with the basket and of him opening the eggs. Kenneth was already packed and ready to go on the trip. His mother said he had been packed for days and was so excited about going. He was even having a hard time sleeping because of the excitement.

The day came for their departure and I met them at the airport right before boarding time. We hugged, and I told him to watch out for his mother because she was so pretty that surely some handsome guy might come along and try to snatch her up. We laughed and kissed good-bye. His mother promised to call me at some point during the weeklong trip to give me the updates.

The second night of their trip, she called me around 11:00 p.m. She was crying so hard that I began to panic and wondered what had happened. I thought she was calling because he was worse or he had gotten hurt. She finally dried up her tears long enough to talk to me. Something very significant had happened to Kenneth. The first night of their stay, he had wandered off without telling her where he was going. She said that he was gone until nearly midnight. She had checked over and over with the service attendant at the hotel but he had not been seen. She was about ready to call the police, but first decided to walk up and down the beach to see if he was out there.

The moon was extremely bright that night. The deserted beach looked so wonderfully inviting with the warm breeze coming in off of the waters. There he was, in the distance sitting in the sand, looking out over the gulf waters. She ran to him and found him crying. When she asked what was wrong, he said he had been visiting with his father for hours. Kenneth had forgiven his father for leaving them so suddenly and without warning. He said that he had talked out all of his problems and had faced his illness and his fears. He was not afraid to die anymore. His fear had not been for himself but for his sister and his mother. He knew how devastated they would be when it was his time to go to be with Jesus. She told me that they stayed on that beach talking for the rest of the night and on into the morning. They had watched the sun rise together. Kenneth told his mother that gorgeous sunrise shining on the golden sand was a sign of his new beginning. Kenneth had become a new person overnight.

When they arrived back from the trip, Kenneth was ready to reenter school and try to get on with his life. His mom was able to get him back in school among his friends and classmates, which we all thought would probably be good for him.

He had only been back in school for two weeks when while riding the school bus home one day, a few of the boys started teasing him about not having any hair (due to the radiation). They had removed his ball cap and were tossing it from person to person on the bus. When his stop came up, he pleaded with them to give him back his hat because he had to leave the bus. Then one of them came up from behind him and hit him hard in the back of the head (as he slapped Kenneth's cap back on his head). As Kenneth was stepping off of the bus, he fell to the ground holding his head and crying. The driver called for an ambulance and then called for Kenneth's mother to come quickly.

His mom arrived even before the ambulance did. When the ambulance got there, they loaded him in the ambulance and took him on to the local children's hospital. Late that evening, his mom called to tell me what had happened and that Kenneth had gone into a coma after he was hit by that boy. I could hardly believe my ears! What kind of person could be so cruel? Kenneth was so sweet and full of life. I just do not understand some people. I am not sure if anything was ever done to punish that young man for hitting Kenneth, but he sure needed it.

A month went by and Kenneth had no changes. I would go by the hospital to see him and talk to him even though the physicians had told us that he couldn't hear me. (This was in the mid 1980s.) I told his mom to talk to him, too. I would say, "How do they know he can't hear us?" There he stayed, hospitalized, with no changes for months until his mom finally asked if he could come home. She said that she could get a nurse to come by everyday to check on him and give him injections when needed. The doctors agreed. At least she could be there 24 hours a day and still get things accomplished around the house. This arrangement worked out so much better for her.

He had been home for a week when I went out to see them. I talked to her for a while and she told me they had taken Kenneth off of the IVs and he was not going to live much longer. He was not receiving any type of nutrition so he was becoming weaker everyday. Of course, this was her decision to make and I dare not give any opinions on the matter. I am not one to judge another, especially when I do not know what it is like to be in their shoes. I can only hope and pray God will spare me from having to make any decisions of this type in the future.

I went into his bedroom (right next to the living room) where Kenneth was lying on a twin bed. His mom was folding laundry in the living room and her daughter was to arrive any minute. I was talking to Kenneth, as I usually did, when he opened his eyes and looked at me.

A cold chill ran across my spine as I tried to remain calm for him. I asked him if he knew where he was and he said, "Yes, I'm home." I asked him what made him wake up. He said, "I heard you talking to me and decided I wanted to talk to you and tell you thank you for helping me go on that trip." "You know, that trip was important to me. I saw my dad!" I told him that his mom had told me everything about the trip. I asked if he felt like sitting up and he said, "Okay". I propped up two pillows behind his head and back. He was not comfortable so he suggested that he use me as a prop so he could sit up straighter. So I sat down near his head and I helped him move around so the back of his head was leaning against me. I held him to keep him upright.

As we talked, I calmly called to his mother, "Mary, will you please come in here?" She said, "Sure, in a minute!" So I said, "Mary, can you come in here now, please?" She dropped what she was doing and walked in and stood at the foot of his bed, only for a second, with a shocked look on her face. Kenneth smiled and said, "Hi Mom." She saw him sitting up with his eyes open and she fell to the floor on her knees and began crying. I said, "I can't come pick you up off the floor so you'll need to get up on your own and come over here." Kenneth and I chuckled. She got up and immediately started asking what, when and how this had happened. I told her what he said about hearing me and decided to "wake up" and talk to me. I asked Kenneth if he was hungry and he said, "Yes." I then asked if he would drink a nutrition shake for me. He said, "Sure." I asked his mom to go get one from the refrigerator and she did. I held it while he drank the entire canned drink through a straw.

Just as he finished the entire shake, his sister came home just in time to see him awake and he talked to her, too. Mom and his sister talked to Kenneth nonstop for a short while when he looked up at me and said, "I'm tired and I'm ready to lie down again. This time mom helped him while I moved out of the way. As he lay back down, he looked at me and said, "I love you." I said, "I love you, too. And thank you for waking up to talk to me." I left the room so his mom and sister could talk to him alone. He turned to his sister and mom and said that he loved them. He then said something special to each one and closed his eyes. He went back into a coma and never woke up again.

When his mother called the doctors to tell them that he had awakened from that deep sleep just to talk for a while, they said, "Well, maybe we need to change our way of thinking. Before now, we had never known anyone who had awakened from a coma and carried on a conversation and then went back to sleep again." They sent for an ambulance to come take him back to the hospital for tests. He stayed in the hospital for the remaining time he had left.

He died a short time later; only one and a half weeks after that great day that he woke up long enough to say what he thought was important for each of us to hear.

Kenneth was a wonderful loving child. He was too young to have experienced so much tragedy in his short life here on earth, but while he was here, he made a difference in the lives around him. Everyone he touched is so grateful for the privilege of knowing him. I am thankful to have been one of those individuals. It has been 20 years since his death and I still feel like it was yesterday. I will always have a warm place in my heart for him and his family.

By a Volunteer and a Friend

Chapter V.

Sometimes accidents happened while we were in the process of completing the wish. No matter what happened, we still managed to be on time to finalize the dreams.

SONNY (Dream—To have an All Terrain Vehicle)
By V. O'C. Davis

Early one morning, I received a phone call from an oncologist at the local children's hospital. The phone call was in regards to a patient who was 13 years old. The child had been asking his doctor to call our organization. The child's name was Sonny. He wanted to get an ATV (all terrain vehicle); precisely a four-wheeler was the request. The physician said that Sonny was in fairly good condition after a series of chemotherapy treatments he had received since his diagnosis of acute myelogenous leukemia (A.M.L.). He said since Sonny had a three-wheeler last year (before his diagnosis) he felt Sonny would be cautious when riding a four-wheeler, if we did indeed get him one.

The doctor went on to say that Sonny sold his three-wheeler and bought a drum set with the money last winter. Now that spring was here, he really missed having an ATV and was very sorry for giving his up. Sonny and his family lived in the country where they owned a large plot of land. Sonny could ride it within their private property and still be close to home.

After receiving the information about Sonny from his physician, we contacted the mother and requested an interview to determine whether Sonny could be a good candidate for an ATV. We have never felt completely safe giving any patient an ATV, but if the physician and parents of the patients were willing to sign releases to that affect they will not hold our organization responsible in case of an accident, we will give the patient his request.

All releases were signed at a meeting with the patient, his parents and the oncologist. Now we had to find a dealership willing to help us with a break on the cost. Luckily, we had a good relationship with a local dealer, so we contacted him. We worked out a deal with him for the ATV but there was no trailer to borrow for hauling it to the small town, as we had done in the past. Since the family lived about 60 miles out of town, we had to contact a car dealership in our area that was willing to donate the use of a pick-up truck to haul the four-wheeler to the home of this child. We found one on the same day.

Sonny would be released from the hospital on Tuesday morning and get home no later than noon. We worked the schedule out around him. The only problem we had at the time was that the car dealer could not let us borrow the truck until the morning of the dream being granted. That pushed us to a smaller time frame to work within. This meant that we had to pick up the truck around 9:30 a.m., go straight to the ATV dealer to pick up the four-wheeler, and then high-tail it 60 miles away, on rural back roads, in time to meet Sonny and his parents at their home. Now, the newspaper and TV media wanted to cover Sonny receiving the ATV. They would be meeting us at the same place and time.

That Tuesday morning started out very well for me. I took my three sons to school and ran back home to get ready for the dream. I could not find anyone else within the organization that could go with me, so I was to do this by myself. My plan was to go back home to apply my make-up, fix my hair and dress properly. Then I would dash to the car dealership for the truck and to the ATV dealership for the four-wheeler and then race to meet Sonny arriving home from the hospital. Okay, that sounded easy enough!

I decided, at the last possible minute to change shoes and wear designer shoes from Italy that I had just purchased the day before. I was moving very fast because I was running out of time. Just as I was about to step down the stairs in my house, my right high-heeled shoe broke throwing me frontward down to the next step where I knew I could catch my fall with my other foot. As I was falling, I stepped down to the next stair with my left foot, and the second shoe broke! I went tumbling down the stairs and landed at the bottom. I was in pain, but also in shock. I looked around and saw my right arm up and behind me. My right leg was draped sideways. I evaluated the situation before I tried to move. At least I was not bleeding anywhere! I knew I was in trouble but I did not have time for this. I had to think fast. "What was I going to do?"

I tried to get up, but I could not walk. I pulled my right arm down to my side and began crawling back up the stairs to the next room to reach the phone. It was very painful, but I kept thinking about the need for me to get to those places because I was running out of time. I knew I did not have enough time to go to the emergency room first if I was to get to Sonny's house on time. As I crawled back upstairs to the phone, I made a decision. I would call my husband at work and ask him to come home and help me. This was so unlike me. I never asked him for help with anything!

I got my husband on the phone and said, "I need help." He had never heard those words from me before. He screamed, "Oh my God! What is wrong?" I told him to go by the car dealership to borrow the truck, then go to the ATV dealership to load up the ATV, and then come home to get me. I would explain everything when he got here. I called both dealerships and told them to get ready for him to come. We were running a little behind the time schedule.

He showed up about 45 minutes later and came running in the house. There I was lying, on the floor! I told him I fell down the stairs, but I was alright for now. I needed him to retrieve my tennis shoes from the closet and carry me to the truck. He was not very happy with me because I would not let him take me to the hospital. I talked him into driving on to Sonny's house and promised that he could take me to the emergency room after we granted the dream.

For the next hour, on the road to Sonny's house, I had to listen to him fussing at me for being so stubborn. We arrived in the nick of time. Since I could not walk, I asked Sonny's mother to please bring out a chair so I could be outside when we gave the four-wheeler to Sonny. I told her that I was injured but did not want the media to pick up on that. I just wanted them to focus on the coverage of Sonny receiving his dream.

Everything was set up and ready when the media arrived. I was sitting outside with a good view of the yard. Sonny's father kept Sonny occupied inside so he would not see us in the front yard. He waited until we were ready for him and then brought him out to us. His parents had helped this day remain a secret so Sonny would be surprised.

As the media taped the events, Sonny and his parents came over to me and I told Sonny that we had a surprise for him in the back of the pick-up truck. He ran over there as the ATV was being taken out of the truck. He was jumping and yelling from shear delight! Sonny talked to the media first. Then he and his father got on the ATV and started it. They took off and drove the ATV up and down a small hill beside their front yard. They kept circling around us, laughing and shouting to us as they went by.

I was so happy we got there in time, and I thanked God for helping everything go so well for Sonny. I had forgotten about my pain because it was replaced by my happiness for Sonny. After all, he was going through so much more pain and rough times than I could ever even imagine. My problems were nothing compared to his. This day was for Sonny and nothing could have stopped me from seeing it happen.

After the interviews and discussions were over it was time to leave. Sonny hugged us over and over as he thanked us for getting his dream. This is what that day was all about! Making him happy even if it was just for a while! Days like this are much needed to help these wonderful children keep going. These special dreams are sometimes just what are needed to get them a little further along in life and show them others do really care what is happening in their lives.

When we left Sonny's house, my husband drove me straight to the hospital emergency room back in the city. The doctors did not understand why I hadn't come right away. When I explained that it was important to see the dream granted first, they were not impressed. It was four and a half hours after my accident by the time I made it to the hospital. After the x-rays, they found that my right foot was broken, my right shoulder had been pulled out of socket and I had a slipped disk in my neck. It sure didn't seem that serious when I was so busy thinking about Sonny.

Sonny got to enjoy his four-wheeler for another one and a half years before he became too ill to ride it any longer. After he was gone, the family called me to tell me that when he died, they sold the ATV to help pay for his funeral. I was glad they had it to sell.

By V. O'C. Davis

MIKE (Dream — To have Art Supplies)
JAMES (Dream — To have a large Gas-Powered
  Airplane)
ROBERT (Dream — To have a Remote-controlled Car)
By a Volunteer and a Friend

Nine year old Mike, eleven year old James and sixteen year old Robert were brothers, and all three were diagnosed with the same crippling and life threatening disease. They were diagnosed with Duchene (one of the worst forms of muscular dystrophy). Even though they had a 14 year old sister, she was untouched by the disease. This is because this deadly disease only attacks the males in families.

People hear the words muscular dystrophy and think that this is a crippling muscular disease and everyone who has it are the same, and treatments are the same. This is not true. There are actually 40 different types of muscular dystrophy. Duchene is life threatening and is one of the worst types to treat. The life span of a patient is far less than most patients with other forms of muscular dystrophy. If a patient diagnosed with Duchene lives to be 20 years old, it is rare.

This story begins when I received a call from the boys' doctor. He gave me the information about the family, their address and phone number. He thought that these three boys needed some positive moments in their lives. The oldest was not expected to live very long. I called the family to ask for a meeting and get directions to their home. They were already expecting my call.

They lived in a rural part of the state about 65 miles from the city. On the way to their home, as I read the directions to their house, I passed by it, thinking it was a two-car garage or a small mechanic's shop. When I backtracked using the map, it led me back to the same location. When I got closer, I just stopped the car and sat on the dirt road staring at the building. It was too small for a house! This building was made from concrete blocks and sat on a slab floor. I knew that the family consisted of three sons and a daughter and both parents. I thought, "How were they living in this small space?" I saw smoke coming from the chimney and realized that someone must be inside. I collected my thoughts and drove on up to the house.

I walked up and knocked on the door, still thinking that this was not a house at all, but I was hoping that someone in there could tell me where to find this family's home. A very nice older woman came to the door and I could quickly see that inside was a home setting. I asked if I was at the right house and she said, "We thought that might be you. We've been watching you for some time now and were wondering if you were going to find us okay." She invited me in and I sat down at the kitchen table and put down the paperwork. That was the grandmother who answered the door. She lived there, too!

There were only three rooms in the home and I could see all of them from the table. There were two small bedrooms, and a kitchen/living/dining room combination. A pot bellied, wood-burning stove sat in the middle by the kitchen and living areas. It looked like this was the only heat in the whole house. We were in the dead of winter and it was cold outside! I know that it must be freezing in this house in the early mornings because it was in the afternoon when I was there and it was cold, then!

While the mother and I were having a conversation, her husband (and father of the children) walked in from outside and said hello. The daughter also came in and started talking to me. We had just begun to talk about each of the boys having a dream granted when in came Mike, the nine year old. He could walk fairly well but his ankles and feet were turned inward. His hands were badly disfigured and his fingers were folded up permanently in the palm of his hands.

He plopped down on my lap and immediately started talking about his art. I could see that he was probably the center of attention in that household! He told me that he "could draw real good with his feet". I was amazed and asked him if he could show me some of his pictures. He took me to a bedroom that had three beds and one chest of drawers with a mirror hanging on the wall. His "art" was in a pile on the floor.

Mike started gathering up, with his wrists and arms, pictures he had drawn and some he had painted with watercolors. I was quite amazed to see that these were very good! I said, "Did you say that you drew these with your feet?" Mike assured me that he can't use his hands and that his toes were the only way that he could hold the pencils and paint brushes. He told me to pick up his pencil and the large sketching pad and go back to the table with him. When I did, he hopped back up onto my lap and told me to hold the pad out for him. He put the pencil in his toes and began to draw. He was very good! Most people I know that have two good hands could not compete with his talent!

I asked him if he could have something, anything that he wanted, what would it be? He immediately said, "Pencils, chalk, drawing paper and lots of paint and paintbrushes." I looked at his mom and she said, "If that's what he wants then it's okay with me." I said, "But Mike, don't you want to go see anything, like travel to see something special?" He said, "No and besides, my brothers can't travel anywhere because they are too sick. I won't go anywhere without them." I was deeply touched that he cared that much about his brothers.

It was not long until all of the commotion woke up James. James is the 11 year old. He started yelling for someone to come and get him out of his bed and put him in his wheelchair so he could join in the action. His father quickly went in to get him and rolled him out to sit with us. James was much quieter than Mike. He was even a little shy. I talked to him for a few minutes in between Mike's interruptions and he warmed up to me. I asked him what he would want if he could have anything that he asked for. Just like Mike, he already had been thinking about it. He wanted to have a gas-powered airplane. I was not familiar with what that was, so James had to explain it to me.

A gas-powered plane is huge, almost the length of an automobile and just about as wide as one. He told me, "You can control the flight by remote but it takes gasoline to power it." The first thing that I thought about and said was, "And James, what happens when it crashes?" He said that if they had a bad crash, it couldn't be fixed. If it was a small crash, then most likely they could repair it "just like the real planes". He assured me that he had been around them most of his life. There was a club in the city that met and flew their planes the first Sunday of every month. He wanted to be in that club, also.

I turned to their father and asked, "How much does one cost?" He claimed that they were around $700.00 each which included all of the accessories. "Oh Boy! That seems like a lot of money for something that could crash on the same day that he got it!" I was concerned about that being his dream. I told him that I would have to check this out and talk to someone before I could promise him a plane. James didn't even seem worried. He just said, "Okay" and went on talking about other things.

Now we are hearing Robert waking up for his meds. Robert was the 16 year old and was bed-ridden. He could only raise his head for a few minutes at a time. The rest of his body was immobile. He was in the final stages of the disease and his time remaining was very short. I went to his bedside to talk to him. I told him about what I did and I just wanted to get some idea of what he might want for a dream. He said that he has always wanted a remote control car. He said that he could play with it from his bed and his brothers would help him to guide it. I was nearly in tears. I said I would see what I could do for him and if he could think of anything else I would like to add it to the list.

It was time to sit down with their parents and talk about everything. I explained that they would need to sign the legal paperwork before I could do anything. I told them I would meet with the doctor again and discuss everything that the boys were asking for but I didn't foresee a problem with any of the requests.

The mother signed the documents without hesitation. She got up to start cooking supper so I decided that it was time to go. She asked me to stay for dinner but I told her that I had three boys at home and needed to get back to see that they were all right.

When I got in the car and started the long drive home, I began to cry. I believe that I cried most of the way home that evening. I was so full of emotions. I was amazed at how close the entire family was. They truly loved one another and each son thought of the others before himself; they all seemed to work as a team in doing most things. The parents were full of love toward their children and I could feel the love they had for me, a total stranger. They practically lived right on top of one another in that small house but it did not seem to matter to them.

In spite of their situation, there was more love in that house than I had ever seen in most other people's homes. They were taking the worst of times and making them the best of times. These children had asked for so little and yet I could see that there were so many other needs that family had. Their family was truly the perfect picture of what a family should be. They may not have had much, but they had each other, which was in reality, so much more than most!

My plan was to go, on the upcoming Sunday, to the area outside of town where the pilots of the gas-powered airplane club met. Maybe if I could talk to some of them, they could give me some insight into what I was looking for. That Sunday, I was there long before anyone else arrived. I had waited over an hour before the first one showed up. At least I had the right Sunday!

A gentleman and his family came to talk to me and were very nice. I told them that I was looking for someone who could get me familiar with the planes and show me what all was needed as accessories. The man gave me the name and phone number of the president of the club. (Later, I went home and called him.) But for now, I watched around 20 people fly their airplanes for hours. This was really interesting!

I made an appointment with him to talk about the planes. We met and he gave me the information that I needed. Then he said, "You know, I could donate one of my planes to your organization and take the tax deduction at the end of the year." I agreed but wanted to know about that plane first. He said it was in excellent condition and it flew very well. I asked him to please let me see it fly before I accepted it for the child.

The following weekend I took my children with me and met him at the airplane club. He flew the plane around and around until it was almost out of gas. The plane actually looked brand new and it flew without any problems so I made a date to come get it from him. It was too big to fit in my car!

The following Wednesday evening, I arrived at his home and met him and his wife. We walked back out the front door and he said, "Follow me to around the house to my shop in the backyard." As he walked ahead of me, I could hardly keep up because he was walking too fast. There were no outside lights on the house so I couldn't see where to walk. It had been raining and it was night-time. There was not even a moon shining to light my way. Besides, I was walking slowly because I had on some very expensive shoes and I was wading through deep puddles of water in the yard. It was wintertime, so I had on a heavy faux fur coat, that later, turned out to be a blessing for me.

The man went into the shop in the rear of the back yard and did not even look back for me or wait for me. As soon as he disappeared into the shop some 30 yards ahead of me, something grabbed and clutched onto my right arm. I could not even see what had me! Then I heard the growling. It was a dog! A big dog! This dog kept biting and pulling my arm. I knew not to scream because the dog may become angrier. I did call out to the man by calling his name several times as loud as I could as not to upset the dog even more. He did not hear me. He had a radio on in the shop! Couldn't he see that I was not coming right behind him?

The dog kept biting up and down my arm never really releasing me so I could not go forward or backward. I tried but I couldn't get away. He had me good and he knew it. Then all at once the dog leaped for the front of my throat. All I could see were his eyes and teeth in my face. I put my injured arm back in his mouth. He lunged for my throat over and over and I just kept giving him back my right arm. It was so dark that I couldn't even see his body. All that I knew was that he was a big dog!

Finally, the man came out to see why I didn't make it to the shop. He saw his dog jerking me around and yelled for the dog to stop, but the dog ignored him. The man ran over and tried pulling the dog off of me but the dog would not let go. He went back in the shop and came back out with a metal pipe. He began beating the dog in the head, yelling at him and pulling on the dog's collar. Finally the dog released me but was still growling and snarling at me. He chewed on my arm for about three to four minutes, but it sure seemed longer! I really didn't know that I was actually hurt yet because I was in shock.

That man walked me on into the shop and he didn't even tie the dog up! He told the dog to sit and the dog sat, but the whole time he was growling under his breath and staring at me. I was nervous about being there in the same building with his dog. I said, "Why is that dog still loose? Why don't you tie him up or take him somewhere else where he can't attack me again?" The man said, "Oh, he didn't mean any harm. He just thought that you were invading his backyard or it could be that fur coat you're wearing!"

This man was living in a dream world! His dog was going for my throat! He meant to kill me! "Oh, he didn't mean it!" I said, "Yeah right! He is still growling and watching my every move. You need to tie him up until I leave!" Now I could see the dog clearly under the shop light. It was a German Shepherd and the man said that the dog weighed 110 lbs. That dog weighed five more pounds than I did!

The man closed the dog up in the shop as we left and he then carried the plane out of the yard. This time, I was not leaving any space between us just in case that dog got out! He put the plane into the back of the pickup truck that I had borrowed from a car dealership. He also brought out all of the necessary accessories for James.

The man then took me inside the house for a visit and to tell me all about the accessories. They offered me a chair and I then sat on the floor. I do not remember why I did that. His wife offered me a cup of coffee, but I declined. They helped me get my coat off to look at my arm. My $300.00 new coat had ripped straight up the back! I saw the coat and said, "That was a new coat! And an expensive one, too!" My arm did not have any open wounds so they said, "You're all right now. He didn't hurt you too bad. He has never bitten anyone before. What did you do to make him mad?" With a shrilled voice, I answered, "Make him mad? I didn't even know he was there until he grabbed me!" I just wanted to go home. I got up, thanked them for the airplane and left.

I backed out of the driveway and as soon as I got two houses away, I began to shake uncontrollably and cry. I couldn't even press down on the brake to stop the truck. My legs were shaking too much. I managed to get my foot on the brake and then slam it into park and the truck stopped. I thought, "Now what I am going to do? I'm shaking too much to drive." I walked back to the house and used their phone. I called a friend and asked her to please come and get me. And she did.

When she saw me, she took me straight to the hospital. My friend arranged for someone else to drive the truck to my house so I wouldn't worry about someone stealing the truck or the airplane.

I had serious injuries and not all of them visible. Besides the bruising from about 150 separate bites to my arm, my right shoulder had been pulled completely out of socket. This was the 2nd time that I had been injured in the same shoulder while granting a dream. (The first time was about a year before.) In the emergency room, the doctor shoved the shoulder back in place. I screamed so loud that my own ears rang. Later, when I went home, my husband asked if I screamed when they shoved my shoulder back into place. I said, "Well, yes, didn't you hear me?"

To this day, I am deathly afraid of German Shepherds and I do not trust their owners for fear they may think "Their dog would never bite anyone". Some dog owners just refuse to believe that their dogs will bite. Hello, people! They are dogs! That's what dogs do to protect their owners and their properties!

It took me about a week to go purchase the other items on the boys' lists and get back with the parents to set up the date and time to bring the gifts to them. I questioned if the boys had asked for anything else. The mom said they hadn't. I asked about the 14 year old daughter's clothes size because I was going to get her some new clothes, too. I found a donor to pay for her things separately. I didn't want her to feel left out.

The day came quickly to take them their dream gifts. Although the requests were so small, they said that was everything that they wanted. Those children were so very excited when I arrived with the presents. Mike was the first one to have everything opened. He had received several hundred dollars worth of art supplies. He was excited to get these things.

Mike then ran over to help his oldest brother, Robert open his gift. Robert got a huge remote control car that cost $250.00. It was very nice and it did several different stunts. Robert was thrilled. Immediately Mike helped Robert steer it and they had mastered the moves in just minutes! The tires were squealing all over the room. They did wheelies and jumps and got it to ride upright on its back wheels. They were laughing and really were having a great time playing together.

James had asked for the plane. It was in the back of the truck that I drove. It was too big to wrap! I told the dad to please roll James out to the truck. Once we were out there, I opened the tailgate to show James his airplane. He was so excited that he almost jumped out of the wheelchair! His dad pulled it out carefully and carried it to the back of the house.

The sister was out there with us. From the cab of the truck, I pulled out a large gift-wrapped box and handed it to her and told her that this was her gift. She said, "What? You got me something, too?" She had tears in her eyes and ran inside to open it. Then the dad came back to the truck again and showed James the accessories that came with the plane. It was everything that they could possibly need. I had even filled the gas can with gasoline before I got there.

The entire family was elated and thanked me over and over. I explained that it wasn't just me who did this. It was all of the wonderful, caring people that worked together to make their dreams come true.

I never mentioned to the family that I had been injured in the process of getting the airplane. That family did not need to know that. I never contacted the owner of the dog or sued them over my injuries either. Many said that I should have, but I just did not feel right suing them. After all, they were kind enough to donate the plane and accessories for James. I just could not do that to anyone who was helping with a dream, no matter how many years I have spent dealing with those injuries.

A few weeks after the dreams had been granted; I called a few grocery stores and individuals to ask for food donations for this family. Right before Thanksgiving, I took the boxes of food out there to them. There was enough food and staples in the boxes to at least get them through the Thanksgiving and Christmas holidays.

I called the mom after the first of January and asked about each child and then asked about James' airplane. "Was it still in one piece?" She laughed and said that it had a small accident, but it had been repaired and was flying just fine again. They were putting it up until spring after it gets warmer outside. I felt a little more at ease about the airplane after that.

Later on that year, they lost Robert and James started getting worse. When I first met them, I could see the different stages of the illness just by looking at all three boys. Now, James was taking Robert's place in line. I could not even imagine what a nightmare that those wonderful people were living through. I was sorry that they were going through such a hard time, but they had a very strong faith in God. Their mother told me many times that this is where their family's strength comes from.

I have seen parents of children that were dying when they did not believe in God or in any other higher power. That means that they do not believe in heaven or hell, either. They think that when a person dies, they are put in the ground to rot or to be cremated and it's over. I say, "What does that leave for them to hope for? Especially when their child is dying! There is no one to pray to or believe in during the hardest times of their lives." Those are the ones who are lost when their child is gone or when any loved one has passed on. They have nothing to ease their fears or to help them through the hardest times. Those are the people that I really feel sorry for.

By a Volunteer and a Friend

Chapter VI.

The chapter will allow you to take a peek at some of the bizarre and unusual events that took place while we were in the process of granting the dreams. Thankfully, these were very rare times.

BILL (Dream — To have an All Terrain Vehicle)
By a Volunteer

Late one evening, I had been visiting one of our dream patients when I met Bill, in the hallway of the cancer floor, at our local children's hospital. Bill had heard from a couple of LPNs, on that floor, that I was someone that he should meet. He didn't waste any time once he heard I was there. He came up to me and introduced himself in the hall as I was leaving. Bill wanted to have a dream granted. He wanted an ATV (all terrain vehicle). A four-wheeler was on his agenda.

Bill was a 16 year old teenager who lived on the outskirts of a larger city. He was diagnosed with ostco sarcoma (a type of bone cancer). I met him just after he had surgery on one of his legs. They had removed part of his leg, from the knee down, and he had just been fitted with a prosthetic leg. He was able to walk around without anyone even knowing that he was wearing the device.

I was impressed with him because he had taken the initiative to come find me and was adult enough to carry on an intelligent conversation. As we sat and talked, I could see that he had such a good outlook on his situation and a very positive attitude about getting well. His mother arrived as we were sitting there and talking. Bill introduced us and I very much liked her, too. She was a positive influence to Bill. No wonder he was doing so well!

Before I left the hospital that evening, I told both of them that I never make promises of a dream until the child's physician agrees and signs a release allowing the dream to go forward. Besides, I hated those four-wheelers! I had tried to discourage him from asking for one, but his mind was set. I did not like giving ATVs to the patients because I thought they were too dangerous. I took down their address and phone number and said that I would get back with them when the oncologist and I had discussed Bill and his dream request.

Over the next couple of days, I did meet Bill's oncologist. He felt that Bill could have the four-wheeler and believed that Bill was very level headed and thought he would be very cautious on one. I called Bill's mother and told her that the doctor had agreed to a four-wheeler for Bill's dream. I would shop around and call them when I found a dealer who was willing to give us a break on the cost. I found one fairly easy—really too easy! The first dealer that I contacted was not only willing to give it to us for half of the cost, but he knew Bill. The dealer said that Bill and his daughter went to school together and were around the same age.

I called Bill and the dealership to set up a time to meet. That following Saturday, Bill and his mother met me at the dealership and he picked one out and test-drove it. Then is when I noticed that Bill was using the prosthetic foot to push down the gas pedal. I said, "Oh no! Is this going to work for you?" I know that Bill thought, "You silly woman!" (but he didn't say it). He was much too kind and so very happy that he just said, "I can use the prosthetic leg just like it is my real leg." That shut me up but it really did not quiet my fears.

When Bill had made his decision, I paid for the vehicle. I had borrowed a small trailer from the dealership to take it to Bill's home. We loaded it up and then Bill rode with me to his house. He was extremely happy and laughed a lot that day.

Weeks had gone by since the dream was granted and I hadn't heard from them so I picked up the phone and called Bill's mother. I was worried about him getting hurt on that machine. Well, everything was fine and Bill was riding the four-wheeler every waking hour. She did say that he was fishing close by and was expected back soon. She said that Bill could call me back when he returned.

Bill called me back within the hour. He invited me to come out to their home because he wanted to give me a bunch of strawberry plants from his garden. We set the date for the following Saturday and we met then. Bill and I were outside, in their unfenced back yard, digging up plants when a little girl wandered up to me. I turned around to see this very small child with one arm in a sling. She was also losing clumps of her hair. This was a sight that I knew only too well! I stood up and asked Bill to introduce us. I asked her where she lives and she pointed down the street about a block away. I asked her several questions about her illness and herself. She told me that she was seven years old and had bone cancer.

Bill came over to me and said that this little girl had lost her dog a few months ago to bone cancer, too. Then during that same conversation, I was told about five more children in this same trailer park that all had cancer of some type and that another neighbor had lost their family dog to bone cancer, also.

I decided to go inside and talk to Bill's mother about this. She confirmed what Bill had just told me. I asked, "What was going on? This is too much cancer for this small area! What had the doctors said about these coincidences?" I could see something very wrong with this picture! She said that the doctors knew about other patients with the same type of cancer but never did anything about it. I decided to go on home since it was getting dark. But before I left, I asked Bill if he knew where all of the patients lived. He knew, all right. I said, "Come get in my car and as I drive you can guide me around to all of the trailers where you know someone is sick inside." And we did just that. It looked like the vicinity was a four-block radius. I took him back home and told him, "I'm not sure what to do, but I will try to find the right people to tell. I'll let you know as soon as I find out something."

The next morning I went to my office, which at that time was on the top floor of the only radiation therapy institute in the central part of the state. I met with the President of the Institute and the Director of Public Relations, explained what I had found and asked what to do with the information. They immediately became as concerned as I was. Some of those patients came here for radiation, so the Director of Public Relations knew a couple of them. I was given the phone number of a man from the Environmental Protection Agency (EPA). I called him and gave him the information. He said he would send someone out to take soil samples from around that area, test it and then get back with me.

It was over a month before I finally heard back from the man at the EPA, but when he did call me, he told me that what they found was substantial. Soil samples had been taken all around and inside of the trailer park. They found a 12-acre lot in the area not only unfenced, but it was right in the trailer park. It was actually a dumping ground for toxic chemicals. Besides finding toxic chemicals, they also found old electrical transformers and car batteries that were lying around in this same lot.

I called Bill as soon as we hung up. Bill knew about that piece of land. All of the kids in the neighborhood played there and, yes, the dogs went with them often. I told him that he needed to drive around the neighborhood on his new four-wheeler and tell the people and kids not to go around that area. The EPA would be contacting each residence to warn them to stay away from that area, but that might take weeks.

I never heard anything back from the EPA employee directly, but all I had to do was turn on the TV news or open up the newspaper. It was all over the news. They were looking for the owner of the property. They knew who he was, but did not know where he was. The EPA said this man was being paid by large companies to dump toxic waste on his land. He had no consideration for anyone else's well being. It seemed that the all-mighty-dollar was what he cared about even more.

Within a month, he was in custody. It was in the news again. When his trial came up, he was sentenced to 12 years. Only 12 years, and how many lives did he take? Years later, the media covered a parole hearing where he might be released, but so many came forward that he did not get the parole. I believe that he ended up serving his entire sentence behind bars. He has been out for many years now. I can only hope that he was sorry for what he did and is now a changed man.

I have seen so many different types of situations over the 14 years of my volunteer service, but it never ceases to amaze me what some people will do. I have a hard time understanding those who do not have a conscience. What is sad is that the older I get, the more people I meet are like that.

I am happy to report that Bill is still with us 20 years later, has a great job and has never had a reoccurrence of bone cancer.

By a Volunteer

SARA (Dream—To Search for her Missing Father)
By a Volunteer

One day, while I was working in the office, I received a phone call from a young girl who said she was a patient at the local children's hospital. She explained that she had a brain tumor and was told that everything that could be done for her had already been done. She went on to say that she had several surgeries but the tumor was in a place where it could not be completely removed. She had already gone through the radiation and chemotherapy treatments, and, yes, it was a malignant tumor, and her outcome was dim.

She said that she was told to contact me because there was something that she really wanted but knew it would be next to impossible to accomplish without our help. She was 16 years old and had never seen nor heard from her father. She asked if we could help her try to find him. She wanted to meet him before she died.

I questioned her about him. Who last saw him, when and where? The only thing she knew was that when she was two weeks old, in Atlanta, Georgia, he came around to see her and then disappeared. I told Sara that usually when people disappear it is because they don't want to be found. If he knew about her birth and believed that she was his child and left anyway, maybe it was because he did not want the responsibility of having a child.

I tried to explain to her, "You cannot expect us to find him and everything will magically turn out like a fairy-tale ending. He probably will not be very happy if, in fact, he is hiding out and we found him, anyway. What if we do find him and he refuses to come and meet with you? You would be devastated! Do you really want to put yourself through this? Sara, surely you can understand that if we find him, you can't expect him to fall madly in love with you after 16 years of separation. Love is very strange, as strange as each individual. You cannot make someone love you. You cannot make a person change just because you want them to. I am trying to tell you the negative side of things to prepare you for the worst. We do not really know what will happen or if we will even be able to find him."

"And what about your mother? How is she going to react toward him? Or him towards her? She cannot be too happy about him running off without helping her with <u>their</u> daughter." Sara assured me that her mother was willing to cooperate with us and help in any way possible. I requested to meet with both of them in the afternoon to discuss this further. The time was set for early in the afternoon so I could still have time to also meet with Sara's neurologist and oncologist. I wanted their opinions before proceeding.

I met Sara and her mother in her hospital room. Sara was a beautiful young lady. She had lost her hair due to the treatments and had a scarf tied around her head. She was so vibrant even without her hair. Her face had a glow to it and she had such a wonderful smile. She even giggled now and then as we talked.

Sara's mother convinced me that she would not interfere if we found her dad. I commented that I certainly did not want to be involved with any trouble that might erupt from us finding him. Her mother signed the waiver allowing us to proceed. From there I met with Sara's physicians, and they agreed that I should give it my best effort with their blessings.

I worked on into the night, putting together information that I was given. I had to type out press releases to the three cities where he was last seen 16 years ago. There were two very good tips to find him. He had served in the Army in the 1970s and he had a very unusual last name.

The following morning, I faxed the press releases to the major newspapers in the three cities, Shreveport, Louisiana; Atlanta, Georgia; and Greenville, Mississippi. I pleaded with the public to please come forward with information or any assistance in finding this man. I wrote that this patient, Sara, wanted to find her father while she was still alive.

I had around 50 to 60 phone calls coming in that next day. Some sounded as if they might have seen him years ago, but no one knew where he was living now. One of the calls was different, though. He was a private detective from Shreveport who said he had free time on his hands because he had developed a heart condition. He desperately wanted to help a good cause while he was still able. He said that he couldn't think of a better cause than this. I explained that we had no money to pay him (for one thing, I didn't know him) and he commented that he would do this job for free.

He wanted to do something good in his life before it was too late. I said, "What could it hurt? Even if you don't find him, it could be worth the effort." We both agreed under certain circumstances, that he must check in with me at least three times a day and more if he found out any information.

Boy, it wasn't but a couple of hours later when I received a call from the private detective! He had good news! He checked with our "armed forces" and then the Social Security Office and found a man by this same name living and working in New Orleans. To verify the information, I called Sara's mother, at her home, to see if the Social Security number we had tracked down could belong to Sara's father. She looked up an old file and called me back. She said, "Yes, yes, that is him. I had forgotten about having his Social Security information until you mentioned it. Now what will happen from here?" I told her to just hang on and don't tell Sara anything yet. We didn't even know if he was still there anymore until someone goes down there and finds him. For all we knew, he could have moved last week!

I phoned the private detective and he offered to go down to New Orleans to look for him and bring him to us if he was found. He said that if we called the dad on the phone, he might just take off again. I was hesitant but finally agreed. I said, "You need to call me any time anything happens. Don't leave me in the dark." He agreed and said he was taking a "big" friend with him in case they ran into trouble. I had an uneasy feeling about this whole situation but I prayed and decided to put it into Gods hands.

I had phone call after phone call from the detective. He did exactly what he said he would do. He called me to tell me the play-by-play descriptions of the events as they happened.

I was told that the private detectives went into the place of business (a restaurant) where the father of the child cooks, but it was his day off. The owner of the business gave him the correct address of the man they were looking for. The detectives proceeded to the residence and encountered a "seedy" woman who answered the door. During their conversation, she said that she did not live there. They asked for this man by name and then the man came to the door. "It wasn't a pretty sight!" said the detective. He saw a man standing there who looked to be in his late 60s (but we knew he was only 49 years old). His uncombed, gray streaked, wiry hair hung down to his waist. He had almost no front teeth (about five teeth were missing). He looked and smelled as if he hadn't had a bath in a while. When the man asked what they wanted, the private detectives explained about the 16 year old daughter wanting to meet him. The man got angry and said that he did not want anything to do with seeing her, even knowing she was gravely ill.

Now, the next scenes are not quite clear to me but I remember hearing the detective say that they took the father back to Shreveport that same night. He did not call me until the next afternoon to tell me that they had bought him a suit and other clothes and made him take a bath. They had taken him to a barbershop and got him "a real nice haircut", too. He also said that he had a dentist friend who was going to see him in the morning and fix his teeth so he would be presentable for Sara to meet. He told me that he would have the dad there to meet his daughter by 9:00 a.m. in two days.

I began making my calls to set up a meeting place for the family and to set up a press conference. A local well-known hotel allowed us to use their lobby for the events to come.

I contacted Sara and her mother and made arrangements for us to meet for dinner that same evening and discuss the following events to come. At the dinner, I explained to Sara that I had no idea how her father would act since we have no control over him. Whatever happened at the meeting with her father was strictly up to him. I did not tell her the negative things about her father, like his looks and actions up to this point. I did tell her that if things went badly, it was not because of anything that she had done wrong. Again, I repeated this to her many times over the next few days.

That night she told me that she really did not expect to ever see him again after this special meeting took place. Sara said that she really just wanted to see him and talk to him at least once in her lifetime. She said that she had never looked like her mother. She just wanted to see if she got her facial features from her father.

That morning finally arrived and everyone was to meet at 9:00 a.m. in the lobby of the hotel. I was asked to go meet her father around 8:00 a.m. in his hotel room accompanied by the two detectives that brought him here. As I entered the room, he was very angry and said, "I'll just mess it all up because I don't want to be here in the first place!" I had a hard time understanding why he was so hostile. I tried to explain that Sara was very ill and probably wouldn't be around much longer. "Couldn't you just pretend to be nice for her sake? What would it hurt for you to be nice and talk with her? If you want, you will never have to see her again. This will be your choice. But please at least act like you are glad to see her just this once!" He calmed down a bit and said he would think about it. I left the room thinking, "What have I done? He just might sabotage this whole meeting. What will Sara think? I know how disappointed she would be if he acted terrible around her."

Well, at 9:00 a.m. here they came to the lobby. The media was waiting. Her father handed her a teddy bear and a bouquet of flowers. (The detectives bought them that same morning.) He sat down in a wingback chair beside Sara. Not one word was said by either of them. I quickly came over to them and made my comments to the media explaining that we had found her father in just a few days. I told the story of how Sara called me and requested this huge favor for her dream. I introduced her father, her mother, and Sara to the media. I told them to ask whatever questions were needed for their stories.

Her father kept mumbling under his breath and complaining that he was forced to come here. I'm not sure if any of the media even heard him. But if they did, they ignored it. After all, it only made him look bad. Boy, if only I could have told them about how awful he <u>really</u> was, but then I didn't want to ruin this day for Sara. Sara was all smiles and did the best that she could that day. She heard his mumbles but she didn't let him ruin this day for her. After all, this was "Sara's Day!"

That afternoon, we arranged for Sara, her mother and father to spend time together away from everyone else. They had lunch together and then went to the zoo. That gave them time to walk and talk without interruptions from others. I was hoping that he would be friendlier when no one else was around. I heard that it went fairly well.

That evening, my husband and I picked up her father at the hotel and took him to the bus station. During that entire ride, he never had anything nice to say to us. I had a hard time understanding this because I thought that the day went better than expected. We bought him a one-way ticket and waited around to make sure that he got on the bus for New Orleans. After he got on the bus, we sat in our car and watched the bus drive off before we left the area. We wanted to make sure he would not get back off and go somewhere to try to cause trouble in town. We had given him Sara's phone number, address, and the address of the hospital where she spent so much of her time. We were hoping that he would keep in touch with her.

The nice private detective who had spent his own money and time to find Sara's father later died of a heart attack. I was sorry to hear this. His wife called me and said that he felt very good about helping Sara and that somehow made it easier for her to let him go.

I kept in touch with Sara for a couple of years after that. She did not have any more surgeries, although the tumor was still there. At least it was neither growing nor causing problems or pain. She said she wanted to try to live a "normal life" while she still could. She said she had written to her father a couple of times, but never got a letter back from him. Of course, this was no surprise to any of us.

Some people go through life never thinking of anyone but themselves. I'm hoping that maybe this man will someday "get it". Maybe this event changed his life for the better. Whatever happens in his life, it was totally up to him. No one can make those changes for him. Maybe he is a good and decent person and is out there helping others. I hope so. That would be a good thing!

As for Sara's mother; she waited a couple of years for him to do the right thing. Even a couple of letters from him to Sara might have made a difference, but it never happened. Finally she decided to sue him for back child support and for the accumulating medical bills. I do not know the outcome of their situation because Sara and her mother moved to another state after that to start a new life.

I received a few letters from them over the next couple of years, but one day my letter came back to me with a "no forwarding address" stamped on it by the post office. That is how we lost touch. I think they moved again. I pray that Sara got the surgery that was needed to rid her of the brain tumor. I wish them well. They were very nice people.

By a Volunteer

TOMMY (Dream—To go to Florida to see the Gulf Waters, Beaches, Disney World, and The Epcot Center)
By a Volunteer

Tommy was like the typical eight year old boy with the exception of a very serious health problem. Tommy had been diagnosed with several types of lung disorders. Normally, not any one of these diseases or disorders were actually life threatening, but when all of them were diagnosed together this does put him in that category. He was on oxygen for about 20 hours a day when I first met him. He had serious allergies and was allergic to everything in sight. He also had other health problems including having severe bouts of asthma.

His mother contacted me by phone, and to ask if it was possible if he could have a dream granted. Once she told me what his diagnosis, I suggested that she first contact his pulmonary doctor to discuss this with him. I also told her that the doctor needed to call me so he could answer some of my questions about Tommy's illness. I could tell that something was not quite right from our conversation, but I did not know what it was. Tommy's pulmonary doctor knew all about our organization and I knew him personally. He was my youngest child's physician. If something was amiss, he would know right away, and he would tell me.

Within a few days, Tommy's mother called me again. She informed me that the doctor said that Tommy could go on a trip. I asked her to come up to our office and pick up the paperwork that she needed to fill out. Then she needed to take it to Tommy's doctor's office to sign his part of the forms. Since I had not heard from the doctor yet, I told her to please ask the pulmonary doctor to call me after he had signed the papers. I would need to have a conversation with him before we could go any further.

She came in and got the information and paperwork. We sat down to discuss her son. She told me that her son wanted to go to Florida to play at the beach. She said that he also wanted to go to Disney World. During our conversation, I told her that I needed to see Tommy and have him tell me what he wanted for his dream. I said that we always talked directly to the patients before we made any final arrangements on a trip, just in case the child changed his or her mind. I was nice to her, as I am with everyone. She immediately "snapped my head off" by telling me that she knew what he wanted, and I did not need to talk to him. Again, I explained the procedures of our organization and reminded her that I still needed the approval of the pulmonary doctor, also. She wasn't very nice and got up and left my office in a huff.

This was a very unusual reaction from someone who was asking for a free trip. I knew there had to be more that I wasn't aware of yet. I finally called the doctor myself to see what he thought. He told me that nothing had even been mentioned to him about Tommy going on a trip or having a dream granted. He did say that if we did send him on a trip, Tommy had to have oxygen with him at all times. He hesitated and then stated that Tommy's mom has been a troublemaker at the hospital several times. He also told me that most of Tommy's allergy problems were due to her chain smoking around her son.

With regards to Tommy's condition, the doctor said that he could be in a life threatening situation just because his mother did not give him the medications as directed and did not see to it that Tommy always had oxygen. The bottom line was that Tommy was in a life-threatening situation and it was out of the hospital's control. He said that he thought if the mother could behave, a trip might be good for Tommy.

I knew that I had to handle this mother with every precaution taken that would be necessary to keep her calm, so not to upset the child. I now believed that the child was not being taken care of properly and I needed to double-check all medical arrangements necessary for a safe trip for the child.

About a week later, Tommy and his mother came to my office for a visit. She brought the signed paperwork with her. The pulmonary doctor did sign his part, too. Tommy was adorable. He had big blue eyes and a very large smile. His hair was so short that he almost looked bald. I asked him what was up with the "no hair look" and he said that it was easier on his mom to keep it short because the barbershop cost too much. She cut his hair at home with hair clippers. He was rolling his oxygen tank around behind him and had the oxygen hose in his nose.

He told me that he wanted to go to Florida and he wanted to see the ocean and beaches. I asked if he wanted to go to Disney World and The Epcot Center while he was there and he said, "Sure!" That was what I needed to hear. I told him that I would see what I could do about getting the trip together and would be calling them soon with the information. I told his mom that I would probably be calling her to help me with the medications needed on the trip and the information on how much oxygen that would be needed, etc. I told her that I would get the information from her and then verify it with the doctor. She seemed to be fine with that.

The trip was scheduled and I had to make the appropriate arrangements for the oxygen to be given to Tommy on the plane ride down there and back. They do not allow oxygen to be carried on the planes because it can explode, just like dynamite. I had to find and work with an oxygen company in Florida to deliver oxygen to the hotel upon their arrival. The oxygen was very expensive and we had to have several canisters of oxygen available for Tommy for his entire stay in Florida. Since he used approximately one whole canister in a day and a half, it would be necessary for the company to deliver the oxygen two canisters at a time. By the time the second canister was almost empty, the mom could call them to pick up the two tanks that she had and they could leave two more full ones behind. Since the trip was for the six days of his vacation he would need four canisters during his trip. Everything seemed to be working out.

The day that I met them at the airport to see them off, I made sure that the stewardess knew about the need for the oxygen for Tommy before they boarded the plane. All of the orders were already in place and there shouldn't be a problem while flying down there. I had called the doctor days before and made a list of the meds his mom was supposed to have on the trip so I could check it before they boarded. I made sure that Tommy's mother showed me all of the medications. She did have everything. I thought, "Wow! Everything was going so well. Maybe she would be all right on the trip, after all." They boarded the plane and I left the airport feeling very good about the trip.

On the second night of their trip, I received a phone call from Tommy's mother around 2:00 a.m. our time. She had been arguing with the oxygen company because they had given her an empty canister. The first one was fine but when she went to hook Tommy up to the second one, it was empty. In the middle of the night, she had called me to tell me that they were rude to her and that she had to make them come out there right away to bring a third one because Tommy was completely out.

I said, "Okay, are you telling me that when they delivered the first two tanks, you did not look at the gage to see if they were full or empty?" She said, "I didn't think to look since they knew we needed two tanks to be delivered at the same time." This made perfectly good sense to me. I am not sure I could have thought to check the gage, either. Since she had already received the third tank of oxygen after the mix up, I told her I would call her back in the morning after I had spoken to the oxygen company.

The following morning, I called the oxygen company to see what had gone wrong. They had a copy of the form that Tommy's mother had signed that said that she had accepted two full tanks of oxygen. They swore to me that they know for sure that both tanks were full. When they picked both of the empty tanks up from their hotel room in the middle of the night, both were empty. They told me that they have the exact amount of oxygen in each tank recorded. They further said that there was no way for any one person to have used both tanks in the time that she had them. One of them would have to be opened up on purpose and just let it run until it was empty. Since I was not there and could not verify what had actually happened, we had to pay for the second tank.

On the fourth day of the trip it happened again. Here we had to pay for two extra tanks at just over $200.00 more than planned and we were running short of money within the organization. We barely had the money for their trip as it was. Where was I going to get more money?

This was not Tommy's problem. He couldn't help what others around him were doing. I just tried to handle the situation as calmly as possible and didn't want to see his mother get angry again. I had no way of knowing who was telling me the truth. No matter what else was happening, Tommy still needed his oxygen to be able to breath.

Other than the oxygen caper, the rest of the trip went all right. They made it back without any further incidents. I did call the oxygen company in Florida again to try to get to the bottom of all of this but they stood by their story that the tanks were full when they arrived at the hotel. I had no recourse except to pay them and apologize.

Before I mailed out the check for the extra oxygen that we were charged with, I made a few calls to other oxygen companies in that area just to see if they knew how reputable this company was in Florida. To my surprise, every other oxygen company in that area said that this company had a great reputation and they had never heard anything bad about them. I wrote the check out and put a note in the envelope saying how sorry we were about the problems that were caused.

Now my suspicions were geared toward Tommy's mother. Why would anyone do such a thing? Surely she knew that we did not have a lot of money to be throwing away. There were always other children that needed our assistance, too. We just could not be wasting money like that.

I called Tommy's doctor and told him what had happened. He reminded me that he had previously warned me about Tommy's mom. I acknowledged that and said, "Well, I guess it could have been worse."

I did not hear from Tommy or his mom until right before the Christmas party which was six months later. Of course they had been invited and we mailed the information to be filled out to her on

October 1st. On the top of the form it said in giant letters, "Return this form by October 30th". Underneath, it said, "We must have November 1st to 30th to find all of the sponsors needed to either buy the children their gifts or donate the $100.00 for us to buy the gifts." Since we had not received their forms, they were not on our list.

It was only ten days until the party when I got that phone call from his mom. She said he was coming to the party. I went over the procedures with her and explained that there was a deadline of October 30 for the forms to get turned in. By waiting two months before contacting us, we, now do not have a sponsor to buy his gift. All of our sponsors were already assigned to patients. I asked what he wanted for Christmas and said that I would have to stop what I was doing and start calling around to find someone who would give us $100.00 for his gift or go buy it and bring it to us in two days.

I knew that this was not going to be easy. I did not have anyone else to call. Everyone who always assisted us each year with the gifts was already contacted. Every bit of the $32,000.00 that was raised (either by cash or donated gifts) for the Christmas party was already spent (or gifts collected) for all of these surviving patients and their siblings. Each child could request a gift or gifts up to $100.00. Believe me, they could always spend the entire $100.00 easy! As it turned out, I had to go buy Tommy's gift out of my own pocket. I could not find another $100.00 in this town at that time. We had already hit everyone that we knew.

She did fine at the party with no complications or complaints. Tommy had a wonderful time and hugged me over and over from sheer delight. He loved his gifts.

Now, six months later, when it came time for the annual trip for the survivors, Tommy wanted to go. Because we were traveling by buses that year, I thought that he should do fine on the trip. I would assign an RN or respiratory therapist (or both if needed) to him and we shouldn't have a problem. His mother was not allowed to go with us, so one problem solved already!

The annual trip that year was to Memphis, TN to The Peabody Hotel to see the ducks march from the rooftop to the lobby fountain where they swam all day (indoors). Graceland and Libertyland Theme Park were the other places that we would visit that day. We made sure that Tommy had two tanks of oxygen for the trip. His mother brought them to us with Tommy. The bus trip was only for one day but we would be away for 18 hours straight. I assigned a volunteer and a respiratory therapist to Tommy for the entire day.

On the day of the trip, everything was fine all day long until the bus ride home. It was 11:00 p.m. and we were traveling by four buses on the freeway when my bus driver was pulled over by another bus driver because of an emergency. Tommy was on that other bus. He had run completely out of oxygen. "I said, "What? This was not possible because the respiratory therapist was supposed to have checked the tanks before we left."

I entered their bus and Tommy was breathing shallow. I personally looked at the gage and it was empty just like they said. We moved Tommy and the respiratory therapist to my bus and hit the highway, looking for a hospital. We had to get off at the next exit that said "hospital". That was 30 more miles down the freeway. We rushed up to the emergency entrance, took Tommy in and I said to get him on oxygen until we could figure out this dilemma we were in. Now we had two empty tanks. The hospital did not have the same type of equipment because the hospital was old and the equipment they had was outdated. What we had was the newer versions.

Getting another tank of oxygen was not the problem. The hospital employees were willing to give us a tank and anything else that we needed. The problem was that Tommy's tubing and hookup would not fit on the older tank. Between the hospital employees and a couple of our RNs, the respiratory therapist, and me, we riffled through the hospital looking through every cabinet and drawer in the place. All we needed was a nozzle to fit his tubing. It did not sound so difficult. But it was! Finally our respiratory therapist had an idea. He thought he could make one up with some of the things that we found around the hospital. It worked!! He was a genius!

Once we got Tommy fixed up with the tank from the hospital, we got underway again. Tommy was riding on my bus now. We had several discussions on the way back. While we were trying to figure out what had happened, Tommy finally "came clean with us". He said that his mom gave him one full tank and one empty tank. The therapist did not look at the gages too well like he was told to.

Tommy said that his mom told him that she hoped that something would happen to him, and then it would be our fault.

I was in total shock. I asked him if he was sure that is what had happened and he said, "Yes." I asked him about the Florida trip while we were on the subject, and he said that his mother opened up the second tank on both nights so they would run out of oxygen.

Now it was sinking into my brain. If something had happened to him on a trip or while in our custody, she could sue us. Never mind that she would lose her child. What a horrible person! Poor Tommy did not have much of a chance of surviving with a mother like that! I asked him where his father was and he said he does not know his father. He was his mother's only child so he did not even have a sibling to talk to. It took strength for me to hold back the tears. I just cannot imagine anyone doing his or her own helpless child like this. Then I remembered the doctor telling me that his mom smoked around him all of the time. She is actually making his life harder for him so how could she possibly care about him?

After this trip was behind us, I contacted the hospital social worker and we met for lunch. We had a long talk about Tommy and his mother. I thought that someone should do something about helping him before it was too late for Tommy. He agreed and said that he would see what he could do.

Around two months later, I received a call from the social worker at the hospital. He told me that they were going to charge the mother with "Munchausen Syndrome by Proxy". They were planning to take the child away from the mother for his protection, but they were dragging their feet. They took too long! The mother heard about it and moved away with her son.

Munchausen Syndrome by Proxy is a syndrome that affects (usually) a parent. The sad thing about this disease is that the parent falsifies history and may injure the child with drugs or add blood or bacterial contaminants to urine specimens to simulate disease. The parent seeks medical care for the child and always appears to be deeply concerned and protective. The child is often seriously ill, requires frequent hospitalization, and may die.

I became ill and had to retire suddenly ten years ago. I lost touch with many people due to my inability to walk without assistance or even to use the phone. I do not know what happened concerning Tommy. I do not even know if Tommy is still alive. We do know that we did good things for him by making some of his days brighter even if it was for only a short while.

By a Volunteer

Chapter VII.

Below are a few of the stories that address the sad times and the good times. Some tell about the interesting events that happened surrounding the patients' dreams and lives.

SKIPPER (Dream — To have a G. I. Joe Aircraft Carrier)
By a Volunteer and a Friend

This is one of those stories where you can definitely proclaim that God had a hand in making this dream come true. I already know that God had a hand in every one of the 833 dreams that we accomplished over the 14 years while I was involved, but this dream was special because the likelihood of granting this dream was nil.

I received a phone call from the head physician of the Pulmonary Clinic at a local children's hospital. I was told that I should contact the parents of a ten year old patient who was diagnosed with cystic fibrosis. The child was talking to everyone about wanting a large toy. So many others thought this would be a simple task until they looked for it and could not find it anywhere in town. The doctor called me and said, "If you can't find it then no one can!" I was given the phone number of the parents.

I called the mother and told her who I was. She said that her son, Sam (nicknamed Skipper) wanted to get a G. I. Joe Aircraft Carrier. Now that sounded easy enough. I thought for a second and remembered that I must have seen that toy a hundred times in different stores. I would remember this because I had three sons who were around Skipper's age. Many times my sons had said, "Look Mom! There's a G. I. Joe Aircraft Carrier!" This toy was so huge that we could never have it in our home because we did not have that much space in our house. (There were 6 of us living in a 2 bedroom apartment.)

I gathered up all of the paperwork and forms to be signed and went to visit Skipper and his mother at the hospital. I wanted to make sure that this was really what he wanted for a dream. I explained that he could go on a trip, go on a shopping spree or have a computer & printer or whatever he really, really wanted more that anything else. He insisted that the G. I. Joe Aircraft Carrier was all that he wanted. His mother shrugged her shoulders and said, "That is all he wants!"

The following day, I decided to pick up the phone and start calling around town to the local stores to find one for Skipper. I called Target. No, they did not have one. I called J. C. Penney and no, they did not have one. I called all of the toy stores in our area and no one had one. I called one of the Wal-Mart Stores. No! I called another Wal-Mart, and another Wal-Mart. Same answer, no one had one. This had turned into an entire day and I still have not found one! I thought, "What is going on. I know that I had seen them and it was not that long ago! Or was it? Now, I remember, it was last Christmas!" This is now October, ten months later. After six hours on the phone, I knew I was in trouble.

Over night I thought about whom I would call next. The following day I started all over again calling around to stores in other towns. I called the Wal-Mart Distribution Center 60 miles away and asked for the manager of distribution. I explained my situation and asked if he could help me to locate one anywhere in the country, from any and all of the Wal-Mart Distribution Centers. He was kind enough to check all of the centers for me. The following day, he called me back to say, "No, no one has had one since last December and none were on order either. While I had him on the phone, I asked him for the maker of the toy and the address and phone number so I could contact them directly. He looked it up, shared it with me and I thanked him.

I called the manufacturer of the toy and to my dismay; it was not being produced any longer. The last production date was over a year ago. Of course I explained my dilemma and they had no answers for me. All had been sold over a year ago. I called contacts that I had in other states. The answers were all the same. No one could find one.

I went home on that third day worn out from the stress of not being able to grant such "a simple wish". Before I went to bed I prayed and begged God to please help me. I knew I could not do this alone.

The next morning, here I am. "Now what?" I thought for a moment and remembered that a couple of days ago a lady working at a Wal-Mart near Skipper's home said she would call me back, and I had not heard from her yet. I picked up the phone and called her. She had been busy calling the same people that I had already spoken to from the Wal-Mart Distribution Center.

The oddest thing happened while we were talking. Another employee came up to her and said she had heard that we were looking for a G. I. Joe Aircraft Carrier. She asked to speak to me. This wonderful kind lady said, "I bought one for my son last Christmas, and he has never even had it out of the box! He really never wanted it. Could I donate it to your organization for this patient?" I was crying tears of joy! I made the necessary arrangements and within a few days, Skipper got his wish.

I feel that God touched this lady to give unselfishly and He led me right to her within hours of me asking Him. Sometimes we get so caught up in our daily lives and the lives of others that we sometimes forget to ask God for help. The Bible tells us that all we need to do is ask and our needs will be met but we sometimes forget how easy it really is. When I finally asked God for help, help was there. I know this and you know this, but we sometimes do not think. I have even learned that God will occasionally answer prayers before I have had the time to finish praying!

By a Volunteer and a Friend

KIMBERLEY (Never Requested a Dream for Herself but Got One Later in Her Life)
By V. O'C. Davis

Kimberley & Steve in a hot air balloon

Early one morning on September 11, 1986, down at the River Park, I had a speaking engagement to promote the upcoming

911 Emergency Services. My job was to inform the public of the importance of having this service around the entire state. I was speaking to a crowd of over 500 people including 80 of our state's legislators and 40 of our local and out of town mayors. It would be their jobs to go home and promote the changes necessary so this could be handled swiftly and with ease.

There was a company that had made a hot air balloon with 911 across the side of it. The owners were going to fly the balloon up and away right after the speech was finished. They were going to fly this balloon all over the state to help promote the changes to be made for the good of everyone.

I had brought a patient and her mother there to ride in the hot air balloon with the owners. The patient was Kimberley, who just happened to have her birthday on that same day of September 11. She was 11 years old on that day, too. What a coincidence!

After the speech, the owner of the hot air balloon tried and tried to get the thing airborne but with no luck. It was entirely too windy and it would be hard to control so they had to call off the flight. Kimberley did not get to go up in the balloon that day but she did get a huge birthday cake from our mayor and the whole crowd sang Happy Birthday to her. It is not every day that a crowd with such importance sings Happy Birthday to someone. Kimberley was very pleased and excited that this was done in her honor.

Kimberley was a cancer patient and was receiving radiation treatments at that time. I had spoken with her mother about our organization but she said she was not ready to ask for a dream yet. I gave her information on our organization before we departed. Years went by before I heard from her again. Kimberley was in remission and was going to college. She seemed to be doing just great and I was so happy for her.

Around the time of Kimberley's 18th birthday, I received a call from a young man, Steve, who had been dating Kimberley. He told me that she had been in remission from cancer for four years. He wanted to ask her to marry him but he needed my help. Just for my own peace of mind, I decided to call Kimberley's mom to confirm his story. Mom did say she felt sure that if he asked Kimberley for her hand in marriage, she would say, "Yes."

I phoned Steve back the following day and asked what I needed to do to help out. He asked if I could find an owner of a hot air balloon who would be willing to allow them to ride in one and let him propose to her while they were airborne. How romantic!

My best friend and a dedicated volunteer of our organization knew a gentleman in her hometown who had one. So she called him to see how much it would cost to hire him, the hot air balloon and the flight team. He gave her the figure and I got back with Steve. Another problem arose. Steve was also a student who was attending the same college as Kimberley. He had no money! I told him I would see what I could do. I called around until I found someone who agreed to try to help me pay for it. I would cover half of the cost from my own pocket and she would cover the other half. I called Steve and told him to confirm one of the dates that I had received from the owner of the balloon. He chose one and the ball started rolling from there.

Steve received a ring that was handed down from generation to generation in his family. I found him a ring box, at my home, so he could properly present it to Kimberley. I also found two people willing to videotape the events on that day, one on the ground (my husband) and one to go up in the balloon with them. My friend was a photographer, so she would be there to take the still shots.

On the day of the event, Steve had a hard time getting Kimberley to the place where he was supposed to meet us. He wanted this to be a complete surprise so he had to make up a story to get her in the car. I know that when she did not want to go, he was deeply concerned. I believe that he said that he started perspiring almost uncontrollably. Then he tried to hide it. Eventually he had made an excuse to get her in the car but she tried to talk him out of going most of the way there. She had other plans that day. He had to drive 30 miles to get to the spot of the take-off. Don't you know that he was about to panic when she did not want to go! I do not remember what he told her that day, but whatever was the story was not a good enough lie. That could be a good thing!

Everyone was on time but them. We waited for them for a while before they got there. Her mother and his mother were both there along with our own set of people. We had about 15 people who came, including the hot air balloon crew. When they arrived, Kimberley saw me and the balloon lying on the ground and thought that I was finally going to get her up in a hot air balloon for her dream. She got excited because she was going to ride in one. She never suspected the real reason she was there.

They got in the basket and away they went! Our group of vehicles followed them on the ground and all around the river's edge. They covered a lot of miles in just a short time. They flew to a large lake and took a well planned dip into the water. From there they went toward the downtown area. Finally they lowered the balloon over an open area where we could see and hear Steve as he knelt down on one knee and asked for her hand in marriage and gave her the ring. She was so surprised that she couldn't speak. We yelled, "You had better say yes after all of this trouble that he went through!" Then we all laughed. She screamed, "Yes, yes, yes!" Then we cheered. Up they went again to fly over some buildings.

They landed only a few blocks from Main Street. After they landed, the owner brought out a bottle of champagne, opened it and poured everyone a glass. Steve and Kimberley knelt down on both knees as the hot air balloon prayer was recited. Then we all poured our glasses of champagne over Steve and Kimberley's heads. This is the tradition for any air hot balloon flight. Kimberley was so happy I believe she could have flown without that air hot balloon!

They set a date for the wedding ten months later. We were all invited to the wedding but it would be in another state well over 300 miles away.

As it turned out, my husband and I were able to drive down and attend the wedding. The wedding was beautiful! For those of us who knew their past history and what they had to do to get this far in life, it was a very emotional and inspiring event. They seem so happy together. I just knew that their marriage would last. They shared a very strong faith in God that would be their foundation for the marriage.

About two months after the wedding, they phoned me and asked if my husband and I could meet them for dinner at a local restaurant not far from our home. They lived 50 miles away and would be coming into town to visit us. Steve and Kimberley wanted to see us and thank us for our help. We met them and had a wonderful dinner and visited for around two hours. When we were about to leave, they pulled out a very nice surprise gift for us. They had purchased a Precious Moments figurine of a little girl sitting on top of a rainbow. The title was "Dreams Really Do Come True". I have this in a special place in my home. Every time that I see it, I think of them.

Steve and Kimberley have been married for over ten years now and their marriage is still very strong today! Kimberley has never had a reoccurrence of cancer. Even more surprising is that they have a baby girl. This is the child that her doctors said would be impossible for her to conceive. With God, "All things are possible."

I am thankful that Steve and Kimberley allowed my husband and me to be a part of their engagement and their wedding. I know that their lives are in Gods hands, and they will never forget the blessings that He has bestowed upon them. Every once in a while when I think about them, or walk by our special gift from them, I will stop what I am doing and say a prayer asking God to keep them safe. I wish them all of the best.

By V. O'C. Davis

JIMMY (Dream—To go to Disneyland)
JOHN (Dream—To Fly in an Airplane)
By a Volunteer and a Friend

A local neurologist contacted our organization by phone to discuss two patients. Both children were three years old and both were diagnosed with malignant brain tumors. He continued to explain that he had spoken with both sets of parents about allowing their children to have a dream granted. He suggested, if the parents agreed to let their child have a dream and it involved traveling, they would need to go on the trip very quickly. He gave us both patients information and agreed to sign all papers allowing them to go. This was extremely important because we would never grant any dream without the written consent of the primary physician.

One family lived here in the city, and the other family lived 70 miles away. The local parents called me before I could even dial their phone number. They had just gotten home from the hospital and were eager to get all of the paperwork signed and out of the way so the trip would happen soon. I told them that the neurologist had already called me and would sign for them to go on a trip anywhere that their son wished to go. I did not tell them that the neurologist said that their child only had weeks to live and may even (possibly) have health problems while away on the trip. They told me that their son Jimmy wanted to go to Disneyland in California. The parents immediately came up to the office and signed all of the legal documents. I told them I would start making arrangements immediately. I called the travel agency and set up the trip for only a few days away.

I promised to get back with the parents as soon as the travel agent finalized the arrangements.

In talking to these wonderfully kind people, I could see that their family was very close and very supportive. They were doing everything humanly possible for their son. I could also see that they had a very strong faith in God and they were looking for a miracle to cure Jimmy.

In the late afternoon, I finally got a break and phoned the other family. These parents were staying overnight at the hospital with their son John. I explained that I had received a call from John's physician and knew that the doctor had spoken to them about John getting a dream granted. I asked them if John had made a decision about his wish. They said when they asked him what he wanted to do as a dream; John told them that he just wanted to fly in an airplane. I decided to take the paperwork to them at the hospital and talk to John myself. I told them that I would be there soon and hung up.

When I arrived, I went straight to John's hospital room. John was very excited because he knew he was going to get to ride in a plane. He was ready to go fly right then! I had the family sign the paperwork and then we talked for a long time. John was so very sweet. At first he was shy, but around me, that changed fairly quickly. I tried to find out where he wanted to fly but he had no ideas. After all, he was only three years old!

He just wanted to "fly"! I asked the parents if he had ever indicated any place that he would like to visit. A destination was critical. He had to go somewhere! Disney World in Florida came up in our conversation because Disney was being heavily advertised on television. John did not care where he went as long as it was by plane. The parents decided to go to Disney World in Florida. I told them that I would see the neurologist the next day and get him to sign the paperwork. I would discuss the trip to Florida with him at that time.

The following morning, I met with the neurologist and he signed papers for both children to travel. He said that everything should be fine but it might be wise to keep in contact with Jimmy's family to make sure he was okay while traveling around in California. He could become critical at any time. I agreed that I would.

I called the travel agency to set up John's trip to Florida when I was told that a plane going to Florida was leaving on the same day and nearly at the same time as Jimmy's flight to California. Even the departure gates were across from one another. I was thrilled and agreed to let her set up that flight. I called both sets of parents and went over the arrangements for the trips. They would be leaving the airport at the same time! I requested they meet me one hour before the flights so we could go over their itineraries and reservations and give them money to spend on food, gas, souvenirs and etc. All final questions could be answered before they boarded the planes.

That day came fast. At 7:00 a.m., I met both families at the airport and introduced them to each other. TV and newspaper reporters were also there to interview both families. We went over all of the details of both trips and I requested that both families please keep in touch with me while they were gone. I asked that they call me collect at the office at least once every evening. I would key the office phone into the home phone so I wouldn't miss their calls. Both of the children were so very excited! Each was telling the other what they were going to do on their trips. It was time to board the planes. It was almost 8:00 a.m. so we said our good-byes and they were off! John was going to Florida and Jimmy to California.

I left the airport and returned to my home. I was still working on two other dreams that would not be finalized for a couple of weeks. Here I had used the money that I thought would pay for the awaiting dreams on the two emergency trips that just left that morning. I needed to find donors who would help us pay for the upcoming dreams.

Our organization was always just a little behind in having enough funds for the dreams at hand. But one thing is for sure, when it came time to pay for each child's dream, the money would always find its way to us. I know that this was because God had a hand in running our organization. He always came through for us. Of course, we did not sit back and wait for Him to magically have the money appear. Not at all! We had to do our part, too. We had to go out there speaking to groups, talking on the radio, having fundraisers, begging the media to cover the dreams so that our name would be on the thoughts of the people who would soon donate money for the children. It was very hard work pounding the pavement looking for donors, but so well worth the efforts.

Instead of going to the office, I went back home to finish typing some letters that I had started in the middle of the night. I still had the office phone rerouted to my home and boy, was I glad that I did!

Only one and a half hours after the planes took off, my phone rang. When I answered the call, my first thought was that I was speaking to the local airport personnel. I did not understand why the airport was calling me. I don't remember the exact words that were said but I thought that I must have left something behind at the airport. The man was not too clear with his words.

It was actually a pilot calling me "while in flight". He stumbled around for the right words. Finally the pilot said, "We are having a problem on board." I said, "You are a pilot? What is wrong?" I was dumbfounded because he had caught me off guard. I have never had a pilot call me before. And my mind was now focused on the next patients' dreams and how I was going to find the necessary funds to grant them.

I collected my senses and finally understood to whom I was talking. He said that my dream child was asleep and they couldn't wake him up. His father was holding him in his lap. As the conversation progressed, I kept thinking that this was about Jimmy on his way to California. After all, even the neurologist warned me there might be a problem. Then the pilot said, "We just took off from Atlanta 20 minutes ago and will be landing in Orlando in 45 minutes." I said, "Why were you in Georgia? That's the wrong way to California!" Then it hit me. It has to be John that we are talking about and not Jimmy! John was not supposed to have any problems! "Do you mean this is John we are talking about?" The pilot confirmed. I then told the pilot that we would have an ambulance waiting for them when they landed in Orlando.

I hung up and called long distance information to find an ambulance company in Orlando. The operator connected me directly to one and I sent them to pick up John. I told them to take him to the main Orlando hospital. We hung up and I then phoned John's neurologist. He assured me that I did the right thing by calling the ambulance and sending them to the main hospital. I asked him to call ahead to the hospital to speak to the medical staff to give them all of the information needed for John. He said he would do this right away.

As soon as I hung up, my phone rang again. It was the pilot calling me, again, to tell me the latest details of the incident. He said they sped up the plane and arrived in Orlando early. They had just landed and were there, now. He said that the plane was on the tarmac and he was looking down at the ambulance. They were raising the door to get the EMTs on board. An EMT then took the phone and told me what they found. John was alive, but barely. He was in a comatose state. They put in an IV and were off to the hospital. I told them to make sure that they find the same physician that was in contact with John's neurologist from Little Rock. They agreed to do this. Everyone was so very nice and so sincere. I felt that John was in good hands.

In the mean time, I looked up the emergency contact information of family members who were listed on the legal documents that the parents signed. (These papers were still with me.) I really did not want to be the one to call them but I had no choice. I quickly said a prayer for all of the family and for John. I asked for the right words when I spoke with the family members because I did not want to frighten them. I reached the grandfather and told him all of the information that I had. He said he would gather up some family members and would immediately head to Florida by car. He said he would keep in contact with me. And he did. He called me several times during the road trip. Orlando was 17 hours away from here.

Only hours after this ordeal began, the Florida's hospital administrator called to say that they had lost John. He died within just a few hours of reaching the hospital. He said that John went into a coma on the plane and never woke up. The doctors believed that he had a brain hemorrhage.

Then he shocked me by asking when I could come pick up the body. "What? What do you mean?" He explained that they were sending the body down to the morgue. He told me that I needed to contact a funeral home in Orlando to pick up John's body and soon. I had never been involved with anything like this before and I was in shock over the whole tragedy. During the conversation I asked them to please let John's parents know that their family was in route to help them and would they please tell the parents to call me soon. Before I hung up, they gave me the names of several funeral homes in the area.

"What was happening with John's parents?" They were so far away from home with no family or friends around them to console them. Then John's grandfather called me. I asked him what I should do and he said to go ahead and call one of the funeral homes and make arrangements to have John's body picked up.

The first funeral home that I called the gentleman asked me, "How are you going to return the body back to Little Rock?" I said by plane. Then I was informed that the body could not be flown back without it first being embalmed. Also, I would need to purchase a casket (or box) to ship him back. "What? I need to talk to the parents first. This should not be my decision to make."

I then called the airlines to talk to them about what I needed to do. The whole time I was thinking that I could use the return tickets to send his parents and John's body home. Wrong! Now I am being informed that I must purchase another ticket for John's body to be flown in the cargo area. And they would not refund the return flight ticket money on his seat! I needed the money badly to help with the expenses. Furthermore; I needed to pay extra for the return tickets because the parents were going home earlier than originally scheduled. We barely had enough money raised to pay for both original trips and now I would have to call around and find more money for the funeral home and the flight home. It was like the "snowball affect".

Finally, John's father called me. Of course, they had no money for these things either. He would have to use his hotel room and rental car at least one night and possibly two nights because they needed to go to the funeral home the following day to sign for the final arrangements. He agreed to all of the arrangements that I had made thus far. "Poor parents", I thought. "How horrible this must be for them." I was so glad that the grandfather was on his way down there for moral support. He seemed to be a very stable and calm man. I was sure this is what was needed right now for the parents. They were being hit from all directions.

Since I had no money for all of these things that must be paid (immediately), I had to come up with a solution, in a hurry. I decided to call the funeral home and the airlines to pay for everything with my personal credit card. Our organization had never even thought of getting one for emergencies before now! The amount charged to my personal account totaled $1,600.00. This, at least, bought me another 25 days to raise the funds to cover the expenses.

At the other end of the United States, that same evening, Jimmy's parents called me to tell me everything was wonderful in California. What a relief! At least Jimmy was doing well. I did not dare tell them about John! When I hung up, I said a prayer for God to please keep them safe. I never even made it into the office that day, at all. I could not get free from the phone long enough to go in. I was thankful that I had everything with me that was needed for this emergency.

Before going to bed that night, John's grandfather called me to tell me that they had arrived in Orlando safely. They were going to stay with John's parents and assist them in getting everything done the following day. I informed him of all that had happened up to this point and that I had the parents and John's body scheduled for the flight home. He said that he would see they got to the airport on time for the flight to come home. I went to bed that night but never slept a wink. I couldn't stop thinking about the day's events and worrying about that poor family and about what they were going through.

The following day things were quiet with the exception that the TV stations and newspapers had found out what had happened. They wanted an interview with me. They came to the office and I explained everything as best as I could. I used this opportunity to ask the public for donations to cover the extra expenses. And yes, people came forward over the next 30 days to donate the money, but just barely enough to cover everything on my credit card.

On the afternoon of the third day another call came in. It was John's parents. They arrived in town and were coming to talk with me. They had some things to say. When they arrived, we sat down together and talked and cried. They thanked me for taking such good care of John. He was home now and the funeral was set for a couple of days away. John's whole family was close and they were all very nice people. My heart hurt just thinking about what they were going through.

John's dad said that John had gotten his wish but I didn't understand what he meant. He continued to say that John had been so excited about flying. He reminded me that John only wanted to "fly like a bird". He didn't care about going to a destination. He said that John got to meet the pilot, see inside the cockpit and even walk around to see the inside of the plane before they took off. John had a window seat while in flight, and he was so very happy about being in the air. He loved the view and loved the clouds. After a couple of hours on the plane he became tired and asked his dad to hold him. He talked to his parents for a while and then fell asleep in the dad's arms. He lay there sleeping for about 20 minutes when his dad decided to move John to the seat next to him. That is when he found out that he couldn't wake him up.

John did get his wish before he was gone. No one knew he would become so ill on the flight. Remember, John was the one who was not expected to have any health issues on the trip. That day, I learned a very important lesson. No one ever knows when it is his or her time to die. Not even the doctors can tell you definitely. Only God knows for sure.

When Jimmy and his parents returned from California, I met them and we talked. I told them what had happened to John. I knew that they were going to hear about it from the gossipers at the hospital anyway. I decided that it was best to hear it from me. At least the story would be accurate.

Jimmy's family and I have stayed in contact ever since that trip. Of course, Jimmy came to all of the Christmas parties and went on every special annual trip. I love these dear people. We have become good friends. Jimmy was only three when he went to California for his dream. He is now 20 years old and has been in remission for about 15 years. Jimmy has become a handsome young man and has a wonderful sincerity in his disposition. What a pleasure it is to know him and to have been an important part of his life! God has surely blessed this family.

By a Volunteer and a Friend

Matt (Dream—to go to Graceland)
"Life goes on"
By Shane, Brother of Matt

I entered this world staring opposition in the face as many did. The difference is how I have chosen to handle it throughout my life. The events in my life I am sharing with you have made me the person that I am today. It has built character in my life and has given me an appreciation for the little things.

Our lives began as children of a lower class family in a small country town. My older brother Matt is four years older than me. His father and our mother divorced when Matt was two and a half years old. Our mother married my dad one year later and then I was born. Our youngest brother John was born one year after me.

As I remember back to the way life was as a child, many thoughts come to mind. I did not know my maternal grandmother because she died from some type of cancer before I was born. Her husband (my grandfather) was an antique collector. He had lots of old cars and other types of antiques. His property was fenced, and he kept the gate locked. He never allowed any children, not even his own, to be on his property after the death of my grandmother. No one ever knew why.

The only way that family members could visit him was to go to his antique store downtown. The only time that I stepped foot on his property was on the day of his funeral. When I saw the store that day, I was able to appreciate the antiques that he had collected, but really regretted that I did not know him better. Unfortunately, his antiques meant more to him than his family.

I also did not have the opportunity to get to know my paternal grandfather because he was killed in a tragic car accident only five days after I was born. I only have seen a few pictures of what he looked like before the accident. Through the stories that I have heard about him, I have been able to put together a likely character that might portray him as he was. From that information, I knew that I did not want to grow up in his footsteps. I also have come to understand the bitterness that my family walks in when they are around one another. That side of the family cannot be in the same room together because of the constant fighting among themselves.

My paternal grandmother is still living and is who I probably owe my life to. Although she had nothing but bad stories to tell us when we were younger, she was still the one I ran to for shelter when things got bad. Sadly out of all of my family members, she was the one who was the most stable. I spent a lot of my childhood around her.

That was where my work ethic started. I had to earn my keep. I don't remember her ever going to church or reading the Bible, but she sure let us know that she was the one in charge! I received my fair share of switches and then some. The Bible has many verses that give guidance for disciplining children. A few examples are Proverbs 13:34, 22:6, and 23:13-14, when paraphrased says "if you love your children, discipline, drive the rebellion out, and train them in the direction they should go while they are young and they will not depart from it as they grow old. You will also deliver their souls from hell." In a nutshell, this is what my grandmother did for me as I grew up. It is what helped me to do right and avoid trouble. She "nipped it in the bud" as the old saying goes. I can't say it did the same for her other grandchildren, but as I look back I am truly grateful to her.

There were two events in the same year that changed the lives of our family forever. Matt was only nine, I was five, and John was four at the time. In August, Matt's biological father passed away from a brain tumor. I did not know Matt's dad because he was not around us. His passing did not affect me, but I am sure Matt was very hurt. In December, our mother passed away with cancer of the liver. I can only imagine how it must have been for Matt. He lost both parents in the same year. This was one of the worse times in all of our lives. We were all so young and really had no guidance from those around us. We soon learned that our mother <u>was</u> the stability in our lives and now she was gone. Things were going to change drastically.

Some memories I have of my mother are very vivid and distinct. There was the time when she had to bail Matt and me out of trouble because Matt was shoplifting. I had to tell the store manager where we lived. I can remember barely being able to look over the dashboard, giving him directions to our house. Another memory was when she would watch Care Bears with us, while we waited on daddy to get home from work. I also remember that she was very sick for a long time. There came a time when we had to live with my grandmother because my mother became bed-ridden. I knew that our mother loved us, although she was not able to care for us toward the end.

Two details about my mother stand out the most in my mind. The first was the last time I saw her alive in her hospital bed. She was happy to see us. Someone had brought her a couple of packages of lemon drop candy - and everyone knows how children love candy! She gave the majority of the lemon drops to us kids. That was the last gift we received from her to show us her love and affection. When I see lemon drop candy or put one in my mouth, I think of her.

The other detail was the night she went to be with the Lord at the age of 37. Everyone knew that it was only a matter of time before the Lord called her home. All of the family from both sides gathered at my grandmother's house. My dad and uncle went in to see her. We were all waiting on them to return. As soon as my dad walked in and I looked into his bloodshot eyes, I knew that she was gone. I remember asking, "Daddy, what's wrong?", and then I began to weep, as I am now. I wept for what seemed like hours as my aunts passed me from one to another as they tried to comfort me. They tried everything they could think of to stop me from crying. The one thing that finally worked was cherry-flavored children's Tylenol. As soon as they gave it to me, I was immediately quiet and fell fast asleep.

After the death of my mom, I remember my dad never staying with one job more than a few months. We began to go to church, but that only lasted a short while because my dad had a car accident and just quit going. My brothers and I managed to catch rides in the church van. I remember the seeds that were planted in my heart at that young age. "For I know the plans that I have for you," declares the Lord, "plans to prosper you and not to harm you, to give you a hope and a future" (Jeremiah 29:11).

I remember moving and changing schools a lot while we were young. We were very poor and did without a lot of things. We lived in one house where the closest thing to a toilet was a five gallon bucket with a toilet lid placed on top. Everyone took turns emptying it on a daily basis. There were several houses that we lived in that we had to share with others (as in rats, mice, and roaches). I remember going through some old clothes when we were moving again, and we found dozens of baby mice in them. Another house we referred to as the roach motel. We would walk in turn the lights on and they would be everywhere. Or if we pulled on a piece of wall paper, and they would come out of the walls.

At this same house during the summer, the grass would get so high (about five or six feet tall) that we would make trails through it to ride bikes and pull wagons through. We also played hide and go seek in the tall grass. There was also the time when my dad sat on the front porch and shot at us with a CO2 BB pistol while we ran around to dodge the bullets. I do not know what made him do such a stupid thing! Now that I am grown, I see what harm could have come from him doing that.

Once, we lived in an old house by the train tracks way out in the country. The engineer always threw candy to us with a note attached. We looked forward to the next time as we waited on the front porch (including my dad) watching and counting down until the train came by again. I think you can figure out who got all the candy.

When we were young, I thought there was no one in the world we could relate to because of the way we grew up, and I thought we were the only ones who had to do without. We had a saying, "We were so poor growing up, that we had to put French fries on layaway at McDonald's just to be able to enjoy them!" The majority of the time our father would send us to the neighbors' houses for sugar, milk, flour, bread, etc. Other times, we charged groceries at the convenience stores, but that only lasted until they figured out that we couldn't pay the bill.

There are some foods that I cannot stand to eat now because those were the meals that we had no choice but to eat. Our only other choice was to go hungry and sometimes we did that, too! Some of those meals were potted meat, bologna sandwiches, sour kraut and weenies. I always looked forward to the trips to grandmother's house because she cooked lots of vegetables out of her garden. My favorite was and still is purple hull peas, cornbread, and sliced tomatoes. After our visit to grandma's house, it was back to the regular diet again!

When Matt was 11 years old, he was diagnosed with liver cancer (the same type of cancer that Mom had). He began receiving chemo treatments. He spent most of the first year in the children's hospital, 65 miles away. At this time, dad began to stay at the hospital a lot. While he was gone, John and I stayed either at friends' houses or with our grandmother. Once in a while, dad would take us to visit Matt. We had many different vehicles that were not dependable over this period of time. One specific time, we came to see Matt, and our car broke down. My dad did not have the money to fix it, so we left it and hitch-hiked all the way home.

I started working at the age of seven and have not stopped since. I would rake leaves and pine needles for whoever would pay me. One time I remember that I doubled my pay. I raked all of the pine needles off of one business property onto another business property. (I was told to do this.) Then I went to the other businessman and asked if he had any work for me. The owner said, "Yes, you can rake all of those pine needles up that I watched you rake over here. And then you can bag them." My response was, "I only did what he told me to do," as I pointed to the other store owner. He said he would pay me one dollar for each bag. I collected seven bags of pine needles. We used that money to pay for fuel to go see Matt.

One summer I stayed with my grandmother and worked to make money. I learned to do yard work and to pick vegetables out of the garden. I found several things out the hard way. I found out that okra was prickly and learned how purple hull peas received their name.

Another rollercoaster ride that we did not enjoy was my dad's dating life. While my dad was staying at the hospital with Matt during his treatments, he began to date again. He met and dated several women both married and single. It was one problem after another.

He would see one woman for several months at a time. We would get used to seeing her around and the story was "We are going to get married soon.", so we began to call her "Mom". This happened time and again. It never failed that just before the scheduled wedding, they would always split up.

One married woman was even responsible for all of us spending the night in jail on my eighth birthday! We went to pick up her daughter from her "husband's house". He invited us in, fed us hamburgers, and then held us at gun point while he made my dad drink heavy liquor. We were told to stay in a bedroom as my dad passed out. The guy proceeded to beat on him. After beating him up, he used black coffee to try to sober up my dad. Once, when he kept my dad awake (but not sober) he finally sent us on our way. As all drunks do, my dad was driving all over the road, so we were pulled over by the police. We were taken to jail and had to wait for someone to pick us up and agree to care for us until my dad was released from jail. We were out of state when this happened, so another married woman came and got us.

Afterwards my dad moved us across the state to another city to be with this woman. Before long they broke up. In the midst of all this, my younger brother and I had become victims of child molestation by an old "friend" of the family. Matt missed most of this because he was always at the hospital. That was sure a blessing for him, but he did have troubles of his own going on.

When the doctors allowed Matt to go home, they were privy to some of the shenanigans of my father. Matt could go home only if he was allowed to stay at my grandmother's house. Everything had to be kept clean around him. Matt even had his own room. In my eyes, he became spoiled because everyone came by to see him and brought him things.

I know that he endured a lot of pain throughout his sickness. He had to take lots of chemotherapy treatments, too. It is truly a miracle, an answer to all of our prayers, that he was cured from this rare form of cancer. I do not know exactly how much he developed his faith in God along the way.

My younger brother and I shared in many of Matt's experiences during this time of sickness and recovery. Our life was not fun for any of us. We all had bad experiences, but we met some very kind and loving people who helped us have a break now and then. They brought positive things into our lives.

This was an organization that was dedicated to granting the dreams of children diagnosed with life threatening illnesses. They had worked hard to make life easier and more enjoyable for the children (patients and siblings) while they were at the lowest points in their lives. This foundation granted some dreams that may have seemed impossible to accomplish, but it happened because of the volunteers' persistence and their strong faith in God. With God, all things are possible. And they believed that, too!

Some children wanted horses or other types of pets. Some wanted to meet famous people or to go to special places. Matt wanted to go to Graceland, the home of Elvis Presley and this organization made it all possible. Matt was born about two weeks after Elvis' death, but he has always loved the music of the great king of rock-n-roll. This program also took annual trips as a group with all of the children together. There were as many as 200 children on each trip. Some trips that I recall were to Universal Studios in FL, Graceland in Memphis, TN, St Louis, MO and Silver Dollar City in Branson, MO. We got to go on some of those trips.

They held Christmas parties every December and invited all of the patients and their brothers and sisters. We got the presents that we requested when Santa called us up to see him. For so many children like us, this was our only gifts for Christmas. We got to go to their Christmas parties over the next eight years.

It was a real blessing to see these children experience things they may not have had the opportunity to experience any other way. There were a number of great relationships that were formed as a result of these experiences that I shared in, even though I was just a brother of a patient.

Even today, more than 15 years later, I still call and visit with so many of the friends that I made during those special times. The encouragement and dedication of so many people helped to build the faith in me needed to overcome situations in my own life. From these experiences came many building blocks in life, not just for me, but for so many others, too. I give thanks to the Lord for those who stepped out in faith to believe in, to give to, and to encourage others during these trying times.

When Matt was 15, he went into remission from his cancer. He was allowed to come live at home with us. After all of the challenging experiences listed previously, my dad began to brighten up. Maybe he saw that others did care what was happening to us. He began to keep a steady job, for which he has now had for about 15 years. He settled down and married a nice woman. They have been married for 14 years, now. We refer to our stepmother by her name, not "Mom", because of the repeated hurt that we went through growing up.

Our parents actually bought a house. My brothers and I attended one school district for the rest of our school days. You might say life returned to normal or almost normal. At least we could identify with others our own age. Life with a "Mom" meant better living conditions, better meals, and more discipline. Although all of these things were big improvements, there were lots of things that we did without simply because we could not afford them, but we were grateful for what we did have considering the alternative (and we had already seen that side before!).

After life began to calm down, my brothers and I began to go to church again. My parents always supported us in going, but never went with us. My stepmother's father was a minister so she could answer any questions that we had. For many years it was just a place to get away from home life. At church, there were always different games and events going on. Obviously, we were drawn to all of them. Life at home was filled with chores or discipline. We were not allowed to stay in the living room and watch much television. Dad was either sleeping or watching what he wanted. Being the boys that we were, when we did get to watch TV, we would start talking or play-fighting so he would send us outside or to our rooms.

Matt reached the legal working age and began to work as much as he could. He worked at Hardee's and a few grocery stores during his high school years. I was younger than Matt and I saw that working got him away from home more. I decided to dedicate as much time as I could to finding yard work around the neighborhood so I could do the same. My lawn mowing business lasted until I graduated high school. It kept me very busy and out of trouble. Praise the Lord!

Matt entered a phase where his peers at school influenced him more. He quit going to church as often. I even remember a time when Matt wanted nothing to do with Christ. He basically denied that Christianity was real. He has since changed his opinion on this subject. He is not at a point to where he has changed his habits, but he does believe. Many people who are in life threatening situations go through different stages of believing and disbelieving in God. I know that he must deal with this in his own way. I am praying that Matt will come through these stages and become much stronger in his faith.

I am proud Matt has good work ethics and goals for his future. After Matt's graduation, he continued his education by going to school as an auto-diesel mechanic. He has always loved working on vehicles. After he graduated from college, he joined the navy to get further training as a jet engine mechanic. He has just recently re-enlisted for another four years. He says he plans on making a career out of it.

Matt has always been shy. I never knew of him having any girl-friends when we were in school. Then while he was in the Navy, I heard that he was getting married! He met his wife through the internet. She lived out of state. When he first met his wife in person, she said he would just sit there and not say much. Whatever he did next must have worked because she married him. Now they have been married about five years and are hoping to have a child soon.

After Matt left for the Navy, our parents decided to let the house go back to the bank because they could no longer make the payments. They decided to move more than 20 miles away. John stayed with them. I decided this was the time for me to go my own way. I was a junior in high school and wanted to continue to graduate with all of my friends I had made over the past eight years. I began working for a grocery store as a cashier and grocery stocker. I had an older hunting buddy who allowed me to stay with him until I went to college.

I always made good grades in high school and became a student in a vocational school in addition to attending high school classes. I received credit towards graduation for it. The field I chose was building trades. I learned the basics of building a house. I now know how to do plumbing, electrical, carpentry, roofing, and heating/air conditioning.

While all of this was going on, I came to a point in my life where I learned there was more to God than what I have known and experienced. I never had trouble with drugs and alcohol because I have seen what it has done to my friends and family. There was an empty void that could not be filled by just going to church and going through the motions or by playing games.

I changed churches and had someone take me under their wing and disciple me. I took part in an Easter drama called the "Passion Play" and it shed new light on many things for me. At this time, I decided to seek after God with my whole heart. I made Jesus the Lord of all of my life and asked the Holy Spirit to come into my life. I surrendered my life to Him and decided to attend Applied Life Christian College. I now know that Jesus came to give us life and life more abundant. We must take hold of God's promises and apply them to our lives.

My experience at Applied Life Christian College paved the way for the ministry I have embarked upon. It has taught me how to live and enjoy the abundant life that Christ has in store for us. It all points back to the choices we make. God has given us two ears and one mouth, so we would listen twice as much as we speak. Out of the abundance of the heart, the mouth speaks.

What kind of situations do we create for ourselves? As a man thinks, so is he. If you think depressing thoughts, then you stay depressed. If you continue to dwell on hurtful situations, then anger builds until you explode. It is not just you who is now hurting, but everyone around you. Then there is the issue of forgiveness; how many times do you have to continue to forgive? The Word says 70 x 70 you shall forgive which means as many times as it takes. We are instructed to be quick to listen, slow to speak, and slow to anger. There is a reason for it.

We (as Christians) are all called to be ministers of the Word no matter what we do. Actions do speak louder than words! Whether you are a doctor, an auto mechanic, or a carpenter you are to live as little Christ's pleasing unto the Lord. You speak to someone by what you do not say. Saint Francis of Assisi said, "Preach the Gospel at all times; if necessary use words."

The ministry path I chose was a short-term missionary. I once asked the Lord to give me a love for people, and He did. He has also blessed me with many talents I use to fulfill his calling and bring glory to His name. I take advantage of every opportunity that comes my way to serve Him and to reach out to others. I believe that the Lord has orchestrated each and every event and person to whom I have met. God can take the bad things and turn them into good for us, if we allow Him. I believe my obedience to Him and the past events of my life has shaped me into who He wants me to be. For that I am grateful!

God has blessed me with a wonderful wife of four years, a house, reliable transportation, a business, a vision for life and now a new little baby girl. My wife and I have a vision to own a horse ranch for trouble teens. The preparations have begun, and it is only a matter of time until it is here.

"With God, <u>ALL</u> Things <u>ARE</u> Possible!"

Shane & friend Amanda at an annual Christmas party

By Shane, Brother of Matt

PART 4

**This section
will let you
experience
the joy
of the
annual trips
and
witness how
God watches
over us.**

Chapter IIX.

In this section, we will tell you how some of the special trips and parties were made into huge successful events for our precious children. Once in a while, others tried to interrupt our plans, but God was there always watching over us.

Our Wonderful Experiences at the Little Rock Air Force Base

The Thunderbirds with some of our patients

Within a few weeks, after Timmy had gone up in the helicopter, I received a call from the Air Force Base. Again, I thanked them. They were calling because they wanted to get more involved in assisting with our dream children. I explained that we do not ever suggest to a child what they want for a dream. The child must tell us what they are wanting, but if we ever had another child requesting to go up in a helicopter or plane, we were happy to know that they would gladly assist us.

During our conversation, I mentioned the Christmas parties we have each year for these children, and they suggested that we have the next one on the airbase. They would devote a hanger for the site of the party and guards could direct our people from the main gate to the hanger. What a great idea!

The Radiation Therapy Institute donated our organization's office space for the next 6 years. This was where many of our patients went for radiation. Our office was located on the top floor next to the office of the Public Relations Director for the institute. She and I became very close friends. She was a beautiful and talented young woman with a big heart. She, like me, had love and compassion for each of these special children. We were always working toward making the children's lives a little easier by having different events throughout the year for them.

The Radiation Therapy Institute had a Christmas party planned for that year. We put our heads together and came up with a great idea. We arranged for both organizations to work together to combine the two parties into one party and have it at the airbase.

The Director of Public Relations had many clever volunteers who were creative in making a C130 cargo plane into "Rudolph, the Red Nosed Reindeer". They put big red jagged horns (made of tree branches) on top of the plane (at the front), painted eyes in the pilot's front windows, painted the nose of the plane red, and had red lights blinking on the nose. This was so very cute!

We actually had the Christmas party in one of the hangers where "Rudolph" was parked inside. Rudolph's tail was opened, and we had tables of catered food and drinks in there for everyone to enjoy.

Santa and his helpers flew down in a helicopter and entered the hanger carrying a huge bag of toys. Santa sat down in a large chair and gave out gifts for each of the patients and their siblings. We had around 250 people in attendance that year. It was a great day for the children, their families, and for all of the volunteers who assisted. We even had the top commander of the airbase and some more top ranking officials attending the party to watch the children enjoy the day.

The airbase had arranged to take us up for a ride in a C130 cargo plane! They flew the plane all day, taking 30 people up at a time. They flew the children halfway around the state and back. The patients had earphones to listen to the pilots talk to them about what they were seeing on the ground. Everyone got to go up in the plane by the end of the day because we all took turns.

The children were thrilled to be able to fly in that huge plane! Many of them had never been in a plane before and were amazed at the sights from the sky to the ground. Even for those who had flown before, this was quite a different type of flight than riding on commercial airlines. This plane was so very big and so very loud! We sat in the belly of the plane and, of course, there were no cushioned seats! What a great experience for these children. I am sure they will never forget that day!

The airbase was such a blessing for both of our organizations. Over the next 13 years, they never forgot about our dream children. When something special was going to happen at the airbase, they always called us and invited the children and families to attend the events. The children were anxious to go out there any time they were invited because they knew something fun always happens at the airbase.

From time to time, the airbase personnel had fundraisers for our organization. Many of them volunteered their services to us, also. Several times, the airbase had The Thunderbirds come in for air shows and invited our patients to come out there to meet the pilots and see the jets up close. Special bleachers were put up in front of the normal crowd just for our patients and families. Our children were always treated very well and with great respect. We can only hope they know what a huge different they made in many of our patients lives. The airbase personnel were an important part of helping these children to gain the strength to keep fighting their diseases. We wish to thank them for caring about these special children and their families.

Our Trip To Memphis, Tennessee

Keith as Elvis on Memphis trip

As with all of our group trips, we started out by planning the itinerary. We sent out forms to be signed by both parents and the children's head physicians with a deadline to be back in our hands

30 days before the scheduled trip. All must agree to allow us to have the children for a full day. If any medications need to be given on that day, our volunteer RNs must have the authority to administer those meds. Some children will require wheelchairs and some will need oxygen. All special needs must be included in the forms.

We always had RNs and LPNs on these trips, as well as respiratory therapists, and physicians. Everyone must be updated on every patient's needs for the day and given instructions on what to do in case of an emergency. Any "what ifs" were to be included in the physicians instructions on the forms. We then discussed those possibilities with our medical team.

We had several state troopers, local policeman, and EMTs with us all day. Many patients needed to be carried (at times) and we needed strong men to be able to do this.

Patients over the age of ten; their parents were not allowed on the trip. A volunteer was assigned to each of them. Patients, ages ten and under; must be accompanied by one parent (unless other arrangements were made) and a volunteer was also assigned to them. We have determined, through experience that some children do not obey their parents very well, but they will respond better to another adult who is not their parent. We used this knowledge to our fullest advantage to keep the children in line. Although, in ten years of trips, we never had one ounce of trouble with any child misbehaving.

Our ground trips would include the siblings of the patients. Ground trips meant that we would travel by buses. Getting more buses for these types of trips was not a problem, but when we had to fly by an airline, getting more seats on a plane was much different. One 747, DC10 or 777 was all we could afford at a time, and they were always filled to capacity on each trip.

Every child was assigned a volunteer for the day. If we were going to a theme park, the child could lead the volunteer into any direction of the park because it was "their day" to enjoy all that the parks had to offer. We had volunteers with walkie-talkies positioned all around the park in case of an emergency.

Every trip had a theme and we designed t-shirts with that same theme. On each trip, we had a different color of t-shirt (like purple, light orange, gray, yellow, light lime green, etc.) so volunteers could watch for our special colors from anywhere in the parks.

When we designed the t-shirts for the Memphis trip, Priscilla Presley was the one who gave us a special photo of Elvis to use on our t-shirts. (Elvis is standing with his legs apart while playing his guitar.) We had to sign an agreement that we would not sell the t-shirts, but would only use them for wearing during that trip and to give one to each child and volunteer as part of the memorabilia from the trip. We agreed and were very much in appreciation for her kindness. The t-shirts also had the Peabody Ducks walking across the shirt and a Libertyland Park Ferris wheel in the background.

We always had media come with us on the trips. Usually there were one or two TV stations, sometimes a radio station, and always one to three newspaper reporters, and all with cameramen. We had our own people taking still camera shots and movie camera footage of the day's events, also. After the trip, we put all of the still photos and movie film together to make a video to give to everyone who participated in the trip. Even the large donors received a copy. Still photos went to the patients and their brothers and sisters along with their videotapes.

We had around 162 children on this particular trip. Our day began early, at 6:00 a. m. Most of the patients were ready and anxiously waiting at the designated area specified on the parents' materials. By 6:30, we were off to Memphis! We stopped halfway to Memphis and ate breakfast at McDonalds. Some parents (from that part of the state) met us there so we could pick up the patients. It saved them from driving all the way into the city.

My husband has a great sense of humor. He loves to act out. He went to the bus bathroom and dressed up in an Elvis wig with long black sideburns, dark sunglasses, and was in a complete Elvis costume. He had on a white jumpsuit with bellbottoms and red sequins. He had a long red silk scarf hanging around his neck to match. He got off the bus and walked around for all of the children and volunteers to see. He has a great Elvis voice and sang parts of Elvis songs and did his "Karate moves" for the kids. The children squealed with excitement. Outside of McDonald's, even people we didn't know came over to see him. Grown women ran up and kissed him! Even the thought of Elvis does strange things to people.

On the road to Memphis after breakfast, one of our "clown" kids Shane (a brother of a patient) put on the wig and sunglasses and stood up before the entire busload of people and started playing around as if he were Elvis. Another very young and talented patient, Nate (age seven) took over the microphone and began to sing Elvis songs. We were all amazed at how good he was! He sang us on into Memphis.

When we arrived in Memphis our first stop was to the Downtown Peabody Hotel. We lined up inside the lobby to watch the Duck Master bring the ducks down from the roof via the hotel elevator. The elevator door opened up and out came the ducks all in a row waddling passed us. They went straight to the indoor fountain in the center of the lobby and jumped in, one by one. The crowd went wild over those adorable ducks. The ducks were Mallards, both hens and drakes. They quacked and quacked and shook their cute little tails as if they knew they were the center of attention (and I am sure they did)!

We had to watch very carefully over the children because many of the smaller ones wanted to try to grab the ducks and pet them. We moved back many little hands while trying to explain why they could not touch the ducks. One little three year old girl decided to go in the water after them, but we caught her just as she put part of her sandal in the water. Those precious children were just as darling as the ducks!

Next we loaded everyone back up into the buses and headed for Graceland. Once we arrived, there were so many things to do and so much to see! We first made our way to the display of Elvis' many cars and airplane. We had our photo shoots set up in front of one of the cars. Each set of patient, siblings, (and/or parent) and volunteers assigned to them were in the photos together. While some were waiting for their turns, they ate lunch at the Heartbreak Hotel Cafe.

After everyone was finished with the photos and lunch, we headed across the street to the Graceland home, grounds, and burial sites. The whole Graceland experience was awesome. We were allowed to go everywhere inside the house except upstairs where the family still lives. Elvis' real cook was actually standing in the kitchen, and we got to talk to her. She was so very nice. She told us about Elvis' favorite meals.

We got to see his huge collection of gold records. The room had tall ceilings and the walls were completely covered with gold records. Some of his famous outfits were glass enclosed for viewing. We went through the target room where he shot his many guns. Bullet holes were all over the back wall, including some in the targets that were placed there.

We saw beautiful horses in the pasture grazing in the picture-perfect green grass. We walked all around the gravesites where he and his family are buried. The grounds are immaculate with gorgeous flowers in bloom.

Seeing all of this was so overwhelming to all of us. Most of these children were born long after the "King of Rock-N-Roll" died. They are still just as interested in him as if they personally knew him. It seems as if everyone loves Elvis and anything to do with him. We were and are today still so thankful that the Presley family was so gracious and kind to us. This will be a day that the children will never forget.

Next, we loaded back into the buses to continue with our trip. It was on to Libertyland (a theme park just outside of Memphis). The rest of the day was for running, playing, and riding the rides, as many as they could and as many times as they wanted. The park was the perfect size for all of them to do whatever they wanted for the last six hours of our trip.

When the park closed at 10:00 p. m. it was time to start the journey home. Every last one of us was exhausted. We thought that we would have a nice quiet ride home on the buses, and for one hour we did. One of our patient's oxygen tanks emptied and the backup oxygen tank (provided by his mother) was also empty! We had to find the nearest hospital and fast. About 30 more miles down the road we found a hospital sign and took off the freeway and made a bee-line to the hospital. The respiratory therapist, an RN, and I ran into the emergency room and asked for a new tank. They had one all right, but the patient's attached equipment would not fit with the small country hospital's outdated oxygen tank. We had to improvise to make it fit until we could get him home to his mother. The respiratory therapist was a genius! He made it work. Well, that problem was settled, the patient was breathing great again, and we were off to Little Rock!

Not so fast! Just down the road, another one of our buses pulled our lead bus over. I was asked to go see what was wrong. As I entered the other bus, an LPN and a RN met me at the door and told me that one of our 11 year old patients' stomach wound had come open and his shunt was sticking out. I had wonderful and very intelligent medical personnel with me. In just a few moments, they were putting the shunt back in place and closing his wound. He was a great patient. This "small" problem hardly phased him at all! He remained calm, and it was over in minutes. They used sterile equipment and were very careful with the procedure.

After arriving back in the city, we met the families in the same designated area as we did that morning. A couple of the RNs and the patient's parents took "our surgery patient" straight to the children's hospital only to find out that they had performed an excellent job of repairing the problem. No changes were needed, and the family was so thankful that we had taken such good care of their child.

It was the Lord that made everything great for the entire day, and all problems were solved quickly and perfectly. I think maybe He allows things to happen sometimes just to keep us on our toes and to keep us thinking. He was always with us on every trip and special event we had for these precious children. We were and will always be thankful that He is with us, watching over us at all times.

In the Middle of the Transplant Drama we had a Picnic at the Governor's Mansion

There was a time, in the mid 1980s, when our Governor was William "Bill" J. Clinton. He and his wife, Hilary Rodham lived in our Governor's Mansion. (Hilary did not use the last name of Clinton until a few years before Bill announced that he was running for President.) They had one child, their daughter Chelsea.

Now I knew most of the Governor's staff both in the Governor's Offices and in the Governor's Mansion including some of the security personnel. We had actually granted the wishes of one of the mansion security employees' children in the recent past. I also knew most of the appointed political officials holding positions in our state offices. I often asked for favors from a few of them when it included assisting a patient with extra activities, to come to a fundraiser, or to be involved in some other capacity. Hardly anyone ever said no because they received good media coverage when they did assist us.

During that period, Governor Clinton and I had been in a battle over Medicaid not covering transplants. The problem, as I saw it, was that Medicaid would pay for a patient to stay in an Arkansas hospital until they died, but would <u>not</u> pay that same amount of money or less to send that patient to another state for the needed surgery and rejection meds. At that time, no one could receive transplants in Arkansas because we had no hospitals capable of performing the transplants. The only transplants Arkansas hospitals were equipped to handle were kidney transplants. Now does that make any sense to you? Well, it did not sound right to me either!

We fought back and forth through the media (newspapers and TV), but neither of us would budge from our views. One day while I was in the State Capitol, I ran into Governor Clinton and asked why he did not want to support those changes. He told me that he wanted to keep Arkansas money in Arkansas (whatever that meant!). I had patients dying in the children's hospital trying to wait for a transplant that would never come. I tried to shame him into changing his position, but it did not work.

I finally started raising money to pay for the transplants that Arkansas Medicaid would not. These children were dying and could not wait much longer. People from all over the state sent money in to help. Thousands of dollars piled in from all over the United States after the national media picked up on the stories. Even "USA Today" carried a couple of our stories. Once the political officials saw that the majority of the people agreed with me, they began helping me, too.

One of our Arkansas State Representatives called and invited me to come before the General Assembly to speak to our State Representatives and ask for a new law to override Governor Clinton to make Arkansas Medicaid cover these surgeries. So shortly thereafter, someone wrote up the bill and sent it through the legislation. Because of this, the legislators overwhelmingly agreed to put a law into effect to make Medicaid pay. That law went into effect only five months later.

In the mean time, I ended up helping 20 patients have their transplants before the law was changed and set into place. All of the money raised paid for these surgeries after I negotiated the prices down from each hospital, surgeon, anesthesiologist, etc. Through those national media stories, we received the attention of the "ears" in Washington D. C. I then received a phone call from the White House when Ronald Reagan was President. He put "The Donor Awareness Week" into effect to help find donors for the hundreds of patients awaiting transplants across the country. The program is still in effect day.

Because of the media coverage many more requests for children to have dreams granted came in. We were actually granting dreams throughout that whole ordeal, but now we were swamped with calls from people wanting assistance. After the media attention calmed down and everything was in place for the transplant patients, I made a much needed decision. I decided I needed to devote my time granting the wishes of children diagnosed with life threatening illnesses only. I made an announcement in a press conference that all of the transplant money raised was spent on transplants. I would no longer be involved in assisting with any more transplants and felt it was time for me to go back working full-time granting wishes. My plate was full!

The Radiation Therapy Institute decided to plan a picnic for survivors of cancer. This was going to be for patients from across our state. They asked me if I would join in and assist in the planning stages and in the invitation list. Of course, I thought that this was such a great idea and agreed to assist in any area I was needed. We scheduled the picnic to be held in the backyard of the Governor's Mansion. The mansion had a huge beautiful backyard with enough room for all of the guests.

Of course, I did not call the Clintons for permission. I knew they were not the ones to make that decision. I worked with the mansion staff and security for all planning for the picnic.

That day came quickly. We had several long grills cooking chicken, hamburgers, and hot dogs. We had loads of other foods, too. Over 500 patients with their families showed up for the picnic. Nearly everyone we invited came. We had a band playing, games for everyone, and many other activities. We had balloons everywhere. Volunteers were everywhere. There were local and statewide political people there to introduce themselves and mingle with the crowd. All forms of media were there, too.

I walked around constantly to make sure everyone was happy and that the day was going as planned. One time, I looked up and saw Chelsea walking around introducing herself to many different people (adults and children). She even joined in some of the children's games. She was extremely nice and very cordial to everyone. I believe that she was around 12 years old at the time. She and my oldest son Patrick knew each other because he taught at a cotillion where Chelsea went once a week for dance lessons.

Before long, Governor Clinton stepped out into the yard and started talking with different people. I did not see him out there because I was busy with the cooks and making sure that we had enough food to go around. He walked up beside me and put his hand on the small of my back and said, "I might have known that you were behind this whole thing, and in my backyard, at that!" We laughed together and then I said, "Well sure! This is Arkansas' backyard. We are all just visitors here!" Not one more word was said. We both just smiled at each other and he walked away. He walked around for over an hour visiting with the guests and volunteers.

The picnic started around 10:00 a. m. and went on until dark. Everyone who came very much enjoyed themselves and was very appreciative of all the hard work that was put into this picnic by all of the volunteers. It was a blessing for us to see that all of these patients had such a great time. Sometimes it is the little things in life that mean the most.

Our Trip to Universal Studios in Florida

Group photo on the Universal Studios trip

As with many annual trips for the children, we started out six months in advance by locating a destination. Universal Studios was chosen as the destination. It would take an entire day to see all the theme park had to offer. We contacted the Public Relations Department at Universal Studios. They were wonderful and very helpful. We set up goals and expectations and would get back with them later for the actual number of people coming on the trip. We found out they would not comp the entire amount for the entry tickets but they would work with us at a discounted price. This was still more than Disneyland or Disney World would do for us.

Usually I allowed our local travel agency to handle the leasing of the planes. I called the travel agency, the same one that I used to handle our dream trips for the past two years. The owner and I knew each other very well since we had patients constantly traveling. He always answered his own phone in his office when I called, but today was different. A woman answered and her voice was very familiar to me. She said, "John Taylor's Travel Agency. How may I help you?"

I said, "Marilyn, why are you answering John's phone?" You see, she worked for a local television station as a public relations person, and we had worked together many times in the past. I actually had considered her as a sort of "friend". In this business, you have many of this type of so-called friends.

She told me that she and another well known public figure in our state had together purchased five travel agencies in our city. I was shocked because John had not told me anything about selling his business. I told her why I was calling and asked if the new company wanted to take John's place and be in charge of leasing an airplane for the upcoming trip. Of course, she agreed and I could tell she was delighted to have this chance to help us.

Over the next few days, she and I talked frequently. I gave her my expectations and a price range to stay within. I have done this so many times before. Usually we ended up leasing a 747 or DC10 airplane. The pilots and stewardesses would volunteer their part so we could keep the cost low. The only other cost of the flight would be the special foods that we were served to and from the destination.

She had contacted several airlines leasing agents to look for the right size of plane that was needed. She also needed to find out the dates that a plane would be available for the trip. Within days, she worked out a deal with a leasing company out of Florida. We would be flying on an American Airlines 747 plane, and the flight was scheduled for July 30th. I assumed the price was within our budget. The type of plane chosen seemed right to me.

Once the plane was leased and a date was chosen, we moved on to the phase of sending out letters and releases to the parents and physicians of our patients. When we received this information back, we had a more accurate count of patients and parents going on the trip. Children ten years old and under could bring one parent (if a parent wants to go). All of the children who signed up to go would definitely be on the plane. Next we decided how many seats were available to accommodate volunteers, medical staff, and media traveling with us. The seating arrangements always worked out because each trip was meant to be.

I was also in the process of raising the funds needed for the trip. An average of $40,000.00 was the goal of each of our past flights. This included the airplane, food for everyone while in flight, souvenirs for the children, entry tickets to the theme park, still photos and video footage, video tapes given to each participant, and money for some of the patients who could not afford lunch and extras on their own.

We started this adventure around February 10th and we were not scheduled to leave until July. We had lots of time before we had to pay for anything, yet. I was in the process of raising the necessary funds when Marilyn called me. She had found an airplane to lease two weeks ago but never said the price. In this conversation, she told me that I needed to write a check to the travel agency for $32,000.00 to secure the plane and dates of the flight. That was more than I had ever paid for a leased plane before. I told her that the price was too high and she needed to keep looking.

One week later, she called me again with the same information. She assured me that all prices had gone up and this price was good. Again she told me that I needed to get her the money fast to secure the leasing arrangements. I was pressured for the money up front. Normally, I didn't pay for the planes until a month before the flight, at the same time that I filed for a flight plan, and turned in the flight roster.

I pushed my donors for as much of the money as I could receive quickly. I was able to find the $32,000.00 within a week, but it was difficult to do. I had to promise civic and other nonprofit groups if they gave over a certain amount, they could have a couple of people from their group come on the flight as volunteers. I explained that we had rules to be followed, and the volunteers must be very responsible. I also had to approve of them before they could come with us. It worked out nicely.

That following week, on March 2nd, I wrote the check out to the travel agency. All details were worked out and the trip was set for July 30th. Everything ran smoothly with all of the other arrangements.

One very busy and hectic day, around 3 weeks later, Marilyn and her business partner showed up in my office without calling first. I thought this was strange, but ignored my first impressions. I was delighted to see them and asked them to come into my office and have a seat. They pitched a plan for my husband and I to loan them $2,500.00 as a personal loan so they could purchase another travel agency. Of course, I told them that we didn't have $2,500.00 just sitting around the house to lend to them. I reminded them that I was a volunteer with no salary, and we had five teenage sons.

They promised we would be paid back within 30 days. My husband was not present and I told them that I would never act on anything without talking to my husband, first. I had no money to loan anyone. He was the only paid person in the family. I hesitantly agreed to present this to my husband to see if he would help. I did say if he agreed to loan them the money, I wanted an agreement drawn up by my attorney stating they had to pay it back within 30 days of the signed agreement. They said they would be happy to sign the agreement.

That evening, I talked with my husband. I really never felt very comfortable with them coming to us like that, but I dismissed my inner feelings. We talked about the fact that I have known Marilyn for at least six years. We discussed her partner, of which, neither of us knew personally, but he was a very well known public figure. (I will call him "Joe". I will not disclose his real name, but I will tell you that everyone in the entire state knew him for at least the last 25 years!) My husband said he would do this as long as the legal paperwork was signed. I was still a bit uncomfortable with this decision, but went along with it. I knew we would need this money next month for our mortgage payments and such.

The following day, I contacted my lawyer, had an agreement drawn up and set up a meeting with my husband, myself, Marilyn, and her partner, Joe. The meeting took place the next day, in my office. They read and signed the legal document, and we gave them a check for $2,500.00.

One month quickly came and passed with no payment, no phone calls, and no nothing! I called Marilyn and she had one excuse after another. I told her we needed the money to pay our bills. It didn't seem to matter what I said. Two months passed, and then three months passed. I kept calling, and she kept making excuses. During some of those calls, we talked about the leased airplane, the flight roster, and the flight plan. I was told that everything was set for the trip to Universal Studios and I don't know why, but I believed her.

Our flight was planned for July 30th. On July 3rd, I received a call from the Florida leasing agency concerning the payment for the plane. That feeling of my stomach coming up in my throat started happening. He asked how much longer must he wait before he receives payment for the plane because we were running out of time. I was stunned. My thought process had just slowed down, and I was looking for the right words to explain that I paid $32,000.00 on March 2nd through the travel agency, luckily by check. Once I found the right words, he said that I had a problem, but he understood the circumstances and he would work with me. I promised to get right on it and find out where the money was.

I called Marilyn at the travel agency, but she would not answer. I left 10 messages in the next two days with no response. Finally I called back for the last time and left word that I was calling the Arkansas Attorney General, and he could handle the problem from here on out. And that is what I did.

The Attorney General said he had a huge stack of complaints against those same two people, but he could not act on them because every case was a civil matter. Individuals had prepaid tickets for traveling on vacations before the sale of the five travel agencies, and the new owners (Marilyn and Joe) were not honoring the tickets or reservations. Now I was really worried! They had our personal money, too.

Because we were a nonprofit organization, the Attorney General could now go after them. He instantly put out a warrant for their arrest. On the same day, the arresting officers went to the place of business, but the travel agencies' doors were locked. No phone numbers were posted on the doors to track them down. No one knew their home addresses, and they were not listed in any phone directories or the Crisscross, either. The Attorney General assigned one of his top attorneys to handle the situation. I had to file charges against both of them for stealing from a nonprofit organization which was a federal offense in our state with mandatory sentences.

In the mean time, Marilyn got word that officers were looking for them, so she called me. She said she was sorry about the missing money and was working on a deal to recover our lost funds. I was furious! I told her I would not drop the charges against them until I retrieved the money for the plane. She asked me to give her two more days. I said, "No! You have had three months already. I will not withdraw my complaint until I have the money (in cash) in my hand! And what about this trip scheduled in three weeks? What I am supposed to do about that?"

I hung up and called the Florida leasing agency to fill him in. He was wonderful! He agreed to proceed with our plans as if we had already paid for the flight. He said not to worry about anything but to go after those two people responsible for stealing the money. We could settle up later. He couldn't have been any nicer, but I really felt bad about doing him this way.

By the end of that day, I was very emotional. I finally remembered to stop what I was doing and I began to pray for a solution. Our trip was scheduled for just 3 weeks away and all plans had been finalized since May. I knew this trip was meant to be and decided to let go and let God handle everything. I left the office and started home.

As I was traveling down a main thoroughfare, I looked over and saw Marilyn driving in the lane beside me. I decided to pull over into her lane and follow her. She did not see me nor did she know what type of car I drove. This was to my benefit. I followed her to the next town and watched her pull into an apartment complex. I then watched her go to the door and unlock it with a key. I wrote down her address and apartment number. I also wrote down what type of car she drove and her license plate number. From a pay phone, I immediately called the Attorney General's Office and gave them the information.

By the time I got home through the rush hour traffic, I had a call waiting on my answering machine. They had already arrested Marilyn and Joe and taken them to the Attorney General's Office. Wow! That was fast!

I called the attorney back and he said, "I have Marilyn and Joe sitting in my office. I have us on a speakerphone. Is there anything that you would like to say to them?" I sure did! I told them, "You both should feel ashamed of taking money away from terminally ill children! Marilyn, I am deeply hurt because you were supposed to be my friend and I never expected this kind of treatment from you. Joe, I don't really personally know you, but I am still shocked that you were capable of stealing money from sick children." At least, Marilyn apologized for her actions while Joe sat quietly, not saying anything, not even how sorry he should have been. Even with all of this going on, I really had no hard feelings toward them, just disappointed because they actually believed they could have gotten away with it in the first place.

Marilyn asked me to drop the charges against them. She said they would give me the $32,000.00 in cash by 10:00 a. m. on the following morning. This is when the attorney chimed in and said I had no say so in dropping the charges because the Attorney General's Office had filed their own set of charges against them for defrauding a nonprofit organization. I did agree to meet them at our bank by 10:00 a. m. to collect the money. I asked the attorney to drop the charges after I had the money in the bank. He just said, "We will see about that later."

During this same conversation, I finally remembered to mention they still had our $2,500.00 and had not bothered to pay us back for the personal loan. The 30 days was over and they were two months late. The attorney was very interested in this and asked them what they were going to do about repayment. Marilyn asked if I could wait one more month for our personal money because the $32,000.00 was all they could get right now. She promised to make it worth our wait. I agreed. Besides, I knew that this was a civil matter and it could not be handled by the Attorney General's Office, anyway.

Marilyn apologized again and agreed to let my husband and I have free round trip tickets for anywhere in the world we wished to go. I said, "This is not necessary. We just want our money paid back to us as soon as possible and nothing more." Again, the attorney spoke up and said, "Vicki, let them comp you tickets because they have caused you a great deal of discomfort." I reluctantly agreed, but I certainly never expected them to follow through! They were allowed to leave for the evening, but the attorney told me to let him know if they didn't show up at our bank with the $32,000.00 in the morning.

Both were there waiting with the money at our bank when I arrived on time. I put it in the nonprofit account and immediately felt a huge sigh of relief. Now this is settled. I thanked them and rushed back to my office and called the Attorney General's Office with loads of thanks. I then called the Florida leasing agency to let them know the money was back and I was wiring him the money that very same day.

Now that everything was back on an even keel, I could go back to granting wishes that were pressing. No, I did not use Marilyn and Joe for the travel agency. I knew other agency owners and just called one of them. I always had one or two on standby just in case problems arose, which were rare.

Our trip to Universal Studios was a great success, as always. No child needed extra medical attention. We had no problems at all. The children were so excited and the volunteers were great. The media provided wonderful coverage. Everything went just exactly as planned.

Oh, yes. I failed to mention that Joe and Marilyn went on the trip and filmed the entire day and later, turned it into a Saturday morning TV show. I had agreed to let them do this at the beginning of our first month of working together. Well, the patients and parents loved being on TV. So what could I say? I was an easy target when it came to making the patients happy!

Months later, in September, the Attorney General called me to ask if I had ever gotten my $2,500.00 back. Of course, my answer was, "No". He told me he was going to have them picked up on the old charges of defrauding a nonprofit because he had not dropped it yet. I was surprised that he could do that. He said he would try to collect my money from them. I told him thanks for all of his efforts.

About two hours later I received a second phone call from the Attorney General's Office. He said, "Can you come up here and pick up your $2,500.00?" I said, "I'm on my way right now."

When I got up there, I was surprised to see Marilyn and Joe sitting in his office. The attorney said, "On the way to my office, we stopped by their bank to pick up your cash." Marilyn handed me an envelope with $2,500.00 in cash in it. The attorney asked that I count it, so I did. It was all there! I thanked them for coming through with my money. Then I thanked the attorney and turned to walk out of his office.

The attorney asked, "Have you and you husband decided where to go and what date you are leaving on your free trip?" Not really believing we needed the trip, I said, "We don't expect a free trip anywhere. We are just happy to get our money back." He said, "You don't understand. Part of their agreement with the Attorney General's Office was to give you free round trip tickets to anywhere you wanted to go. Where do you want to go?" I said, "Okay, we would like to go to London from December 11th to 23rd." Marilyn agreed to get us the tickets no later than November 30th. Before we left, the attorney said, "Vicki, if they don't have these tickets to you by November 30th, I want to know." All agreed and we went our separate ways.

Without surprise, November 30th came and went without tickets or phone calls. On December 5th, I received another call from the Attorney General's Office. "Did you get your tickets?" I said, "No, but it is really okay with us. I just want to forget the whole thing." He would not let it go. He called Marilyn and she said she had our tickets, and I could come by and pick them up. He said, "No. You bring them to me and I will see that Vicki gets them." So she did that very afternoon. I went up to his office and picked them up right before closing time. As the attorney and I were looking closer at the tickets, we saw where these were not complimentary tickets issued by an airline. Marilyn and Joe had to purchase these tickets for $3,600.00.

That night when I got home, I surprised my husband and said we needed to hurry up and pack. We were leaving for London in six days. We laughed and could hardly believe we were actually going on the trip. We hadn't even made plans or reservations beforehand. For us, this was a once in a lifetime trip. We could never have afforded such a great trip on our tight budget.

That trip was the most excitement that happened for us in a long time. He and I had the time of our life traveling all over England and Scotland by rails for twelve days. Because it was December and very cold, we could stay wherever we chose. All of the hotels were almost empty. Even the restaurants catered to our every need because there were no other customers. We could not have planned it any better. It was like the whole country opened up just for us.

I know that this was God's gift to us. Whatever we did and wherever we went, it was all just perfect. The trip was like a wonderful dream to us.

When we returned, I called Marilyn and thanked her for giving us this wonderful vacation and told her we could never have done this without the paid tickets. The rest of our trip was put on credit cards, but we had months to pay it off. I told her how sorry my husband and I were to have gone through such an ordeal and said that it should have never happened in the first place. She apologized and asked that we remain friends. I agreed.

I haven't spoken with either Marilyn or Joe more than twice since this all took place because there was no need to call them. Almost every time we turn on the TV and see Joe on the air or hear Marilyn's distinct voice during commercials, we are reminded of that stressful experience. We have run into them only a few times over the last ten years. All of us have always remained cordial.

I do thank God for seeing that everything worked out for the best for our special children. For whatever reason He allowed this to happen, we are all much wiser today. I also wish to thank the Attorney General's Office. For without their involvement, none of this would have worked out so well. I am sure that this type of situation will not ever have to be dealt with again by any of us. I think that everyone involved has learned a very important and valuable lesson.

Our Washington D. C. Trip was Cancelled and Replaced With a Trip to St. Louis, Missouri

Group photo in St. Louis by The Arch

Some wheelchairs & volunteers in St. Louis

Our Group at a Cardinals game in Busch Stadium

Our special annual trips sometimes take weeks of planning out the entire day around the city that we have chosen. This year's special one day trip was planned five months in advance. I had been in touch with staff members of the White House concerning other matters when it was suggested we bring our group of patients to Washington, D. C. for our annual trip this summer.

Our recently elected President of the United States was our own state's last Governor, William J. Clinton. During our discussion, our conversation included plans of a special tour through the White House and President Bill and Hilary Clinton could be on hand to greet the children. What a great idea!

During the planning stage, we contacted other attractions around Washington, D. C. The Washington Monument, the Smithsonian Institute, and the Hard Rock Cafe would be other destinations on that trip. We also planned to lease buses to get us to all of the selected attractions. An approximate count of children and adults was given to each place, and the costs were then decided.

We contacted Southwest Airlines about chartering a plane. Once the cost of the plane and date was set, I got back with my contacts at the White House and the other destinations to finalize all arrangements. Everything was set and ready for the event months in advance.

Our next step was to send out invitations to all of our surviving patients under 18 years of age. At this point, 93 patients were invited. Legal forms to be signed by the parents and physicians accompanied those invitations for a speedy return. All went smoothly and the final count was in. After all forms were mailed back to us, we had 75 children remaining on the list to go on the trip.

We recruited 18 RNs, doctors, respiratory therapists, EMTs, and physical therapists to accompany the patients. In addition to the medical staff, we had many Arkansas State Troopers, local police officers, and other volunteers to lift the children in and out of wheelchairs, up and down stairs, in and out of the plane, pushing wheelchairs uphill, etc.

Mid January was our starting point. Our trip was planned for May 11th, beginning at 5:45 a. m. Now all plans were final, and we eagerly waited for that day to come. The children and their parents were thrilled at the thought of visiting The White House and meeting our President.

Meanwhile, I was working with The Shooting Gallery Foundation from New York City, New York and Miramax Films from Houston, Texas to hold a premier (first showing) of the movie "Sling Blade", written, directed, and starring Billy Bob Thornton who is from Arkansas. The movie was also filmed in Arkansas and had hired some local actors. Other well-known actors in the movie included Robert Duvall, Dwight Yoakam, J. T. Walsh, John Ritter, and Lucas Black.

Included in my duties for the premier were booking the actors to film the 30 second spots to be aired on radio and TV, procuring a caterer, selecting the foods and champagne, finding an ice sculptor, booking the theater with a 180 degree-angled screen, hiring seven security guards, locating auxiliary lighting, microphones and speakers, printing of all materials needed, and so much more! All of these services were, of course, donated, as well as, all persons involved were volunteers. This involvement took months to conclude and the Sling Blade Premier was a smashing success.

Also, during this same period, we were granting wishes and starting the planning stages of the annual Christmas party for December. I hardly had a moment's rest because I was working 12 to 14 hour days with very little sleep. My family life was suffering as well. I barely got to visit with my teenage sons. We just saw each other briefly in passing because their lives were full too, with school and outside activities. My husband was wonderful and very supportive, as always. When his day at the office was finished, he just tagged along with me and helped when he was needed. If it weren't for him, I probably would not have stopped to even eat meals!

The Sling Blade Premier was also a fundraiser to assist our patients with dreams and the upcoming trip to Washington, D. C. Lots of preparations were made to ensure the success of this premier, all of which I was in charge. I had a busy schedule, but everything always came together because I knew that ultimately, God was the one who was completely in charge of all successes in my life, as well as everything to do with our organization assisting children with life threatening illnesses.

Three weeks before the planned trip to Washington, D. C., long after all plans were finalized; I received a phone call from a woman who said she was our First Lady, Hilary Clinton's personal advisor. She wanted to go over our visit to the White House and our meeting with the President and First Lady. Of course, this was expected and I agreed to everything as she spoke. She said that there would be a press conference where the Clintons would address the patients. I fully expected this, too.

Toward the end of the conversation, she said that Hilary would be speaking to our group during the press conference and asked that I speak, also. Then came the shocker; she asked that I announce that Hilary played a big part in the founding of our organization. She asked that I elaborate on how Hilary was a key figure in the founding and early operations of our group. I said, "Just what do you want me to say? Now, I do not mind telling that Hilary helped us in the beginning when she worked for the Rose Law Firm. She was the one who had filed the corporation papers in 1983, but she did not attend meetings, raise funds, or grant wishes of any child. And why did you wait until three weeks before the trip to call me about this?"

The woman made it very clear that I had to cooperate with her on this matter. I was getting very upset. I asked her to have Hilary call me personally to discuss this matter further. If this was expected of me, I wanted to hear it from Hilary. She answered in the negative. I again asked that she talk to Hilary and have Hilary call me. I assumed that Hilary would call me back and say that this was a misunderstanding and all was fine. After all, she knew she had not assisted the organization in any capacity after the legal papers were filed. Also, this trip had been scheduled almost four months ago. This was a last minute detail that they forgot to tell me. When the conversation was over, I hung up and sat there at my desk in complete shock.

The White House staffer working with me had never mentioned anything even remotely close to this before. Although I knew many people who worked at the White House, I did not know this lady (Hilary's personal advisor). I even thought that she might be doing this on her own without Hilary knowing it. I actually cannot even remember her name today.

I picked the receiver back up to my ear and dialed the White House staff member I had worked with to plan this entire trip. I asked her if she knew this lady and she said, "Not really." I told her what had just happened and complained to her and then asked (very nicely) if she could get to the bottom of this matter and quickly, since our trip was scheduled for departure in three weeks. I still needed to pay for the plane and buses before the deadline.

Around 30 minutes later, I received a call from Hilary's advisor again. She said, "Hilary is too busy to talk to you about this, but she wants me to tell you that she wants to take this opportunity to promote her Heath Care Plan with your group present. She told me to make it perfectly clear to you that if you do not cooperate with her suggestions, the trip was off."

I was seeing stars before my very eyes! I had always tried to present myself in a Christian manner but I suddenly forgot my place and said, "Surely, this can't be right. Hilary is denying these terminally ill children the joy of visiting the White House and Washington, D. C. just because I won't lie for her?" Her response was, "Well if that is the way you see it, maybe you don't need to bring the children up here."

I said, "She knows that you are calling me? And she doesn't even have the guts to call me herself to tell me?" I took a deep breath and said something so terrible that I can't even repeat it now. I hung up and then, with tears in my eyes, said (out loud), "What have I done? Oh, Lord, please forgive me. I just said the most horrible thing. What is wrong with me? I just blew off the entire trip because of my own anger!" She caused me to talk to myself out loud. I figured I was only one in hundreds of people the Clintons have affected in this same way.

After a few moments, I calmed down a little and called my White House staff member back again. I told her what had just happened and asked her to see what she could do to fix my mistakes. I knew the future trip was canceled, but I thought maybe she could gloss it over where it was not as bad as I thought it would be.

She called back the following morning. It was that bad! She told me that Hilary's personal advisor had canceled our trip. No way were they going to let us come now! She told me that I should have lied and said that I would say whatever they wanted and then when we were there, just not do it. I was not smart enough to lie to them and then do what I wanted later. I have always believed that being honest was better. I try to base honesty with everything I do because it is the right thing to do. Only a dishonest person would lie to get their way.

On this occasion, I had done a really bad thing. Not that I had lied or even intended to, but that I had said something that a Christian should never say. It was too late to take it back. I had already rung that bell! Now I had to figure out what I was going to do about the trip that was already scheduled and almost paid for. I started praying for an answer. I called volunteers and told them how awful Hilary was and that I was even worse. I asked them to pray for a solution.

Later that day, I called my friend who was the editor of our statewide newspaper. I told him what happened. He decided that the public should know what the Hilary Clinton had done. He printed a small article in the newspaper the following day, even though I asked him not to. The following day, the "USA Today" newspaper had a two liner article about the White House denying sick children a visit to the White House.

Within two days, I received a call from the City Administrator of St. Louis, Missouri asking if we would like to come there for our trip. How kind he was! He had seen the article in "USA Today". I filled in the rest of the story to him. He thought that St. Louis could make up for what Hilary had done.

My husband and I had actually gone to St. Louis two times in the past three years, so I knew what that city had to offer. This was God's gift to us, allowing us to have an alternative to the trip to Washington, D. C. I immediately agreed this trip was still going to be a great trip for our patients.

The City Administrator and I planned out the day's events, keeping the same time and date scheduled for Washington, D. C. I called Southwest Airlines and told them what had transpired over the past few days and requested the same plane for St. Louis, MO. They were eager to assist us with the changes. Even our price for the fuel was lowered. It ended up saving us money to fly somewhere closer to us. We did not even need to lease the buses for transportation from one attraction to another. We were now offered a train free of charge in St. Louis.

The St. Louis City Administrator and I spoke several more times as we planned out the itinerary. I had to then notify all of our volunteers and patients for the new trip itinerary. Most were just fine about changing the destination, but were very disappointed in Hilary Clinton for acting out as she did. No one seemed to blame me for my part because I refused to lie.

On the flight we had 47 patients over the age of ten. We had 28 who were under ten years old and accompanied by one parent. Our total count was 153 on that flight, including RNs, doctors, physical therapists, respiratory therapists, EMTs, state troopers, local police officers, media for TV and newspapers, photographers, and other volunteers.

Our day started at 5:45 a. m. with everyone checked in as they received and changed into their special purple t-shirts. Then they were matched up with their assigned sponsors and patients and/or parents. Everyone then boarded our plane and the first roll call began.

Just after we left the ground, Southwest Airlines gave each person a very well rounded breakfast which was a great way to start the morning. Southwest Airlines is known for never serving food except peanuts and drinks. They made special arrangements to feed everyone. We were blessed to have them care so much about our children and volunteers.

After we arrived at the St. Louis Lambert Airport, we headed straight for the Metrolink to board our "Special" train for LaClede's Landing. We were blessed with our own train to travel around in, compliments of the city.

The entire city of St. Louis had opened up their city and their hearts for these well deserving children. We started out at 7:45 a. m. at the Arch which opened just for our group, long before it was opened to the public. Some of the children were somewhat frightened by the small cubicles that carried us up into the top of the Arch, but everyone did manage to overcome their fears and climb in. The view from the top of the Arch was so beautiful and very much worth the efforts. We could see where we had been and where we were going next.

From the Arch, we walked down to the river. McDonald's Restaurant is on a river boat where all of us ordered an early lunch. It gave us a chance to rest at the same time. After lunch, we gathered across the street in the park with a beautiful green lawn for group pictures and roll call again. The photos of the group turned out perfectly because we had the Arch in the background. We could not have planned it any better.

The hardest part of the day was next. We had a huge outside staircase that we had to climb on our way to Busch Stadium for an afternoon game. The flight of stairs had at least 35 to 45 steps straight up the hill. We thanked God for our heavy man-power. Our state troopers and local policeman really earned our respect as we watched them lift those children and their wheelchairs, just as they had done that morning, in and out of the plane. It took two and sometimes three men just to carry one wheelchair up those steps. We had about 15 children in wheelchairs on this trip. Some of them were very heavy!

Busch Stadium was packed. People were everywhere! It took us a while to get our tickets at the will call gate. We eventually found our group of seats and made sure each child was comfortable in their seats. As the last of us finally got seated in the stadium, someone yelled, "Look at the marquee!" There we were being shown on the huge lighted sign inside the stadium overlooking the ball field. Our section was a sea of purple t-shirts. We waved and screamed at the camera. The sign then said, "Welcome, Arkansas Children's Dreams, Inc. from Little Rock, AR." We were all astonished that they cared enough to welcome our group.

Watching the Cardinals play ball was the highlight of their day. Some of the children ate again at the ball park, but I do not know where they put all that food! The children started "the wave" over and over again. After the game, it was time for another roll call to assure us that we had not lost anyone, yet. Now it was time to head back to the Metrolink to catch our "Special" train. Even the name "SPECIAL" was on the sign on front of our train.

The same person that helped me with all of the arrangements (the City Administrator) was present with us for part of the day. He was a jolly person, so very kind and so friendly. He even brought his teenage son with him. I think he really enjoyed visiting with the volunteers and patients. I could tell he was a wonderful, caring person who loved people. He must have been very good at his job, too.

While waiting for our train to arrive, we did another roll call and still had everyone present. As we boarded our train, we were off to the St. Louis Lambert Airport! Our plane and crew were waiting. We boarded the plane and had our last roll call for the day. No one was missing and not one child had gotten ill all day long — not even the ones who ate too much!

What a blessing that day was for all of us! The day was absolutely perfect in every way. Many of the patients told us this was the best trip they had ever been on. We never had one moment that we thought about the White House or the Clintons. The day was too great to ruin it with negative thoughts about anything.

We arrived back at the Little Rock Airport by 8:00 p. m., right on schedule. Southwest Airlines had gone over and above their original plans for the children. They fed us on both flights. These stewardesses and pilots had volunteered their entire day to fly us to and from St. Louis, and they were so great with the children! Even the pilots told us jokes now and then.

The entire day was full of surprises, where emotions ran high and the patients were full of energy. We know that these one day excursions were very special for everyone involved. It gave the patients new hopes of living longer and fuller lives. It also gave the volunteers a new meaning for the word "volunteer", where they could see they were making a difference in the lives of these very special and deserving children.

One of the most amazing things that had ever happened on a special flight with all of our patients happened on this trip. A round rainbow appeared, at the left wing of the plane after take-off from the Little Rock Airport at 6:00 a. m. As we leveled off, above the clouds, it became a huge rainbow and moved out about half of a mile away. In the center of the rainbow was the dark shadow of our plane.

You could see it from every window on the left side of the plane. It followed us all of the way to the St. Louis Lambert Airport.

A few patients and volunteers invited me to go to their side of the plane to see it. I had flown in airplanes for most of my life and I had never seen anything like that before. I told them this must be a sign that God is watching over us. It was truly an unusual sight to see!

On our return flight at 7:00 p. m. from St. Louis to Little Rock, it reappeared again and stayed with us for the entire flight home. The children and adults said that they had goose bumps just from looking at it.

I have always said that our special flights with our patients had to be the safest flights we could ever be on. For those who saw this amazing sight now believe as I do; God was watching over our organization, our special children, and our loving volunteers.

A few days after our return, I got a phone call from a TV station who knew about what Hilary Clinton had done to the children. He told me to watch the six o'clock news because I would be very interested in the contents. At six o'clock, there she was! Hilary was speaking before a group of children in wheelchairs with their caregivers standing beside them, promoting her Health Care Plan.

PART 5

**Special needs
in the
community
became a task
that no one
volunteered
to oversee
until
I became
involved.**

Chapter IX.

Many lessons in life are learned by accident or chance as long as you have an open heart and mind.

Feeding the Homeless and the Hungry

I firmly believe that when a person is living a life close to God, He will lead them in the correct directions. He will put issues before them to solve. He will also give them the right tools and information that is needed to solve the issues.

I pray daily and many times all day in between my commitments. Driving is always a good time to spend praying. Never do I believe there is no answer or solution to the problems put before me, but because I am a human, I do have moments that I briefly question God, "Are you sure that this is what you what me to do?" These moments pass quickly as He leads me to go on. I trust He is with me and is guiding me all of the way.

One day in the 1980s, I was riding in the car with a businessman in our city. He started pointing out boxes in the alleys. He told me that homeless people were living underneath. I had no idea that we had people living in the streets. He stopped the car beside a large box, got out and knocked on the box. A man peered out asking him what he wanted. The businessman looked at me smiling and gave the man some money. He got back in the car and we drove on. I was silent for a little while. I thought, "I really didn't know anything about my city! Where is the help for these unfortunate souls?" He broke the silence by explaining that there is never enough food or shelter for all of the homeless people out there.

That night, I had trouble going to sleep. Didn't I already have enough to do just raising funds, granting wishes, and assisting with transplants? I also had a family to care for and I thought my plate was already full. I questioned, "God, Why did you take me to see this? Surely you can't mean for me to do something else?"

The following day, I made phone call after phone call to talk to the shelters, the food banks, and some of the churches. I didn't like what I was hearing. So many people were being turned away because of the lack of food and beds in the existing shelters. Even the churches were so overwhelmed that they could not even take care of all of their own parishioners! It was almost November and this winter was expected to be extra cold. I wondered, "What is going to happen to all of those people?" I think I only lasted about two days before I started calling grocery stores begging for food for these people. Tyson Foods sent me cases of frozen whole chickens and turkey breasts. Local grocery stores gave me lots of food. I had to borrow freezer space in my neighborhood and among my friends. Cases of canned goods, drinks, and staples such as flour, sugar, corn meal, etc., all started piling up in my living room. My living room was so packed that there was only a small path from the front door all the way back to my kitchen. I had only been begging for a few days and look at the food! I thought, "Why isn't someone else doing this? I'm only one person!"

We did take care of all of the people that fell through the cracks of the local shelters and food banks, but this was only a temporary solution. I had gathered up volunteers, and we cooked the food and went out to find those who needed it. We found homeless people in boxes in the alleys and some just on the streets around downtown. We found entire families living in their cars parked in the alleyways. We catered hot meals to them once a day until another solution was found.

The local media followed us around. Finally a new shelter opened, and another food bank opened. Within four weeks we could not find too many left on the streets. Only the ones who chose to stay out there were left on the streets. We knew that they had a place to shower and eat so we thought our job was done.

Not so fast! Another call for help came in from the Governor's office and told us the food banks had run out of food again. People living crowded in their homes were without assistance. It was almost

Thanksgiving and here we are again! I called every one of the donors from the last month and begged once more for food that could be cooked in the homes of the recipients. Within a few days, I had my living room full and my neighbors' freezers packed again. It is now late November and only one week away from Thanksgiving.

I gathered up my children, and we packed boxes with enough food to get each family through both Thanksgiving and Christmas for the entire family. There were about 150 families that year that were on our list. I found them through their churches and from the food banks' lists. Many were aliens from Mexico living as several families in one small house. Others were just not making ends meet because the wages were too low for the size of their families. Food and clothing were usually forgotten because their money was barely providing a place to live and paying for the utilities.

We were told about the families before we ever met them. We found clothing for those who needed it and then dropped off both food and clothing for some families. I found donors who purchased children's toys and brought them to my home one week before Christmas. My children and I wrapped the toys and took the Christmas gifts to each of the homes.

A business owner called me two weeks before Christmas and asked if I would like to attend a Christmas party that he was giving for all 50 of his employees and their families. He asked that I bring my own children, too. He offered me the leftover catered food to give to the families in need. We went to this very nice catered affair and everyone was so kind to us. The owner gave a wonderful holiday speech and then asked me to come speak to the employees about the last few weeks of my hectic life. I gave a brief synopsis of the feeding of the homeless and the needy, and thanked the owner who graciously offered any leftover food.

At the time, I did not know what I had done and neither did the owner of the company. The music was playing, but no one got up to get their food. People talked, laughed, and seemed to enjoy the party, but not one person ate any of the especially prepared food! I soon realized that they were giving their share to the families and children. Totally embarrassed I stood up and thanked everyone, and also apologized for ruining their dinner. I was immediately assured that they were all willing participants and were happy with their decisions. The owner and I laughed as we loaded the hot food into my van. I went home and called volunteers, and we gathered up the portions for each family in need. The food was still warm when we finally got the last of it delivered.

I believe that these well deserving families did have many blessings to be counted because others cared enough to share with them.

In one of my weakest moments during my long illness I received this prayer from a dear friend who prayed for me to recover every day. Even though I had read this numerous times throughout my life, this time I really got it! I pinned it up over my headboard and read it every day. I would like to share it with all of you.

PRAYER OF ST. FRANCIS OF ASSISI

Lord, make me an instrument of thy peace.

where there is hatred, let me sow love;

where there is injury, pardon;

where there is doubt, faith;

where there is despair, hope;

where there is darkness, light;

where there is sadness, joy;

O Divine Master, grant that

I may not so much seek to be

consoled, as to console;

To be understood, as to understand;

To be loved, as to love;

For it is in giving that we receive;

It is in pardoning that we are pardoned;

It is in dying that we are

born to eternal life.